T0294519

Designing Museum Experiences

Designing Museum Experiences

Mark Walhimer

ROWMAN & LITTLEFIELD
Lanham • Boulder • New York • London

Published by Rowman & Littlefield
An imprint of The Rowman & Littlefield Publishing Group, Inc.
4501 Forbes Boulevard, Suite 200, Lanham, Maryland 20706
www.rowman.com

86-90 Paul Street, London EC2A 4NE

British Library Cataloguing in Publication Information Available

Library of Congress Cataloging-in-Publication Data

Names: Walhimer, Mark, 1964- author.
Title: Designing museum experiences / Mark Walhimer.
Description: Lanham : Rowman & Littlefield, [2021] | Includes
  bibliographical references and index.
Identifiers: LCCN 2021030229 (print) | LCCN 2021030230 (ebook) | ISBN
  9781538150467 (cloth) | ISBN 9781538150474 (paperback) | ISBN
  9781538150481 (ebook)
Subjects: LCSH: Museum visitors. | Museums—Pschological aspects.
Classification: LCC AM7 .W34 2021 (print) | LCC AM7 (ebook) | DDC
  069/.1—dc23
LC record available at https://lccn.loc.gov/2021030229
LC ebook record available at https://lccn.loc.gov/2021030230

∞™ The paper used in this publication meets the minimum requirements of
American National Standard for Information Sciences—Permanence of Paper
for Printed Library Materials, ANSI/NISO Z39.48-1992.

Dedicated to museum staff and volunteers
who, every day, make the world a better place.

The museum of the future is generous. Instead of categorising and packaging artworks and experiences for express consumption, it endorses the potential of uncertainty. It nurtures the transformative possibilities inherent in the contact between artwork, audience, museum and society.

The museum shows confidence in its users and creates conditions that allow visitors to see their own resources for perceiving art and the world. It does not simply collect the shapes of the world in the form of artworks and objects—it shapes the world. It is a reality-producing machine. It engages in public discourse and policy-making.

A polyphony of voices, actions and possible encounters, the museum of the future is a power that can change the world.[1]

—Olafur Eliasson

NOTE

1. "What is the museum of the future?" https://www.tate.org.uk/tate-etc/issue-35-autumn-2015/what
   -museum-future.

Designing Museum Experiences Advisory Board

In preparing to write this book, I reached out to experts in the fields of user-centered design and museum diversity, equity, accessibility, and inclusion (DEAI), as well as experts in the area of informal learning research about visitor motivations and behavior based on visitor needs and interests and community impact. Thank you to the following advisory board members for your time and expertise in reviewing drafts of the manuscript and providing your invaluable feedback to help me accomplish my goal of creating a research-based "how-to" book about creating visitor experiences that are multicultural and follow the best user-centered design practices.

- Camille Bethune-Brown, Curator and Black History Historian, San Diego, California
- Laura-Edythe Coleman, PhD, Assistant Professor and Director of the Arts Administration and Museum Leadership Graduate Online Program, Drexel University, author of *Understanding and Implementing Inclusion in Museums* (2018)
- Fernando Costa, Assistant City Manager, City of Fort Worth
- Sergio Dávila Urrutia, Coordinador de Diseño Industrial, Universidad Autónoma Metropolitana Unidad Azcapotzalco, Ciudad de México, México
- Corinne Gordon, Historic Farm and History Specialist, Wood County Park District, Bowling Green, Ohio
- Seph Rodney, PhD, author of *The Personalization of the Museum Visit* (2018)
- Peter Scupelli, Nierenberg Associate Professor in Design and Director of the Learning Environments Lab, at the School of Design, Carnegie Mellon University
- Susan B. Spero, PhD, Museum Studies
- Ariadna Téllez, Director, Program Management at frog
- Neil Williams, Director, Experience Design, Customer Advocacy, Manulife and Former Visiting Lecturer of Museum and Exhibition Design, University of Lincoln, Hong Kong

Contents

Part I. Shifting to the Visitor (Why)

Part II. The Museum Visitor (Who)

Part III. Supporting the Museum Visitor Experience (How)

Part IV. Future Museum Visitor Experiences (When)

Part V. Visitor Experience Toolbox

List of Figures

List of Tables

Acknowledgments

In 2013, I walked into Ibero University in Mexico City, wondering if I could teach at a university level. Since then, my students have given me more than I could have ever expected. I have learned that my expertise in museums is also an expertise in customer experience (CX). I have been teaching at Tec de Monterrey, Ibero, and at Georgia Tech in the industrial design departments. Thank you to my students for all that you have taught me.

During one of my lectures, a student asked a seemingly simple question: "How do you create an experience?" The question took me aback. I had to come up with a simple answer at the time, but it wasn't complete. This book is the not-so-simple answer.

Thank you to the readers of museumplanner.org and your always insightful questions. Thank you to my clients. It is my honor to be part of your museum work. Thank you to Amparo, Benjamin, Señor and Señora, Janice and Ron, and Anne and Meg, with my love.

Thank you to Charles Harmon for believing in thinking differently about museums, to Karen Trost and Keith Miller for their tireless editing, to Alvaro Alvarez for the diagrams, and to the book's advisory board for their knowledge and commitment to helping people in the museum field understand their visitors and how to connect visitors with museum experiences.

—Mark Walhimer

Preface

Since I started working on this book, we have experienced the COVID-19 pandemic, the Black Lives Matter protests, the furloughs of tens of thousands of museum staff due to the pandemic, and an increased focus on diversity, equity, accessibility, and inclusion in museums. These events make the work of creating visitor-centered experiences through the methodology of a customer experience (CX) approach even more important.

In preparing to write this book, I read more than twenty museum-experience-related books and was surprised that not one used the research-proven[1] approach of applying CX methodologies. This approach is long overdue. During my twenty-year career as a museum specialist and consultant, I have taken part in opening more than thirty museums and have consulted on more than one hundred museum projects worldwide. I structured this book to follow the same process as my consulting. First, we identify the problems and give the client the freedom to dream big. Then we address the questions from a new viewpoint, achieved by walking a mile in the visitor's shoes (sometimes literally).

The more I work in the museum field, the more I realize that my role as a museum consultant is to come to a detailed understanding of the museum's vision. The more clearly I understand it, the more successful my work will be. If I can create a nonjudgmental environment during our work together, participants feel more comfortable dreaming big (which I refer to as "blue sky" thinking). I pay close attention to the details and adjectives people use; these serve as the core elements for the design of powerful, visitor-centric museum experiences.

Once my client can move beyond logistical questions and start to think "blue sky," we are able to gain a new perspective. The goal is to develop a museum that can connect with visitors emotionally as well as intellectually, empowering them to change their behaviors, and ultimately their lives.

A few years ago, I conducted a workshop with a group whose goal was to create a typical science center in a twenty-five-thousand-square-foot building for a community of about fifty thousand people. The group was looking for assistance with program creation, exhibition design, and gallery development. I asked each group member to take three pieces of scrap paper and write one thing they hoped to achieve on each piece. If any of the participants put down "world-class," "high attendance," "award-winning," or something similar, I asked them to rewrite those generic objectives as "subjective objectives" that used more emotional and personal descriptions.

Once the group members had rewritten and rethought their descriptions, we posted them on the wall and looked at them as a whole. It became clear that they were *not* aiming to create a typical science center. What the founder and staff had in mind was more of an educational think tank for teaching innovation. Without our discussion about subjective objectives, the group probably would have continued on a path toward a typical science center. Instead, we planned an innovation center—a place for teaching science innovation. This approach led to a visitor-centric, community-based plan unlike any other science center in existence. The workshop participants' process resulted in a solution specific to their community.

Time and again, I've seen museum management ask specific logistical questions about cost and visitation without realizing that this narrow, results-oriented mindset is part of a system-wide issue.

Museum management rarely appreciates the full power of their museum. It is essential that they expand their thinking and dream beyond their current limitations. Logistical questions about issues such as cost per square foot are of no help in understanding the emotional connection between museum and visitor. Instead, I'll often point to a photo of a representative visitor and ask the workshop participant questions such as "Do you see that visitor visiting your museum?"

This book is written for people interested in starting a museum, people currently working in museums, and people interested in bettering their museum practices. Some readers may be unsure of the value of a customer-centered approach and may think this is only "marketing lingo." However, a CX approach can result in increased museum visitation by more diverse, emotionally engaged audiences who can protect the museum from market disruptions[2] such as the COVID-19 pandemic. A customer-centered museum constantly changes to meet the needs of audiences, resulting in emotionally invested visitors who trust the institution and will remain committed despite market disruptions. The visitor-centered approach also increases the likelihood of local community impact.

Each museum is unique to its local community, so the staff, board of directors, and visitors need to be representative of the larger local community as well. All groups must be included without implicit bias.

By the end of this book, I hope you will be able to see the visitor experience as the most important part of a museum, view the museum experience from the visitor's point of view, and have empathy for the museum visitor. To create a customer experience is to create a consistent, thoughtful, and emotionally connected museum at all touchpoints.

WHO SHOULD READ THIS BOOK?

This book is written for anyone interested in creating impactful educational experiences. This includes but is not limited to the following.

- Museum staff, board members, volunteers, and service providers: the people who define strategies for customer experiences, services, products, marketing, or technology.
- Community leaders: mayors, city council members, city managers (hired by the city council), city administrators (hired by the mayor), community development directors, urban planners, librarians, and directors of parks and recreation.
- Emerging museum professionals: newly graduated students looking for their first museum job and museum staff and volunteers with less than three years' museum experience.[3]
- Students: these include those studying museum studies, architecture, industrial design, marketing, business, interior design, and education. Students are the future of the museum field and of inclusive experiences.

WHAT IS IN THIS BOOK?

This book is organized into five parts. The first four parts are based on the basic questions essential to information gathering used by journalists, researchers, and investigators. (If you're reading this, you should already be familiar with "what" you're looking for, and "where.") Part V is a collection of visitor experience tools that you will need to help create a meaningful museum visitor experience.

Part I: Shifting to the Visitor (Why)
Part II: The Museum Visitor (Who)
Part III: Supporting the Museum Visitor Experience (How)
Part IV: Future Museum Visitor Experiences (When)
Part V: Visitor Experience Toolbox

Each chapter includes some or all of the following:

Next Steps: questions and exercises related to the chapter content
Key Concepts: terms used and defined in the chapter
Additional Resources: sources of additional information on the chapter topic
Notes: references and citations of source materials

The book also contains several workshop examples designed to help engage the right people at the right time to create impactful experiences.

You'll find the book's companion website at https://www.museum-experiences.com/.

The diagrams and other illustrations in the book are available under a Creative Commons license (when possible) for you to download and include in your own presentations. In addition to the website, readers can sign up to take online seminars and online courses at https://museumcourses.com.

FREQUENTLY ASKED QUESTIONS

Do I have to do all of the items in this book to orchestrate experiences successfully?

Many frameworks and tools are covered, but you will likely gravitate to those that meet your unique needs. For example, for one project you may need to create personas (chapter 4), but for another you may need a journey map (chapter 8). Try out different approaches, mix and match, and build the toolkit that works for you.

You didn't mention [insert tool here]. Does that mean I shouldn't use it anymore?

The constant addition and modification of methods and tools in our toolkits is an essential part of designing a meaningful museum visitor experience. The methods and tools presented in this book have proven to be effective for both simple and complex projects, but please check https://museum-visitor.com regularly for new tools and methodologies.

Does this take a lot of time?

The more complex the problem, and the larger the organization, the more time will be needed. That said, you will find that the approaches covered here can be used to run fast and lean.

Isn't this just service design?

This book is a synthesis of best practices, including service design, user experience, customer experience, lean design, and systems thinking. You will find references to each of these methodologies distilled into best practices that are applicable to the museum visitor experience. At their core, what they have in common is user-centered design. This book will lead the reader through a hands-on process of putting thinking into action.

NOTES

1. "Customer Experience," McKinsey, accessed Nov. 13, 2017, https://www.mckinsey.com/global-themes/customer-experience.
2. Thales Teixeira, "Products Don't Disrupt Markets; Customers Do," accessed Oct. 27, 2020, https://podcasts.apple.com/us/podcast/s5e9-thales-teixeira-products-dont-disrupt-markets/id1359935118. For more research papers regarding the effectiveness of the customer experience approach, visit https://museum-visitor.com/toolbox.
3. "Emerging Museum Professionals," Mountain-Plains Museums Association, accessed Nov. 30, 2020, https://mpma.net/Emerging-Museum-Professionals.

Foreword

We must remake the world. The task is nothing less than that.

—Mary McLeod Bethune

The world is in a constant state of evolution and change. Museum methods are too. Over the past year, the closure of physical museums due to the COVID-19 pandemic challenged us to reimagine our institutions and reignite our audience engagement in innovative ways. With resiliency and agility, museums are redefining what it means to be a museum in contemporary society. We are more than a place, a building, a noun, a repository. We *are* relationships. We *are* community. We aim to *be* art and not just *see* it, to *inspire* history in the making and not just study it.

Museums will help remake our world by engaging with the agents of change—our visitors—in new ways, while responding to current challenges, facilitating urgent conversations, and meeting our community where they are. *Designing Museum Experiences* offers a clear path to transforming museums that are committed to an equitable society, to investing in the healing of their communities, and to eradicating racism and bias through more meaningful engagement with their visitors. The book challenges museums to live up to their fullest potential. By answering four key questions, the book leads us through this current paradigm shift, this necessary undoing, and this universal recommitment in the museum field to radically centering visitors in all we do. It is a step-by-step guide and do-it-yourself toolkit to making museums inclusive, equitable, visitor-centered spaces. This is a visionary book that aligns with museum best practices. Several terms can be interchanged for visitors—audience, guests, community, customers. The point of the book is that museums are all about *them*, not us.

For so long, museums have been object-centered and artifact-driven. We preserve art and historical artifacts. We teach with them. We place lights upon them and stanchions around them and vitrines over them. We distinguish ourselves based on which ones we hold in our collections. We have not as a whole, however, given equal attention to the people who experience museums. We have not placed them center stage in our museums. This book reminds museums that they can live up to their promise and purpose by recentering visitors in the museum experience. The visitor experience starts before they set foot on your grounds and now in the post-COVID world, sometimes an online experience with your museum is all the visitor will have. Author Mark Walhimer reminds us that museums can be all their communities need them to be. This book, written by an expert on visitor studies, offers a guide to how museums can make a difference in the world, one visitor at a time.

Throughout his career, Walhimer has helped to shape, transform, and reinvent countless museums across the globe. He has created new models and templates for visitor engagement. He knows the trusted cultural, educational, and civic roles that museums play. He has written this book with the future of museums in mind. No other book gives this kind of practical guidance on solving the problem of visitor experiences.

He offers a thought-provoking approach to designing museum experiences, centered on change, connection, and compassion. Museums have tremendous influence in society. They must adapt and adjust to the needs of visitors. Getting out of the way in order to prioritize the visitor from design to delivery, museums must have an emotional connection with visitors.

You will think differently about museums after reading this book. But it will not stop there. This book will lead you to take action, the right action to understand and design experiences to meet the intellectual and emotional needs of visitors. When followed, the guidance from this book will enrich and enliven museums for all visitors in lasting ways that make society better. This book will help remake the world of museums.

LaNesha DeBardelaben
President & CEO, Northwest African American Museum
National Board President, Association of African American Museums

Part I
Shifting to the Visitor (Why)

1

A Changing Landscape

Museums are facing one of the largest paradigm shifts since they became public institutions more than two hundred years ago. Traditionally, if a museum deemed an object such as a piece of art or a historical artifact worthy, the visitor was expected to show reverence for and learn from that object. The information moved in one direction: from the museum to the visitor. Today, museums are shifting the focus to the visitor experience. Visitors now cocreate and cocurate their journey with the museum, and that process is upending the way museums and exhibits are designed.

More and more, museums are incorporating the visitor into the very fabric of the experience: Visitors provide content, both during the exhibit and in the online environment. Their identities are shaping the journeys and spaces museums develop. In Carsten Höller's seminal 2011 exhibit "Experience" at the New Museum in New York City, visitors were active participants. They hurtled two stories down a corkscrewing metal slide. They floated in a sensory-deprivation pool. They put on goggles that turned the world upside down. In a sense, the visitors *were* the exhibit: they were the objects on display; they were experiencing their own reactions as part of the exhibit (see figure 1.1). As Höller said, "For every person who comes in, it will be like exposing a film to the light and seeing what image develops."[1]

Figure 1.1. A museum visitor at Carsten Höller's immersive exhibit. *Guy Bell/ Alamy Live News.*

Museums certainly remain keepers of the objects of culture, but the meaning of those objects is shifting to the visitor. Museums are beginning to recognize that meaning is subjective, and depends on the visitor's identity, social background, and environment. Curators are no longer the only important voices. That role must now be shared with the public. Instead of art and artifact warehouses, museums are becoming "content warehouses," with the role of providing factual information and context for the visitor to curate. Museums are starting to ask, "How can the information we provide become relevant to every visitor?"

One museum that has made the shift successfully is the Oakland Museum of California (OMCA). The OMCA's Gallery of California History designed an exhibit called "Sent Away, but Not Forgotten" about the internment of Japanese Americans in California during World War II (see figure 1.2). First installed in 2012, and reopened from 2016 to 2017, the exhibit included a re-creation of a typical prison cell in which Japanese Americans would have been confined. Accompanying the spatial re-creation was an audioscape of the voices of the Japanese prisoners. As they moved through the exhibit, visitors spent time within the cell itself. When visitors left the prison cell, they encountered a bulletin board with the question "What will YOU do when they round us up?" Next to the question were posted recent events, such as the 2017 immigrant travel ban. Visitors were encouraged to write responses to the question and add them to the bulletin board, allowing them to connect emotionally to the experiences of others, as well as contribute in a tangible way to the exhibit itself.

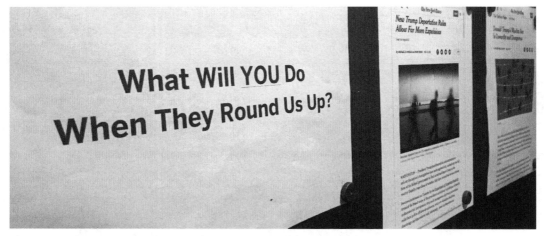

Figure 1.2. "Sent Away but Not Forgotten," the Japanese Internment exhibition at the Oakland Museum of California. *Jeffrey Inscho.*

Teachers leading school groups to OMCA received pre-visit packets that outlined activities, including taking photos during their visit and posting photos and reactions online. The museum in turn reposted the work of students as museum content. Museum information became visitor content, which was then used to inform the museum content, creating a museum–visitor cocreation cycle.

The objects on display in the OMCA exhibit were artifacts of a historical event. Once visitors experienced the objects within the context of the event, they could determine the objects' relevance to their lives, curating and creating their own content from that provided by the museum.

FROM STATIC TO DYNAMIC

The International Council of Museums defines a museum as "a nonprofit-making permanent institution in the service of society, and of its development, open to the public, which acquires, conserves, researches, communicates, and exhibits, for purposes of study, education, and enjoyment, material evidence of people and their environment." There are currently more than ninety-five thousand museums in the world, thirty-five thousand of them in the United States.[2] More than 850 million people visit American museums annually, greater than the number who attend all major sporting events combined.[3] Museums are considered the most trustworthy source of information in the United States. They are rated more highly than local newspapers, nonprofit researchers, the US government, and academic researchers.[4] The large number of visitors and the high level of perceived trustworthiness is a powerful combination.

Traditionally, museums have had a hierarchical structure, reflecting the norms of society. Imagine a stereotypical museum director standing in the lobby of his museum waiting to receive a potential donor. It is nine thirty in the morning, and school buses are dropping off groups of students on field trips. Middle school students stream past the director, who straightens his shoulders and adjusts his tie. Look at the impact my museum is having on these kids, he thinks proudly. He can't wait to tell the donor about his museum's influence on the education of today's youngsters.

But what about the impact of the students on the museum? What about their identities and journeys and dreams? The goal of this book is to shift that museum director's thinking to identifying with the students and viewing them as co-owners or partners in the museum's content.

Museums must change from being places containing artifacts requiring expert interpretation to places that provide impactful experiences and emotional connections that lead to life-changing personal insights. They must become agile content creators able to change as their visitors change. Only if this shift takes place can museums remain relevant to the populations they need to serve in today's rapidly changing world.

PLACEMAKING

As well as a shift in how museums think about visitors, there has been a shift in how people think about museums. Rather than monolithic institutions, they are now seen as ever-changing community centers. This shift involves placemaking, a multifaceted approach to the planning, design, and management of public spaces that utilizes a local community's assets, including its location, history, social attributes, and potential. Placemaking is a philosophy as well as a process; it involves the intention of creating public spaces that promote people's health, happiness, and well-being. We will take a closer look at placemaking in chapter 10.

MUSEUMS AND THE INTERNET

I recently received an email asking about the role of the internet in modern museums. My first thought was that it has changed everything, but then I started to think more deeply about what had changed, and how. The National Museum of African American History and Culture (NMAAHC), which opened in 2016, has proven to be a huge hit with audiences. In fact, it was so popular that the authorities had to implement a system of pre-purchased timed tickets in order to reduce the crowds.[5] This collection of artifacts and audio and visual materials clearly filled a void—visitors of all ethnic backgrounds and nationalities desired that in-person experience. However, the museum also crafted a highly effective online presence. They were one of the first museums to have a significant web presence before the physical building opened, and their Memory Book app allowed visitors to get involved by providing their own written or oral stories, as well as images.[6] The collection and experience housed within the building was complemented and enhanced by the online presence, and it is hard to imagine one without the other.

Taking off from the Museum of African American History's groundbreaking online presence, the 1619 Project, developed by Nikole Hannah-Jones, was a multimedia extravaganza documenting four hundred years of the Black experience in the United States. Its first iteration was as an insert in the

New York Times, which swiftly sold out (Hannah-Jones noted that people were stealing the inserts from papers for sale—it had become a hot commodity). Its online presence was an elegantly presented series of articles, images, and audiovisual materials charting the history and lived experiences of Black people in the United States, but it also included live events, written material passed out on streets, podcasts, and other engagements with the material. The response was overwhelmingly positive, and Hannah-Jones won a Pulitzer Prize for her introductory essay.[7]

This type of synergy between physical structures and objects, online presences, video, audio, live events, and texts will be a growing part of the future museum experience: it will become hard to tell where a "museum" begins or ends. People will still go to a brick-and-mortar museum for the in-person experience, but that experience is now only part of a broader museum visitor experience. The museum has become an entity without walls.

Society has often been referred to as a four-legged stool. Government, businesses, and associations form three of the legs; the fourth one is museums and other nonprofits.[8] Today these distinctions are becoming blurred, with online entities like Google and Wikipedia taking on some functions previously filled by businesses and nonprofits. Museums now exist within an ecosystem of galleries, libraries, archives, and museums (sometimes referred to as GLAMs).

Prior to widespread use of the internet, museums often tried to be encyclopedic, stand-alone entities presenting broad content areas in art, science, and history. As warehouses for artifacts, objects, and specimens, museums of the past had a societal role similar to schools. With the growth of the internet, the world has suddenly become much smaller. Knowledge, once only available in museums or the schoolroom, has become readily accessible online. A school museum visit used to be a "nice experience" for students; now it is seen as a necessity to increase test scores. The visitor's time at a museum is often the pinnacle of a journey that starts on the internet and returns to it after the in-person experience. Museums are still archival machines with the purpose of preservation, but how they interact with the public has changed dramatically.

THE SHIFTING MUSEUM VISITOR

When I started working in museums a quarter of a century ago, the most typical visitors were a nuclear family with two parents and two children. Nowadays, such a family unit is a much smaller segment of museum visitation. School groups, young couples on dates, and teenagers looking for something to do form a larger proportion of visitors every year. Visitors in these categories are often looking for entertainment as much as education. Museums are moving from serving as encyclopedic repositories to presenting readily digestible information that targets different visitor groups. For example, the Metropolitan Museum now offers four separate hour-long tours designed specifically for businesspeople on their lunch breaks.[9]

This desire for entertainment has spurred considerable discussion within museums: how do you continue to attract younger, more entertainment-oriented visitors while still being an establishment at the highest level of education and research? In part, the answer to this question involves following the trend in the formal educational system, which is becoming more informal and less academic. Examples of this shift include museum schools and school-sponsored fairs.

THE MUSEUM VISITOR AS CUSTOMER

In 1998, B. Joseph Pine II and James H. Gilmore described a monumental shift in society to what they termed an "experience economy."[10] The experience economy followed the agrarian economy of ancient times, the industrial economy of the nineteenth and early twentieth centuries, and the service economy of the late twentieth century. Pine and Gilmore argued that, in today's experience economy, businesses must orchestrate memorable events for their customers, and that the memory of the experience becomes the product.

Experiences are economic offerings that differ from other services or products. Consumers unquestionably desire experiences, and businesses are responding by explicitly designing and promoting them. Think about your experience in a well-designed café. It's no longer just about grabbing a cup of coffee. As you enter, you are greeted courteously, and the barista calls out your order by name. The entire environment has been carefully crafted, including the lighting, the colors of the artwork on the walls, the selection of music, and even the typeface used in the menu. You are enveloped in an experience that feels personal.

Museums must now compete in the same realm. Visitors will compare their experiences at your museum to those at businesses such as cafés and hotels. The standards have changed, and museums must acknowledge that they are now competing in a dramatically altered landscape.

The customer experience (CX) is the overall impact of the interactions between a person and a company at all touchpoints. As part of my preparation for writing this book, I asked a variety of museum enthusiasts about CX as it related to the museum. Their response was somewhat shocked: "Museums do not have 'customers,'" they exclaimed. "They have *visitors*." However, like it or not, the museum visitor, whether in person or online, is a customer. Together, the museum staff and volunteers, museum collection, and museum exhibits share the content of the museum to create the CX. This experience should be crafted to align with the museum's identified mission, vision, and values.

Thinking about the museum visitor as a customer and the experience as a product should come naturally in today's customer-centric world. A museum offering an experience is not unlike a business offering a service or product. The importance of experience lies in the fact that traditional products can be better sold when wrapped up with experiences. However, it is not an easy task to switch from selling products or services to selling experiences. It requires a general economic shift, similar to the one described earlier, from an industrial to a service to an experience economy.

An experience happens when services and goods are designed and offered in such a way that they create a memorable event for the customer. While commodities and services are products that are external to the customer, experiences are much more internal and personal. Their relationship with customers occurs on an emotional level, and sometimes even a spiritual one. Because each individual has a different experience, it is not easy to develop an experience that transcends the individual consumer. We will look more closely at emerging trends in design thinking and emotional design in chapter 5.

CONCLUSION

In order for museums to survive and thrive, they need to adapt to a changing market just like other businesses. Museums now vie for their visitors' attention with other destinations and businesses in an increasingly competitive marketplace. Museums must adopt the typical customer-centric processes of business to attract visitors, and shift the focus from artifacts to the museum visitor experience. Although the missions of museums and businesses are very different, a visitor-centric approach is essential if museums hope to thrive in today's ever-changing world.

NEXT STEPS

Thinking about your favorite museum, answer the following questions:

1. Why is it your favorite?
2. Does it focus more on artifacts or the museum visitor experience? Give an example to support your answer.
3. Has it changed over the years you have been visiting? If so, how? If not, what changes, if any, are needed?

KEY CONCEPTS INTRODUCED IN THIS CHAPTER THAT ARE DEFINED IN THE GLOSSARY

customer experience (CX)
experience economy
visitor experience
placemaking

ADDITIONAL RESOURCES

Dercon, Chris. "What Is the Museum of the Future?" Tate Etc. Sep. 22, 2015. https://www.tate.org.uk
    /tate-etc/issue-35-autumn-2015/what-museum-future.
"OpenGLAM Principles." OpenGLAM. Accessed Feb. 24, 2021. https://openglam.org/principles/.
Leber, Jessica. "The Future of Museums Is Reaching Way beyond Their Walls." Fast Company. 2015.
    https://www.fastcompany.com/3044731/the-future-of-museums-is-reaching-way-beyond-their
    -walls
Oakland Museum of California (OMCA): https://museumca.org.

NOTES

1. Randy Kennedy, "Is It Art, Science, or a Test of People?" *New York Times*, Oct. 25, 2011.
2. "Museums around the World in the Face of COVID-19," UNESCO, 2020, https://unesdoc.unesco.org
    /ark:/48223/pf0000373530; Giuliana Bullard, "Government Doubles Official Estimate: There Are
    35,000 Active Museums in the U.S.," Institute of Museum and Library Services, Oct. 13, 2015, https://
    www.imls.gov/news/government-doubles-official-estimate-there-are-35000-active-museums-us.
3. "Museum Facts," American Alliance of Museums, accessed Oct. 31, 2017, http://www.aam-us.org
    /about-museums/museum-facts.
4. Graham Black, *The Engaging Museum: Developing Museums for Visitor Involvement* (Philadelphia: Rout-
    ledge, 2001).
5. Benjamin Freed, "More Than 600,000 People Have Already Visited the Smithsonian's African Amer-
    ican History Museum," *Washingtonian*, Dec. 13, 2016, https://www.washingtonian.com/2016/12/13
    /more-than-600000-people-have-already-visited-the-smithsonians-african-american-history
    -musuem/.
6. Memory Book app, National Museum of African American History and Culture, accessed Mar. 21, 2021,
    https://nmaahc.si.edu/explore/initiatives/memory-book.
7. "1619 Project," *New York Times*, Aug. 14, 2019, https://www.nytimes.com/interactive/2019/08/14
    /magazine/1619-america-slavery.html.
8. "[McKnight] points out their differences: not-for-profit corporations are usually formal and hierarchical,
    whereas associations tend to be informal and horizontal; not-for-profits use the special knowledge of
    professionals and experts to perform their functions, while associations generally use the experience
    and knowledge of member citizens." John L. McKnight, *The Four-Legged Stool* (Kettering Foundation,
    2013).
9. Holland Cotter, "Got an Hour? See the Met These Four Ways," *New York Times*, Dec. 8, 2016, https://
    www.nytimes.com/2016/12/08/arts/design/got-an-hour-see-the-met-these-4-ways.html.
10. B. Joseph Pine II and James Gilmore, "Welcome to the Experience Economy," *Harvard Business Review*,
    Jul. 1, 1998, https://hbr.org/1998/07/welcome-to-the-experience-economy.

2

Shifting to the Visitor's Perspective

Nobody cares how much you know until they know how much you care.

—Theodore Roosevelt

Every day around the world, people make the journey to the front doors of approximately ninety-five thousand museums.[1] Each of those visitors has a unique experience, constructed not just by the museum staff, boards of directors, and volunteers, but by the visitors themselves. Museums serve as an informal means of communication, and communication is key to the relationship between museum and visitor (see figure 2.1).

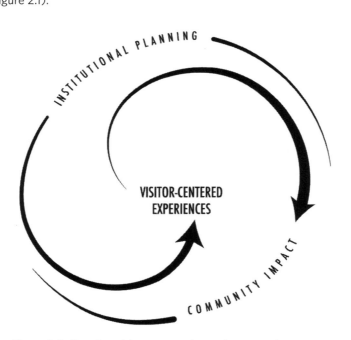

Figure 2.1. Creating visitor-centered experiences cycle.

Several forms contribute to the matrix of communication: museum to visitor, visitor to museum, visitor to visitor, and museum to museum. This is all part of the museum transformative experience (see figure 2.2).

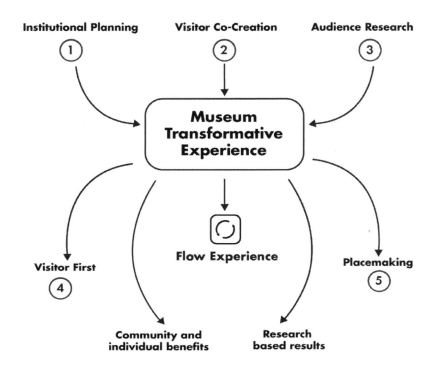

Museum Transformative Experience

Institutional Planning ① **Visitor Co-Creation** ② **Audience Research** ③

Museum Transformative Experience

Flow Experience

Visitor First ④ **Placemaking** ⑤

Community and individual benefits   **Research based results**

---

1 Institutional Planning
Integrated Mission Vision and Values
Part of compassionate society, taking moral leadership

2 Visitor Co-Creation
Community Representation
Museum visitation, staff trustees and volunteers reflect on local and digital communities

3 Audience Research
Audience Segment

4 Visitor First
Use of collection, exhibition and programming to benefit society (civil society)

5 Placemaking
Multiple touch points of civil society, GLAMS (Galleries, Libraries, Archives and Museums) collaborating for the benefit of civil society

Flow Experience
Sense of time altered
Effortless involvement
Sense of control
Concern of self disappears

Figure 2.2. Museum transformative experiences.

In 2009, after completing my work on the expansion of the world's largest children's museum, the Children's Museum of Indianapolis, I took an extended trip. One of the places I visited was Japan, where, after a chaotic week in Tokyo, I decided to travel to Naoshima, an art island off the coast of the small, slow-paced village of Uno.

I'd heard of Naoshima from a photographer friend, but all I really knew was that it was a collection of art installations that encompassed an entire island. To reach Naoshima you have to take a small boat. Free of expectations, I boarded the boat and set off into the unknown. Upon arriving at the island, I received a map of the Benesse Art Site Naoshima with the locations of the Chichu Museum, the Art House Project, and the Benesse (House) Museum. I began my journey by walking through the small fishing community of roughly three thousand inhabitants to the first art house project.

My reaction to the first installation was shock. Here, in the middle of this tiny village, a rustic home had been converted into a contemporary art installation. The juxtaposition of Tatsuo Miyajima's *Sea of Time '98*—a collection of glowing LED numbers "floating" in a reflective pool—and the surrounding two-hundred-year-old traditional fishing hut forced me to change my perception of my surroundings (see figure 2.3).

Figure 2.3. "Sea of Time" by Tatsuo Miyajima. *Everett Kennedy.*

I was fascinated to learn that the inhabitants of Naoshima had assisted with the construction of the art house. The artist was able to convey to the local people the importance of maintaining the traditional exterior to create a vivid contrast with the technology housed in the interior, resulting in an amalgamation that spawned wonder and contemplation.

By the time I arrived at the third art house, I'd gotten the hang of it. I welcomed the surprise of each one and looked forward to the next. There is a walk of about half an hour between each of the art houses. Strolling through the fishing village thinking about the art houses expanded my perceptions. I'd look at random objects along the way and wonder, "Is that an art installation?" The world had become art.

Shifting to the Visitor's Perspective
11

My mind was expanded even further when I arrived at the Chichu Museum, designed by Ando Tadao. The museum includes work by James Turrell and Walter De Maria, and a large Monet *Water Lilies* collection. I'll never forget how the curved walls of the *Water Lilies* gallery transported me. There I was, standing on a Japanese island, by myself, immersed in Monet's ethereal studies of light and color. The paintings are placed adjacent to the Chichu Garden, a replica of Monet's garden in Giverny, which provides amazing context. The juxtaposition of the work of James Turrell, an artist primarily concerned with light and space, and the architecture of Ando Tadao was equally mind-blowing. The brutish concrete structures of Ando Tadao served as a perfect counterpoint to the ethereal, perception-enhancing work of Turrell.

That night I stayed in a traditional guest house in Uno. I don't think I've ever felt so far away from home, both literally and metaphysically. I have always been bothered by art museums that "show" art without an understanding of an artist's perception. At the Benesse Art Site Naoshima, I was seeing the world as an artist. All of my senses were enhanced, and I'd been transported to another world. The combination of the physical journey, the art, and the architecture expanded my expectations of what a museum could be.

I'd often thought of museums as a refuge, but this experience was different. On Naoshima, it would have been much easier to build and set up art inside a traditional modernist building and use buses to transport people from the dock to the museum. Instead, for each visitor the walk through the village becomes a journey of discovery, changing their perceptions even before they arrive at the "front door."

In practice, the entire island becomes an art site. This is an important aspect of placemaking (see chapter 10); although they are not all located on peaceful islands, all museum experiences exist in a particular context. It is important to understand that context and its impression on the visitor before they reach the front door.

Many museums could learn from the Benesse Art Site Naoshima. The island provides a physical perimeter for the art experience and juxtaposes a traditional fishing village with a modernist art museum experience. Most museums consider their perimeter the entrance to the parking lot, but the visitor's journey can and should be expanded much further.

After the visit to Naoshima, I visited the Benesse (House) Museum website[2] to learn more about Tadao Ando, the Art House Projects, and the Chichu Garden. Thus, my journey to Naoshima was composed of a pre-visit experience, an in-person experience, and a post-visit experience. I cannot stress enough the importance of empathy for the visitor's journey from before they enter the front door, throughout the visit, and after the trip home. The value of all three is emphasized throughout this book and described in detail in chapter 8.

WHERE IS THE FRONT DOOR?

The Naoshima experience was an example of transformative museum design. Now let's look at an example from the other end of the spectrum. In 2017, I was teaching a class in the Industrial Design Department at Georgia Tech in Atlanta. I always make a point of visiting area museums, and I decided to start with the Michael C. Carlos Museum at Emory University.

One Sunday afternoon, I drove to the Emory campus and followed the signs to the museum parking lot. However, after I parked the car, I stood looking around for a minute. I didn't know which direction to start walking; no signs indicated the way. Finally, I chose a path at random, but shortly found myself standing in front of the medical school. I stopped a group of students and asked them where the museum was. They pointed to my left and behind me, saying that the paved pathway led to the museum entrance.

The path ended in a T-intersection, with further paths heading to the left and right. In front of me was an industrial-looking building with a dark triangular cutout. I thought, "That can't be the museum," and walked to the right, which led to the side of the building. I was halfway around it when I realized it was indeed the museum building. So I walked back around to the front of the building, which faces the quadrangle. Peering through the door, I finally saw a sign reading "Michael C. Carlos Museum." Without the sign I would not have known this was the museum. The exterior signage is faint and hard to read, especially when the building is in shadow (see figure 2.4).

Figure 2.4. Exterior of the Michael C. Carlos Museum. *Photo by the author.*

I pushed open the door and stepped into a hallway that was empty except for a monitor displaying information about the museum. Assuming that the museum entrance must be straight ahead, I walked about twenty steps down the hallway, where I found a men's room. I decided to go in, because the museum entrance was still nowhere in sight.

Beside the bathroom was an unmarked bronze door similar to the one at the entrance to the building. I walked through it and found myself in a small room. Turning around, I realized there was an elevator behind me. I entered it and looked for something to guide my way, but there were only two buttons, marked "1" and "2." Feeling like a character in a Kafka novel, I pushed button number two. When the elevator doors opened, I again found myself in a small room. After going through a second door, I finally saw an entrance desk to my right in another small dark room, with hallways to the left and right.

The lighting was dim and the ceiling high for such a small room. The dark terrazzo design on the floor did nothing to brighten the space. My first thought was, "They must be closed." Then I wondered if the power was out. I stepped toward the entrance desk, feeling a little exposed in the narrow yet cavernously tall space.

A young woman was seated behind the desk, but the desk was low, and looking down at her made me feel uncomfortable. Sconces to the left and right provided low, eerie illumination that cast shadows across her face.

After I paid the eight-dollar admission fee, she stood up to hand me a ticket and a map. However, the light was so dim by the desk that I had to step to the right to read the map.

The museum's collection is wonderful, and I enjoyed perusing it, but I continued to have difficulty navigating through the space. I found myself shunted disconcertingly this way and that, and was constantly disoriented. The galleries consisted of a series of small, dimly lit rooms, with stairs leading to additional small rooms. At the end of my visit, I counted the doors I had gone through to exit the museum. There were six from the second floor to the lower level, not including the elevator I had taken.

Now, I recognize the postmodern statement of the building, which was designed by Michael Graves. The architecture is playing with the typical classical or modernist architecture and is a critique of the power of "museum." But all of this is lost if I cannot navigate the building. In the end, the building got in the way of my museum experience.

After I left, my feelings about the collection were overshadowed by the feelings of discomfort, confusion, and even mild panic as I tried to navigate the building. Checking online reviews of the museum, I found many comments that echoed my feelings (see table 2.1).

THE IMPORTANCE OF EMPATHY

In 2017, I was hired by the Wow! Children's Museum in Lafayette, Colorado, to facilitate a museum expansion workshop and create initial museum-planning documents. At such workshops I often conduct an exercise: I ask the participants to empathize with a local community member. For this one I created the persona of an eight-year-old Latinx girl. (A significant percentage of the community the museum will serve is Latinx.)

I asked the group to have empathy for the girl, understanding and being sensitive to her feelings, thoughts, and experiences.[3] I invented a name for her—Adrianna—and showed them photos of her and the place where she lived. I told them that she lived with her parents and two older brothers about three miles away. Her parents both worked full-time and made around $40,000 a year. Adrianna, her brothers, and her mother spoke good English; her father only spoke Spanish. I gave each workshop member three Post-it Notes and asked them to write down their ideas about how Adrianna would get to the museum.

After about ten minutes I asked them to put their Post-its up on the wall for the group to review. I separated the notes into groups: "School Group Visit," "Parent Takes Her," and "Community Group."

Table 2.1. Online museum reviews.

The Review Highlight on Trip advisor	**"Great Museum — difficult parking"** They allow non-flash photography, but about half the galleries on the first floor are very dark. In fact, I tripped on the bottom step going to the upper gallery since I couldn't see it! For the size of the museum, the $8 admission is rather steep, so I can only recommend it if you are really into this kind of art. And then there is the parking problem. There is parking behind the museum, but like many major liberal universities, it's not for you, but university staff! There are two garages about a 5-10 minute walk away, but they are very difficult to find and you have to go in the visitor entrance, which is even harder to find than the garage!" (traveler, 2011)
Google Review	"Just when you think the exhibit hall ends there is another hallway of interesting artifacts (yet still a small museum)! A couple of their exhibits are currently under construction, so we were slightly limited in our self-guided tour. I wish there was closer (and free) parking and more staff-guided tours." (Lindsey, 2017)
Foursquare	"Do not bring in a bag, or expect to have to check it. The rooms are small, and make me feel claustrophobic. The exhibits are pretty." (Kat, 2015)
Trip advisor	"Finding this museum is not easy, parking not fun, and having to pay for it even less so. But once you get there [it] is great." (plum9195, 2013)

Then I asked the group to examine the journey that Adrianna would take to the museum's front door. What transportation issues might she face? What financial issues might she face? What cultural issues might she face? By looking at these issues, the group was able to recognize potential obstacles that might prevent certain members of the community from accessing the museum. Once those obstacles were recognized, they could be addressed.

Creating a persona can be tricky. It is important to steer away from stereotypes involving race, culture, gender, and sexual orientation; however, it is equally important to recognize that certain people or communities may have difficulties accessing the museum. For this reason, focus on creating a number of personas, and vet each one for bias.

It's impossible to discuss empathy without discussing bias. Empathy includes exposing biases, both overt and implicit. Having biases is an ingrained human trait that helps us make decisions. The issue is how implicit bias—bias resulting from the tendency to process information based on unconscious associations and feelings, even when they are contrary to your conscious or expressed beliefs[4]—can create a distorted view of cause and effect.

THE EMPATHY MAP

One way to foster empathy in the museum planning process is to create an empathy map. Before creating an empathy map, it is important to have complete information on the user. If they cannot be in the room with you to participate in the process, make sure to have as much information from thorough interviews as possible.

To construct an empathy map, you first need to create a comfortable atmosphere for the group. Allow at least forty minutes for this meeting. Ideally, the users you are mapping will be in the room, or you can do a short presentation about what you learned during your interviews with them. Photos of the users are also good. The empathy map itself can be created in about twenty minutes, but you will need the additional time for the presentation and wrap-up. Framing it as a game will make this process more interesting to participants.

Figure 2.5 presents an empathy map: the series of questions you need to ask yourself about your museums users in creating your own empathy map. The empathy map is designed to start with the observable phenomena of things the user sees, says, does, and hears, and end at the center with what it feels like to actually *be* them. Start from Who at the top left and work clockwise:

- *Who* are you empathizing with? Identify the user segment, such as a potential corporate sponsor.
- What does the user *think*? What might be on their mind that they are not yet ready to share or do not feel is important?
- What does the user *feel*? Their feelings can be divided into pains and gains.
  - Pains could be other uses for the funds.
  - Gains could be increased visibility and enhanced company reputation.
- What does the user need to *do*? The goal for this user segment might be to give a large donation to the museum.
- What do users *say*? They may ask how the contribution might benefit their company or how the museum's objectives relate to their own.

This discussion describes the creation of a single empathy map, but it is helpful to have a general idea of visitor segments before starting the process. For instance, you might say, "We are going to create empathy maps for five types of visitors: child, teenager, twenty-something, thirty-something, and retiree." In this scenario I find it best to break the session into parts—the group can create two empathy maps before lunch and the rest after lunch. If there are enough participants, you can even create separate groups, with each one working on a single empathy map, and then combine them.

An important aspect of employing empathy maps and creating personas is identifying "real people." Those involved in the museum planning process need to go out and interview community members face to face, at their homes if possible, to identify context, which is an important aspect of empathy.

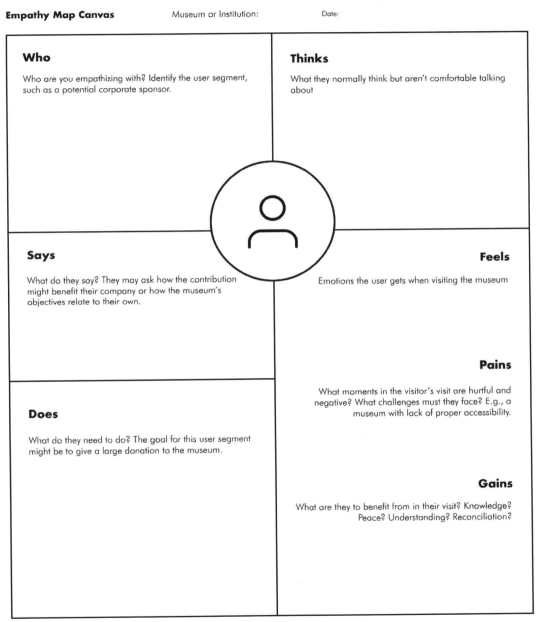

Empathy Map Canvas   Museum or Institution: Date:

Who

Who are you empathizing with? Identify the user segment, such as a potential corporate sponsor.

Thinks

What they normally think but aren't comfortable talking about

Says

What do they say? They may ask how the contribution might benefit their company or how the museum's objectives relate to their own.

Feels

Emotions the user gets when visiting the museum

Pains

What moments in the visitor's visit are hurtful and negative? What challenges must they face? E.g., a museum with lack of proper accessibility.

Does

What do they need to do? The goal for this user segment might be to give a large donation to the museum.

Gains

What are they to benefit from in their visit? Knowledge? Peace? Understanding? Reconciliation?

Figure 2.5. Empathy map canvas, adapted from "Updated Empathy Map Canvas" by Dave Gray, https://medium.com/the-xplane-collection/updated-empathy-map-canvas-46df22df3c8a.

Creating personas like Adrianna and utilizing empathy maps can take our own biases out of the creation process. I recommend two useful interview tools:

1. Half-listening. This involves listening for the reasons behind people's decisions when interviewing them. Are emotions involved in their decision-making process? What are those emotions, and what experiences caused them? If participants have questions or concerns about this process, I refer them to Project Implicit, a Harvard research project about social attitudes regarding race, gender, and sexual orientation.[5]
2. Ethnographic research. This type of research involves acquisition of in-person data during the interview process, such as zip code, brands worn, house value, amount of debt, and schools attended. Use any quantitative data you can gather to understand *how* and *why* decisions are made.

Some people might say empathy is too "touchy-feely," but this is exactly how you impact communities (and individuals) and build diverse audiences, which in turn creates museums as community resources. Individuals impact the community, the community changes, and the museum iterates to meet its changing needs.[6] See the online Museum Toolbox for additional examples.

CONCLUSION

Shifting to the museum visitor's perspective involves communication—museum to visitor, visitor to museum, visitor to visitor, and museum to museum—and increased appreciation of that perspective by museum staff through thoughtful exhibit design. Museum design should take into consideration not just the experience within the exhibits but the journey to the museum and the online aspects of the museum experience. Empathy, which is the ability to put yourself in someone else's shoes, also plays an important part in enhancing the museum visitor experience. The next chapter covers another shift, from museum objects to the narrative created by their impact on museum visitors.

NEXT STEPS

Make plans to visit a museum you have never visited. Decide on the day you will visit and perform the following steps:

1. Visit the museum website. How many clicks does it take to find the address? The hours of operation? The admission price?
2. Visit the museum's social media pages. Does the design and voice of the social media presence match the website design and voice?
3. Visit the museum. Pay attention to the signage directing you to the museum. Be aware of your feelings as you find and enter the museum. Write down, step by step, the process of reaching the front desk, including your feelings along the route. After your visit, evaluate your experience. List three exhibits or artifacts and explain how they impacted you. Describe how the museum surroundings affected your experience.

KEY CONCEPTS INTRODUCED IN THIS CHAPTER THAT ARE DEFINED IN THE GLOSSARY

empathy
empathy map
ethnographic research
half-listening
implicit bias

ADDITIONAL RESOURCES

Benesse Art Site Naoshima: https://benesse-artsite.jp.

Children's Museum of Indianapolis: https://www.childrensmuseum.org/.

Gray, Dave. *Gamestorming: A Playbook for Innovators, Rulebreakers, and Changemakers*. Sebastopol, CA: O'Reilly Media, 2010.

Michael C. Carlos Museum: https://carlos.emory.edu.

Wow! Children's Museum: https://wowchildrensmuseum.org.

NOTES

1. "Museums around the World in the Face of COVID-19," UNESCO, 2020, https://unesdoc.unesco.org/ark:/48223/pf0000373530.
2. "History of Benesse Art Site Naoshima | Benesse Art Site Naoshima," Benesse Art Site Naoshima, accessed Nov. 13, 2017, http://benesse-artsite.jp/en/about/history.html.
3. See https://www.merriam-webster.com/dictionary/empathy.
4. See https://www.dictionary.com/browse/implicit-bias.
5. "Project Implicit," Harvard University, accessed Feb. 24, 2021, https://implicit.harvard.edu/implicit/.
6. Gary Campbell and Laurajane Smith, "Fostering Empathy through Museums," *Museum Management and Curatorship* 32, no. 3 (2017): 298–300, https://doi.org/10.1080/09647775.2017.1326450.

3

From Object to Narrative

> The museum of the future is generous. . . . It nurtures the transformative possibilities inherent in the contact between artwork, audience, museum and society. . . . A polyphony of voices, actions and possible encounters, the museum of the future is a power that can change the world.
>
> —Olafur Eliasson, artist[1]

In 2014, the Institute of Museum and Library Services (IMLS) estimated that there were 35,144 active museums in the United States.[2] This number, more than double their previous working estimate, included museums in a wide variety of disciplines, such as botanical gardens, technology centers, zoos, and wildlife conservation centers. The largest categories were historical sites and preservation societies, which together accounted for nearly half of all museums.

For Susan H. Hildreth, former director of the IMLS, the burgeoning number of museums is a clear sign of how important museums are for culture and education. In her view, they serve as "places where Americans go to pursue the discovery of art, history, science, technology, and the natural world."[3] While her sentiment is certainly accurate, it cannot be denied that the role of the museum is changing with changes in society. So why has the attendance rate dropped in recent years? Are there other roles that museums are supposed to be filling in today's society?

DECLINING MUSEUM ATTENDANCE

While museums are still important as cultural and educational hubs, the number of visitors has been dropping steadily for a number of years. In 2017, the *Guardian* analyzed the situation in the United Kingdom, pointing out that one of the most important reasons for the decreases in attendance at museums such as the Tate Gallery and the British Museum is economic strife. Author Jonathan Jones suggests that visits to museums and art galleries are expressions of hope and self-esteem, and thus the decline can be viewed as a sign of despair. He concludes that it is not the internet or a lack of interest that is drawing youth away from this cultural context, but a general lack of public funding that limits free public museums and galleries, and makes it more difficult for the middle class to enjoy a museum visit.[4]

Visitation in the United States shows a similar decline, but the reasons for the drop in attendance are more complicated than one might expect. A 2018 study by the National Endowment for the Arts suggested that, taking into account the rise in population between 2002 and 2015, US museum visitors declined by around 20 percent.[5] The study also showed declining attendance at arts activities, including jazz events, classical music performances, opera, plays, ballet, and art museums or galleries. The percentage of US adults who had attended one of these activities in the past year dropped from 39 percent in 1982 to 33 percent in 2012.[6]

The numbers look slightly different when comparing museums of art and other types. The 20 percent decline is true for art museums, but it does not fully hold for history museums and other history-related institutions nationwide. A study by Edge Research, which examined 507 institutions on behalf of the National Trust for Historic Preservation, showed that 62 percent had seen an increase in visitors in the last five years, and 24 percent reported no change. More recently, 42 percent saw an increase in attendance and 45 percent reported no change. While these numbers paint a more optimistic picture of the future, note that they only cover attendance at historic sites; the numbers for larger traditional museums are unclear. However, the author of the study indicated that total attendance at all types of museums is not keeping up with the rising population of the United States. In that sense, the attendance rate is dropping at around 5 percent annually.[7]

While education and family income affect attendance, the numbers do not seem to correlate with a decline in the middle class or any changes in education. It seems that museums are losing their relevance in today's world, so worries about how they should engage with the public remain.

WHAT NEEDS TO CHANGE?

One reason traditional museums might be losing popularity has to do with the changing needs and expectations of the public, specifically regarding topics that once existed exclusively in the museum realm. For example, there has been a change in what is considered a "cultural activity," even among those who attend museums and art exhibitions. *Culture Track '17*, a report by cultural innovation engine Culture Track, reported that more than one-third of museumgoers and more than half of theatergoers do not consider museums a cultural experience. Interestingly, the report states that "audiences were more likely to consider a street fair or food and drink experience culture than an opera or ballet."[8]

The study indicates that, although their perceptions of cultural experiences may have changed, most people have an intuitive understanding of culture. Respondents understood cultural activities to be those that "transform perspective," making us think and challenge accepted norms; "build community" by bringing people closer, especially those who might not have that much in common; "educate the public" by broadening horizons; and "foster empathy" by bringing together people of different backgrounds, showing that diversity has a value of its own. All of these are valid views of culture. The question becomes whether traditional museums are equipped to provide their visitors with the cultural experience they want.

The study found that the main motivation driving people to cultural activities is "fun." There are, of course, many types of fun, but this response indicates that museums, art galleries, and similar institutions must compete with other types of enjoyable activity, such as that offered by the entertainment industry: movies, escape rooms, waterparks, and so on. In a world where people have such easy access to all sorts of entertainment, museums must take this response seriously and better understand their market and competitors.

CURATING EXPERIENCES, NOT JUST OBJECTS

The traditional museum model has tended to be inward-looking, with curators and directors deciding what they want to work on, raising money for it, and then putting on an exhibition. More financially viable institutions are currently thinking in terms of customer service and personalized experiences, similar to the experience of walking into your local café and being greeted by name. Another analogy is museums as libraries—gathering spots where people visit regularly, not just for special events: "Go for the yoga, stay for the exhibit." Let's compare two museum experiences, both in Mexico City.

Museo Jumex

My wife and I recently visited the Museo Jumex in Mexico City. In the four years we have lived there, Mexico City has seen an explosion of new and renovated museums, including the excellent Museo Tamayo and Museo Soumaya, reflecting the hunger of the city's rapidly expanding middle class to understand the world. Our visit to the museum, located in the Nuevo Polanco shopping district, began at eleven a.m. on a Sunday morning. We made our way to the third (top) floor, where we found a large text panel titled "A Place in Two Dimensions: A Selection from the Colección Jumex + Fred Sandback," curated by Patrick Charpenel. The panel described the intentions of the exhibit, which were to establish that more than one perception or reality can exist in the same place at the same time. My wife and I were intrigued.

We entered the gallery to the sound of five women in their thirties with shopping bags on their arms talking loudly and taking photos of one another. Because the women were literally shrieking with excitement, my first instinct was to go over to them and discuss a "museum-level of speaking," but it seemed pointless. They were probably in the area to shop and had a completely different mindset when they entered the museum. Unfortunately, their presence obscured the art behind them—works by Carl Andre, Ellsworth Kelley, and Jeff Koons—creating a negative first impression of the exhibition.

We rounded the corner to find a piece by American artist Richard Artschwager, a favorite of mine. Though I liked the piece, I suddenly felt lost. I tried to think back to the text panel, but I was unable to draw a connection between one gallery and the next, and I couldn't figure out how they were tied to the space. I stood back and tried to make sense of what I was looking at: works by many different artists from different periods were hung next to one another, but there was no harmony or even fruitful discord that might spark conversation; it was just chaos.

My puzzlement increased when I saw *Spring of Wood*, a small, delicate sculpture created in 2001 by Yoshiro Suda. This piece was featured on posters above the lobby entry desk, in the museum's shop window, and on the gallery level. If it was so important, why was there no interpretation, and why was it installed on the floor and hung below and in line with the thermostat, fire-alarm pull box, and video camera hanging on the wall (see figure 3.1)? I watched as visitor after visitor approached the piece, unsure of where to look, until they finally pointed to the floor. It seemed unfair to both viewer and artist to place such an important piece in a cluttered corner.

Hoping for clarity, we went to the front desk and asked for a list of the pieces on display, but were told that they only had one copy. We could look at the list but couldn't take it with us. After wandering around the haphazard collection for an hour or so, we left exhausted and confused.

The artwork displayed in any museum requires context; artists build upon their predecessors. If the public is not made aware of this history, the museum experience turns into something akin to a shopping expedition, with visitors taking away only the most superficial impression. The United States has the luxury of a long history of modern art experiences, and Mexico City has several wonderful museums with impressive interpretations and critical approaches to curation. This approach was lacking in Museo Jumex.

A museum experience shouldn't reflect the eclectic whims of those who purchased the art, but should be evocative of the careful thought and planning that goes into creating an exhibition and the inevitable history that exists within each piece. Because all artwork belongs to a continuum of art history, the art requires available educators and on-floor interpretation. The best art collections communicate a greater sum than their parts, sharing a message that is not apparent in the individual art

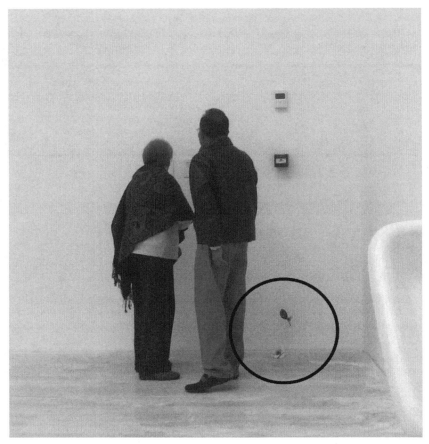

Figure 3.1. "Spring of Wood" by Yoshihiro Suda at Museo Jumex. *Photo by the author.*

pieces. I was not able to connect with the message of "a place in two dimensions" as I walked through the Museo Jumex collection.

In addition, museums in developing countries such as Mexico carry a greater responsibility to educate the public on the importance of museums as a touchstone to civil society and culture. Mexico has a rich and diverse history of contemporary art, none of which was made clear at this Museo Jumex exhibition.

Museo Nacional de las Intervenciones

The eighty-year-old religiously conservative father of a Mexican friend suggested I visit the Museo Nacional de las Intervenciones. A former Aztec site, it was deconstructed and reconstructed as a monastery, then turned into a fort, and finally into a museum. What I love about the museum is the way it cradles all its layers and uses modern technology to tease out meanings. By incorporating the history of Aztec, Spanish, French, and US interventions, as well as the more recent return to Mexican ownership, the museum helps visitors understand how the sense of self is created.

As you approach the entrance, you see the walls of what had been the fortress. The ancient, pitted walls are part of the experience, and form a lovely tactile contrast with the polished modern entrance.

As you cross the threshold into the museum, you enter another world; there are gardens to your right and a terrace to your left. A long walkway brings you to the entrance of what had been the monastery.

Visitors are shown the museum's overall messaging through a deftly designed map of the museum and the gallery content. The galleries are aligned in roughly chronological order, showing the different nations that colonized Mexico, the Mexican response to that colonization, and the effects on Mexican identity. The museum presentation uses touchscreens, pushbuttons, text panels, art, and artifacts to present that content (see figure 3.2). One outstanding aspect of the design is that you can walk into and out of the content; if the content becomes too "heavy," you can sit down and just look at a painting or the garden. After you have had time to relax and gather your thoughts, you can get up and move back into the weightier content.

I believe that museums are not neutral; they have a point of view. When I visit the Museo Nacional de las Intervenciones, the museum's view of the world agrees with my view of self and my persona. A museum constructs points of view to support the organizational culture and the individuals of the culture. However, I have found that this museum also aligns with the personas of many Mexicans I have talked to. It is enjoyed by all ages. Comparing my experiences at the Museo Jumex and the Museo Nacional de las Intervenciones, I realize that they are both attempting to hold and make sense of disparate elements. However, the faulty design at the Museo Jumex exhibition led to a sensation of chaos and unease; the carefully crafted visitor experience at the Museo Nacional de las Intervenciones led to participation and deeper understanding. In fact, the latter fulfilled the mandate the former was striving for, showing that more than one perception or reality can exist in the same place at the same time.

Figure 3.2. Evocative spaces in the Museo Nacional de las Intervenciones. *Photo by the author.*

MUSEUM REINVENTION TO BECOME VISITOR CENTERED

There is often a faulty assumption that museums are about objects. Museums protect the objects in their care; they research and store objects in their care, and display and interpret those objects. However, the objects should never be the focus. Museums should be about people; in fact, I might go so far as to say museums should be about *changing* people and communities. The people who work at the museum, the people who visit the museum, the people of the community where the museum is located, the history of the people at the location, and the context of the community are all central to any reinvention of a museum.

THE SANTA CRUZ MUSEUM OF ART AND HISTORY

When I think about museums that have reinvented themselves, the Santa Cruz Museum of Art and History (MAH) comes to mind.[9] As I often say to clients, it is not the museum building, and it is not the project budget; it is the institutional culture that is the most difficult to create. The transformation Nina Simon fostered at the Santa Cruz Museum of Art and History is an example of the necessary institutional culture required to bring about museum reinvention to become visitor centered.

I have known Nina Simon since her work at the Tech Museum in San Jose and her work with the *Museum 2.0* blog. In my mind, it is not possible to separate the reinvention of the Santa Cruz Museum of Art and History and Nina Simon. In all of Nina's work, it is not about the building, or even about the exhibits; it is about methodology, outlook, voice, and institutional culture. Nina Simon's work with the *Museum 2.0* blog became a sketchbook for her to think about museums' participatory nature.

Nina's methodology is consistent with design thinking and customer experience, starting with brainstorming, moving to an atmosphere of sharing ideas without judgment, allowing and encouraging response and interaction of the ideas, and then iterating, testing, and prototyping those ideas. Central to the process was community involvement and feedback, creating environments of sharing without judgment; creating environments that allowed failure and personal and community growth.

At the Santa Cruz Museum of Art and History, it was not the architecture of the museum or branding (logo, graphic design, museum name changes) that brought about the shift to the visitor-centered approach; it was the dedicated museum staff. Nina helped craft the nimble, supportive institutional culture required to be visitor centered and bring about community change. Too often, museums spend enormous sums on architecture, exhibitions, and rebranding. However, those funds can often be more effectively used in creating visitor-centered and community-centered experiences.

THE VISITOR-CENTRIC EXPERIENCE

Like the Santa Cruz Museum of Art and History, over the last decade a number of other museums have begun to concentrate on a more visitor-centric museum experience. In *Creating the Visitor-Centered Museum* by Peter Samis and Mimi Michaelson, the visitor-centered approach is defined as "making museum collections and programs accessible and relevant to new and existing audiences, regardless of visitor age or background, and whether novice, experienced, or expert." The transformation to a visitor-centered museum connects objects to the audience, promoting "immersion, cognitive impact, inclusivity, and social relevance" and offering more active participation to a new, modern audience. On a macro level, these institutions all share a number of themes: formative visitor research, multiple in-gallery interpretation methods, connection with the community, a visitor-centered mission, firm leadership with buy-in, and new types of teamwork. The authors note that "these institutions success-fully combine visitor evaluation and interpretive approaches to encourage connection with objects and stories, a sense of play, and deep conversation within the galleries."[10]

Shifting to a visitor-centered approach involves digital experiences as well. Individual digital channels such as an app or a new webpage are not enough. As Samis and Michaelson note, "the most successful digital initiatives are those that make sense in the real-world journey and experience your visitor is already taking, and fit seamlessly with that experience."[11] With this omni-channel approach, visitors get the experiences they need outside any specific time, place, digital channel, or device. All changes made to the visitor's journey should seem like a single experience, providing content that makes the most sense at that particular time and place. The context dictates the information that is needed, so not all of it should be presented all the time.

The COVID-19 pandemic has forced businesses across the world to embrace digital technology. Museums are no exception, and find themselves having to leapfrog toward a digital future.[12] For example, the Morgan Library in New York City had planned to display their extensive collection of Giovanni

Battista Piranesi drawings in May 2020. Then the pandemic hit, and a traditional in-person exhibition was no longer an option. Quickly recalibrating, the museum hosted an online walkthrough of their collection. John Marciari, head of the library's Department of Drawings, showed images of the drawings and discussed Piranesi's innovations and contributions to architecture. The sold-out hour-long talk was followed by a lively discussion among participants, who joined from far-flung geographical locations.[13] The expertise and technical apparatus necessary to offer such presentations will leave museums with tools to expand their reach long after the pandemic is over.

The American Museum of Natural History (AMNH) is another institution that is taking steps to extend the experience to "reach beyond their walls." The AMNH already has an amazing social media presence, but they have now started to offer educational programs as well. Over a hundred thousand people have enrolled in their online courses. One segment of the target audience is teachers, who will hopefully extend the AMNH's message regarding science, history, and environmental problems to their students. The AMNH is also one of the first museums in the United States to offer its own PhD program, and is currently developing an MA module. This educational approach is augmented by seminars offered to the general public, which can even incorporate a cocktail party or some other social activity. AMNH also offers mobile apps, some of which are described in chapter 13.

Many visitors appreciate the advantages of an analog approach, especially with cultural activities. The main reasons for this are that they feel more authentic, focus more on relevant activities, simplify the approach, and provide a better connection to the content. On the other hand, the primary appeals of digital are access to more detailed information, shareability of the activity, a deeper understanding of the content, and freedom from geographical shackles.

When describing new trends and digital changes, it is important to note that today's museum visitor experience does not start and stop at the museum, but extends from pre-visit to post-visit. The visitor's journey is the entire process of planning, visiting, and later sharing their experiences as photos or discussions at home. We will take a closer look at the visitor's journey in chapter 8.

CONCLUSION

In 2017, the American Alliance of Museums (AAM) projected how museums will look in the year 2040.[14] They predict that there will be a significant demographic shift: there will be as many seniors over the age of sixty-five as children under the age of eighteen. They speculate that there will be more than two thousand "museum schools" for more than half a million students in the United States alone. The AAM predicts that museums will operate as well-being and cognitive centers as well as guardians of history and educational institutions.

The museum of the future is envisioned as closely connected to the community. Rather than a separate, closed-off entity, it will be more akin to a community center, or an extension of today's public spaces and parks. It is also predicted to become an important place for socialization. This role will become increasingly important as people have more free time due to technological and societal advances and a rise in part-time work. Museums will receive visitors coming there to work, study, and teach. AAM's picture of the future museum also includes an increased role in education, presuming a continuing decline in conventional education. With this picture in mind, it is clear that museums must shift from the objects they curate to the experiences of their visitors.

NEXT STEPS

Think of your favorite "traditional" museum. What would be the challenges to adapting a visitor-centric approach? What would be the benefits?

KEY CONCEPT INTRODUCED IN THIS CHAPTER THAT ARE DEFINED IN THE GLOSSARY

visitor-centered approach

ADDITIONAL RESOURCES

American Alliance of Museums: https://aam-us.org.
American Museum of Natural History: https://amnh.org.
Culture Track '17: https://2017study.culturetrack.com/home.
Institute of Museum and Library Services (IMLS): https://imls.gov.
Museum of Modern Art PS1: https://www.moma.org/ps1.
Museo Jumex: https://www.fundacionjumex.org.
Museo Soumaya: www.museosoumaya.org.
Museo Tamayo: https://www.museotamayo.org.
National Trust for Historic Preservation: https://savingplaces.org.

NOTES

1. Chris Dercon, "What Is the Museum of the Future?" Tate Museum, 2015, https://www.tate.org.uk/tate -etc/issue-35-autumn-2015/what-museum-future.
2. Giuliana Bullard, "Government Doubles Official Estimate: There Are 35,000 Active Museums in the U.S.," Institute of Museum Library Services, May 19, 2014, https://www.imls.gov/news/government -doubles-official-estimate-there-are-35000-active-museums-us.
3. Ibid.
4. Jonathan Jones, "The Drop in Museum Visitors Reveals a Nation without Aspiration or Hope," *The Guardian*, Feb. 2, 2017, https://www.theguardian.com/artanddesign/jonathanjonesblog/2017/feb/02/ all.
5. Seph Rodney, "Is Art Museum Attendance Declining Across the U.S.?" *Hyperallergic*, Jan. 18, 2018, https://hyperallergic.com/421968/is-art-museum-attendance-declining-across-the-us/; Bohne Silber and Tim Triplett, "A Decade of Arts Engagement: Findings from the Survey of Public Participation in the Arts, 2002–2012," National Endowment for the Arts, Jan. 2015, https://www.arts.gov/sites/default /files/2012-sppa-feb2015.pdf.
6. Silber and Triplett, "Decade of Arts Engagement."
7. National Trust for Historic Preservation, "Reclaiming the Past in Bricks and Mortar: New Study Reveals Millennials' Desire to Connect with Historic Places," Saving Places, 2017, https://savingplaces.org /press-center/media-resources/new-study-reveals-millennials-desire-to-connect-with-historic -places#.Xc2bVldKhPY.
8. *Culture Track '17*, Culture Track, 2017, https://2017study.culturetrack.com/.
9. The Santa Cruz Museum of Art and History, https://www.santacruzmah.org/.
10. Peter Samis and Mimi Michaelson, *Creating the Visitor-Centered Museum* (Milton Park: Routledge, 2016).
11. Ibid.
12. Daniel Grant, "Pandemic Pushes Museums Deeper into Digital Age," *Wall Street Journal*, Jul. 31, 2020, https://www.wsj.com/articles/pandemic-pushes-museums-further-into-digital-age-11596196801.
13. "Sublime Ideas: Drawings by Giovanni Battista Piranesi," Morgan Library and Museum, Jun. 24, 2020, https://www.themorgan.org/programs/sublime-ideas-drawings-giovanni-battista-piranesi.
14. "Introducing Museum 2040," Center for the Future of Museums blog, American Alliance of Museums, Oct. 31, 2017, https://www.aam-us.org/2017/10/31/introducing-museum-2040/.

Part II

The Museum Visitor (Who)

4

Personas, Diversity, and Possibilities for Behavioral Change

curate (noun): Spiritual charge; care of soul; the office of a parish priest or of a curate.

cure (noun): Act of healing or state of being healed; restoration to health from disease, or to soundness after injury. From Middle English *cure*, from Old French *cure* ("care, cure, healing, cure of souls"), from Latin *cura* ("care, medical attendance, cure").[1]

In the past decade or two, museums have shifted from their original conception as libraries of artifacts to multicultural institutions that can provide transformative experiences to individuals and communities. They now operate both online and in person, making emotional connections with visitors through an empathetic understanding of visitors and communities. The relationship between museum and visitor is a dialogue that has existed for centuries (see table 4.1). Visitors enter the museum (the "place of the muses")[2] for entertainment, relaxation, inspiration, or an answer to a question. As curator, the museum's role is to educate, inspire, provide enjoyment, and perhaps change hearts and minds.

Ideally, a museum and its visitors work together to create a community of curation. The museum serves both civil and civic roles; as a place of cocreation, the museum exists to inspire, entertain, and educate visitors. The visitor also has civil and civic responsibilities that in turn affect the community (the local context of the museum). The museum has a responsibility to the visitor and the community, as well as the larger society.

Similar to the Massive Open Online Courses (MOOCs) now being offered by colleges and universities, museums are moving toward democratized content that is available and searchable online. They are in the process of becoming part of the semantic web,[3] with content that exists both in person and online. The important distinction here is using the term *content* instead of *documents* to stress relevance to the visitor. The new "semantic museum" combines artificial intelligence and machine learning with traditional offerings to change the role of museum from data warehouses of raw material to continually updated content that is relevant to visitors' lives. For more on the progression of museums through various generations, from collections of objects to semantic museums, see table 4.2.

Table 4.1. Museum Historical Timeline

530BCE	Ennigaldi-Nanna's museum, located in present-day Iraq, is the first museum known to historians.
323–246 BCE	The Mouseion in Alexandria, Egypt, is part of the Library of Alexandria.
1464	Stacks of the library at the Church of All Hallowen in Bristol, England, are open to the public.
1471	The Capitoline Museum in Rome, Italy, can be traced to 1471, when Pope Sixtus IV donated a collection of ancient bronzes to the people of Rome.
1506	The Vatican Museum in Rome traces its origins to the public display of the sculptural collection by Pope Julius II.
1543	The first physic garden (botanical garden) was the garden of the University of Pisa, created by Luca Ghini.
1568	The Botanical Garden of the University of Bologna was founded on the initiative of Ulisse Aldrovandi (1522–1605). It is considered the first natural history museum.
1576	First record of a Kunstkammer, the cabinet of curiosity of Rudolf II, Holy Roman Emperor (ruled 1576–1612), housed in the Hradschin in Prague.
1635	Jardin royal des plantes médicinales (Royal Medicinal Plant Garden), created by King Louis XIII in 1635. It later became the National Museum of Natural History (France) in 1793.
1660	The Royal Armouries in the Tower of London is the oldest museum in the United Kingdom. It opened to the public in 1660, though privileged visitors had been admitted since 1592.
1662	Georgius Everhardus Rumphius created a botanical garden on Ambon Island, holding more than 2,000 plants.
1671	The city of Basel purchased the Amerbach Kabinett, a private collection, in 1661, and opened Kunstmuseum Basel to the public in 1671, making it the first municipal museum.
1683	The Ashmolean Museum opens in Oxford, England, and is the first natural history museum to grant admission to the general public.
1734	The Capitoline Museum in Rome becomes the first public museum.
1752	Tiergarten Schönbrunn in Vienna, Austria, is the first zoo.
1753	The British Museum in London was founded in 1753 and opened to the public in 1759. Sir Hans Sloane's personal collection of curios provided the initial foundation for the British Museum's collection.
1764	The Hermitage Museum in St. Petersburg, Russia, was founded by Catherine the Great and has been open to the public since 1852.
1773	The Charleston Museum in South Carolina was established in 1773, making it the first American museum. It did not open to the public until 1824.
1793	The Louvre Museum in Paris, France, a former royal palace, opens to the public.

Table 4.1. *(continued)*

1805	Charles Willson Peale formed the Philadelphia Museum and School, the oldest museum and school in the United States. Later renamed the Pennsylvania Academy of Fine Art.
1846	Founding of the Smithsonian Institution, the world's largest museum complex, with nineteen museums and a collection of 137 million objects.
1888	Urania, a scientific society, is founded in Berlin in 1888. Its aim is to communicate the most recent scientific findings to the broader public. It is considered the precursor of today's science centers.
1899	Opening of the Brooklyn Children's Museum, the world's first children's museum.
1906	American Association of Museums formed. It was renamed the American Alliance of Museums in 2012.
1916	Association of Art Museum Directors formed.
1919	The British Museum forms the Department of Scientific and Industrial Research to study the causes of deterioration to art and to suggest appropriate remedies.
1924	American Association of Zoological Parks and Aquariums formed, which later becomes the Association of Zoos and Aquariums (AZA).
1940	American Association of Botanical Gardens and Arboreta formed, which later becomes the American Public Gardens Association.
1942	United Nations Educational, Scientific and Cultural Organization (UNESCO) formed.
1946	International Council of Museums formed.
1959	The Science and Technology Education Innovation Center opens in St. Petersburg, Florida. It is considered the first science center in the United States.
1962	The American Association of Youth Museums formed. It later becomes the Association of Children's Museums (ACM).
1969	The Exploratorium opens San Francisco, CA.
1973	Association of Science-Technology Centers (ASTC) formed.
1982	Epcot opens at Lake Buena Vista, Florida.
1987	"Body Works" opens at the Pacific Science Center. Visitors enter their information and the exhibits are "customized" to their needs. The exhibition gathers data of the current participants.
1989	First meeting of the European Network of Science Centers and Museums.
1989	Bill Gates forms Corbis, purchasing digital rights to art with the goal of providing in-home digital art.
1993	Museum of Computer Art (MOCA) founded.
1995	The website of the Museum of the History of Science in Oxford goes online, becoming one of the first online museum exhibitions.

(continued)

Table 4.1. *(continued)*

1996	Institute of Museum and Library Services formed.
2001	Wikipedia goes online.
2005	First use of the term "crowdsourcing," by Jeff Howe and Mark Robinson.
2011	Google Art Project goes online with images of artworks from galleries worldwide, and virtual tours of the galleries in which they are housed.
2014	The 9/11 Museum's "Timescapes" is an early example of a semantic museum. The exhibit uses an algorithm to update the historical content.
2016	The History Museum of Petrozavodsk in Russia is a sematic museum prototype, combining smart building technologies, the sematic web, and the Internet of Things.
2020	COVID-19 forces museum closures and a surge of online museum events and online museum programming, including non-fungible token (NFT) artwork.

Table 4.2.   Museum Generations

Museum 1.0 (530 BCE–1899) A collection of objects on display for study by scholars and the wealthy. Museums did not become public institutions until 1660.

Museum 2.0 (1899–1908) In 1899, the Brooklyn Children's Museum's "Interactive Museum" opens with a "teaching collection" of art and objects for handling by children. In 1908, Deutsches Museum visitors are encouraged to manipulate "interactive" exhibits.

Museum 3.0 (1969–1987) This "open-ended" era began in 1969 with the opening of the Exploratorium, which featured multilayered and inquiry-based exhibits.

Museum 4.0 (1987–present) The "semantic museum" was inaugurated in 1987 by the Pacific Science Center's "Body Works" exhibit, in which visitors entered their information and the exhibits were customized to their needs. Semantic exhibits gather data about the current participants.

A prototype of the semantic museum was created at the History Museum of Petrozavodsk State University,[4] combining the Internet of Things, smart building technologies, and the semantic web. The prototype made the smart building technology of the museum building an active participant in the visitor's experience, allowing the museum's collection to be personalized across in-person and online experiences. Recently, many institutions have started publishing their collections as linked data. Examples include the Rijksmuseum in Amsterdam, the German National Library, and the Getty Institute, which publishes many vocabularies and datasets.[5]

Museums have progressed from private institutions containing scholarly works to the democratization of museum content relevant to the lives of visitors, the community, and the larger society. Heterogeneous cultural-heritage information links video material, photographs, newspaper articles, and museum objects through shared vocabularies and authority files. For example, the Linked Jazz project associated with the Semantic Lab at the Pratt Institute aims to gather and make sense of the relationships among jazz musicians. The project uses audiovisual presentations, visual networking, and other tools to present an enormous amount of data on early jazz musicians and their connections with each other. The result is a searchable database accessible to anyone with an internet connection. It has proven useful to scholars of jazz music and jazz practitioners, as well as interested jazz aficionados.

PERSONAS

One of the most valuable tools in helping you walk in the visitor's shoes is the *persona*, or representative user. We have already looked at the persona of Adrianna, presented in chapter 2. Before you start developing personas, you should complete the Empathy Map (see figure 2.5). Once you have reviewed and gained an understanding of its findings, you can move on to creating a persona for each of your visitor segments. In creating a persona, the most important data to collect is an understanding of *why* the user makes decisions. You need to understand both the qualitative data and the user's feelings in order to create behavioral change.

I often ask workshop or class participants to help me put together personas. We create a page for each one using large posterboards, writing down age, gender, and description. I also ask the group to name each persona using a common local name, which creates greater empathy with the user than referring to them as something like "retired sixty-seven-year-old male." Participants begin to identify with each persona, thinking, "Do I know anybody like this?" This type of empathy is what you are seeking to achieve. Next, I ask the participants to look for a photo of each persona and start to refer to them by name. If a persona is accurate, it can take on a life of its own, and may even begin to be referred to as an identified user group. Two years ago, I did this exercise with a museum group, and to this day they still refer to their personas by name.

When I conduct this exercise with students, I pause at this point and ask the students to go out on campus and look for people who resemble each persona. We talk to them and, after asking permission, take their photo. This part of the exercise always results in more accurate understanding of the user, and students love it! However, the exercise can be humbling because it often reveals that assumptions about people are incorrect. After we return to the classroom, I split the students into groups, assigning one persona to each group and telling them to make changes to it by using the photo of, and information from, the person they selected. A three-hour studio class is plenty of time for the class to create, interview, and revise their personas, and the revisions are usually quite extensive.

The persona shown in figure 4.1 was created as part of strategic planning work for the Discovery Center at Murfree Spring.[6] The project objectives were (1) to create linkages between the Discovery Center and the adjacent Murfree Spring wetlands through the design of an underutilized outdoor exhibition area and (2) to encourage greater visitor diversity. We started our work by understanding the area demographics; at 72 percent White and 18 percent Black or African American,[7] the current museum visitorship was not representative of the area demographics.

Angela Tyson

Age	34
Occupation	Working Mom
Status	Married
Location	Murfreesboro, TN
Tier	Activist
Archetype	Caregiver

Friendly   Clever   Go-Getter

"I feel the Discovery Center has opened up to people from our Community, but for the most part I still only see white folk."

Interests

Music   Football

Celebrities   Swimming

Goals

She is looking for science-related experiences for her daughter. She is looking for a relaxing place to stroll and get away from work pressures

Behavioral Considerations

"She is trying to balance long working hours with trying to give her daughter the experiences she needs to succeed. She is worried about a rise in hate crimes in the city."

Frustrations

Lack of science-related experiences that show Black people in positions of authority.

Audience Segment

Primary Stakeholder

Fundraiser

Connector

Influencer

Wealthy Donor

➔ Working Mother

Figure 4.1. Sample stakeholder persona.

Then we did area audience research while creating empathy maps of area residents. We established as a primary visitor a ten-year-old Black girl named "Malia." Malia's parents work full-time, making around $60,000 per year. She has an older brother, aged fourteen, and a younger sister, aged eight. Malia is curious about the natural world and has a particular interest in how animals interact.

Based on research into how to reach Malia, our strategy became the creation of mobile "pop-up" science pods staffed by teenage Black staff and placed in areas where Black people shopped. "Sarah" became our persona of a staffer who would reach Malia through one of the science pods. A series of stepping-stones was created: Malia meets Sarah, who encourages and gives Malia motivation visit the Science Center, and provides Malia with a future opportunity to work at the Science Center in a capacity similar to Sarah. Another stepping-stone is Malia's mother, Angela, who brings Malia to the pod locations in the shopping area and serves as facilitator (see figure 4.2). Other participants in the stakeholder map shown in figure 4.2 include James, who becomes a connector to help translate the impact of the community outreach to preidentified potential donors, and Dominic, a wealthy local donor. The overall strategy is mapped to a Bubble Diagram, and later a Service Blueprint and System Map

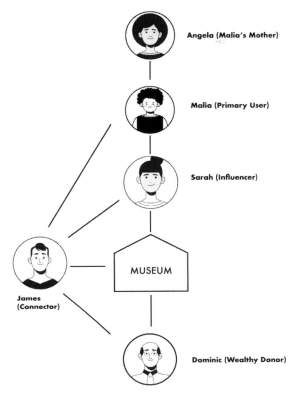

Figure 4.2. Stakeholder map.

(we'll look at these in chapter 7). The next step in the process would be prototyping and testing of the ideas in community and iterating the strategy and tactics. As complex as this strategy might sound, the entire process took less than three months, and resulted in increased Black attendance at the museum.

Note that your situation will necessarily be different. Each museum project, community, and visitorship is unique and requires individual strategies and tactics.

FALK DIERKING MUSEUM IDENTITIES

In *Identity and the Museum Visitor Experience*, John H. Falk includes the following persona categories (paired with quotes from actual visitors).[8]

- Explorers: Visitors who are curiosity driven, with a generic interest in the content of the museum. They expect to find something that will grab their attention and fuel their learning. "I remember thinking I wanted to learn my science basics again, like biology and that stuff . . . I thought [before coming], you're not going to pick up everything, you know, but you are going to learn some things." Malia from the previous example might be characterized as an Explorer.
- Facilitators: Visitors who are socially motivated. Their visit is focused primarily on enabling the experience and learning of others in their accompanying social group. "[I came] to give [my] kids a chance to see what early life was like . . . it's a good way to spend time with the family in a noncommercial way. They always learn so much."

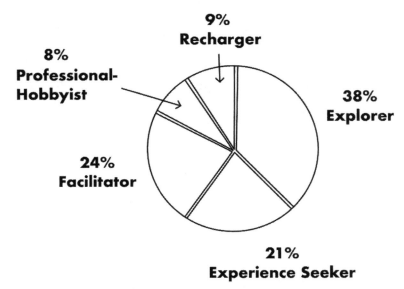

Figure 4.3. Visitor identities, adapted from J. H. Falk, *Identity and the Museum Visitor Experience* (2009).

- Professionals/Hobbyists: Visitors who feel a close tie between the museum content and their professional or hobbyist passions. Their visits are typically motivated by a desire to satisfy a specific content-related objective. "I'm starting to put together a saltwater reef tank, so I have a lot of interest in marine life. I'm hoping to pick up some ideas [here at the aquarium]."
- Experience Seekers: Visitors who are motivated to visit because they perceive the museum as an important destination. Their satisfaction primarily derives from the mere fact of having been there and done that. "We were visiting from out of town, looking for something fun to do that wouldn't take all day. This seemed like a good idea; after all, we're in Los Angeles and someone told us this place just opened up and it's really neat."
- Rechargers: Visitors who are primarily seeking to have a contemplative, spiritual, or restorative experience. They see the museum as a refuge from the workaday world or as a confirmation of their beliefs. "I like art museums. They are so very quiet and relaxing, so different than the noise and clutter of the rest of the city."

Falk and Dierking describe these five roles as temporary and changeable. Users can have different motivations on different days, and their roles may even shift during a single visit.

You can refer to your empathy map (figure 2.5) and persona (figure 4.2) throughout the museum planning process when faced with a decision and ask yourself, "What would my user do?" Empathy maps and the personas you create from them can be used in a broad range of activities, including strategic planning, feasibility studies, exhibition design, fundraising, and marketing.

The Importance of Diversity

In developing personas, it is important to take diversity into account. Diversity is a broad term that can refer to abilities and disabilities, culture, socioeconomic status, gender, sexual orientation, and many other areas. Museums must make sure that they are accessible both physically and culturally to a broad spectrum of visitors.

Ability and Accessibility

Signed into law in 1990 by President George H. W. Bush, the Americans with Disabilities Act (ADA) is one of America's most comprehensive pieces of civil rights legislation. It prohibits discrimination and guarantees that people with disabilities have the same opportunities as everyone else to participate in the mainstream of American life.[9] The ADA extends beyond architecture to include ways in which people will use their environments, including museum exhibits. You will find resources for museum accessibility standards and guidelines at the end of this chapter.

An emerging concept in museum design is universal design: "The design of products and environments to be usable by all people, to the greatest extent possible, without the need for adaptation or specialized design." The National Institute on Disability and Rehabilitation Research includes seven principles of universal design, each of which includes specific guidelines: equitable use, flexibility in use, simple and intuitive use, perceptible information, tolerance for error, low physical effort, and size and space for approach and use.[10] Whether you're designing visitor flow at the front entrance or something as seemingly simple as situating a bench, it can be helpful to refer to the seven principles.

Culture, Socioeconomic Status, and Accessibility

Many factors influence accessibility, including culture, language, and socioeconomic status. These vary significantly from country to country, and from community to community. As part of the groundwork, it is crucial to have a thorough knowledge of the existing pattern of visitorship at the institution, as well as a knowledge of the community within which the institution exists.

What languages are spoken? Which segments of the community fall into lower socioeconomic classes, and thus may not be able to afford entrance fees? How does economic status affect transportation? Is museum-going part of the culture of the different segments of the community?

You should also take a look at the current makeup of the museum staff and stakeholders, including yourself and members of the planning committees. Are the demographics of the surrounding community adequately represented? If not, you may wish to work at creating balance so all voices are represented at all levels.

Be aware that certain communities may have historical issues that affect museum-going. For example, in the United States, the history of enslavement and ongoing systemic racism means that many Black Americans remain disenfranchised. Some members of Latinx communities in the United States are fearful of attending public events because of their precarious immigrant status. It is essential that museums take into account the concerns of all the stakeholder communities, and ensure that the institutions are safe, accessible, and welcoming places for all.

It is important to use actual data in this evaluation, rather than received notions of categories. Use all the resources available to gather this data, including census information, city government documents, and in-person surveys. Once the data are gathered, you should be able to see areas you can target for improvement. For example, if the community has a sizable population of recent immigrants from Syria, a museum may wish to include signage and advertising in Arabic. As another example, if the German American proprietors of a quilt museum are having a hard time attracting members of the Latinx community, they might consider an exhibit on Central American textiles, and invite members of the targeted community to participate in developing it.

POSSIBILITIES FOR BEHAVIORAL CHANGE

Behavioral change refers to ways to empower people, ways to elevate people, and ways to motivate people of all abilities and cultures. Whether they acknowledge it or not, all museums are about behavioral change at some level. Because each museum emerges from a specific cultural milieu, it is not possible for a museum to be completely objective. People are subjective; therefore, museums are subjective. The goal of museums is similar to journalism. Like journalists, museums strive to present the "truth" to the public as accurately as possible and allow visitors to discuss the content and come to their own conclusions. That said, the way in which museums present information also provides a viewpoint.

To get clients and students thinking along these lines, I like to ask them the following questions:

- What is the problem you are solving?
- What is your objective?
- What are you communicating?
- What is the likely behavioral change in the user?

All of the above—strategy, tactics, and tools—should be based on empathy for the visitor. Only through understanding, or "walking in the visitor's shoes," can the emotional connections necessary to a successful museum visitor experience be created among visitor, museum, and community.

CONCLUSION

I love museums and appreciate their power to change people's lives. If museums can have a positive impact on only 1 percent of museum visitation in the United States, that's 8.5 million people.[11] However, it is extremely important that museums take into account the diversity of the community and ensure that they are giving everyone equal opportunity to access the facilities. In order to accomplish this, it is helpful to understand and recognize the demographics of the community, and to create empathy maps and personas with the aim of fostering inclusion.

NEXT STEPS

Think about a change you would like to create in your community. List the stakeholders in the process. Now begin to have empathy for each of the stakeholders by understanding their desires and motivations. Sketch out how your identified community issue might be changed by interrelationships among the stakeholders. Refer to the stakeholder map in figure 4.2 to answer the following questions:

- Who is your primary visitor (like Malia in the figure)?
- Who are the people that affect the actions of your primary visitor (Sarah and Angela)?
- Who can support this change and what are their motivations in creating change (James and Dominic)?

KEY CONCEPTS INTRODUCED IN THIS CHAPTER THAT ARE DEFINED IN THE GLOSSARY

Americans with Disabilities Act (ADA)
universal design

ADDITIONAL RESOURCES

Bundeskunsthalle: https://bundeskunsthalle.de.

Burgstahler, Sheryl. "How to Apply Universal Design to Any Product or Environment." University of Washington, 2015. https://www.washington.edu/doit/sites/default/files/atoms/files/Universal _Design%20Process%20Principles%20and%20Applications.pdf.

Innovation Hub: https://arhub.org.

The following is a listing of museum accessibility standards and guidelines:

Americans with Disabilities Act: https://ada.gov.

National Park Service Accessibility Guidelines: https://www.nps.gov.

Web Content Accessibility Guidelines (WCAG) 2.0: https://www.w3.org.

Smithsonian Guidelines for Accessibility: https://si.edu/access.

United Nations International Accessibility Standards: https://www.un.org/esa/socdev/enable /designm/.

International Telecommunication Union (ITU): https://www.itu.int/en/Pages/accessibility.aspx.

Hearing Loss Association of America (HLAA) Hearing Loops: https://hearingloss.org/?s=hearing +loops.

AppleVis (AV) Low Vision Apps: https://www.applevis.com/apps/ios/apps-for-blind-or-low-vision -users.

Federal Communications Commission (FCC) Closed Captioning Rules: https://www.fcc.gov/consumers /guides/closed-captioning-television.

Of these, the National Park Service guidelines are often used as the highest standard of accessibility compliance.

NOTES

1. See https://www.merriam-webster.com/dictionary/curate.
2. Callimachus, *Hymns and Epigrams; Lycophron; Aratus*, translated by A. W. Mair and G. R. Mair, Loeb Classical Library, vol. 129 (Cambridge, MA: Harvard University Press, 1921); Callimachus, *Aetia Iambi Hecale and Other Fragments; Musaeus; Hero and Leander*, translated by C. A. Trypanis, T. Gelzer, and C. Whitman, Loeb Classical Library, vol. 421 (Cambridge, MA: Harvard University Press, 1973).
3. In addition to the classic "web of documents," the World Wide Web Consortium (W3C) is helping to build a technology stack to support a "web of data"—the sort of data you find in databases. The ultimate goal of the web of data is to enable computers to do more useful work and to develop systems that can support trusted interactions over the network. The term *semantic web* refers to W3C's vision of the web of linked data. Semantic web technologies enable people to create data stores on the web, build vocabularies, and write rules for handling data. Linked data are empowered by technologies such as RDF, SPARQL, OWL, and SKOS. See https://www.w3.org/standards/semanticweb/.
4. Dmitry G. Korzun, Aleksey Varfolomeyev, Svetlana E. Yalovitsyna, and Valentina Volokhova, "Semantic Infrastructure of a Smart Museum: Toward Making Cultural Heritage Knowledge Usable and Creatable by Visitors and Professionals," *Personal and Ubiquitous Computing* 21, no. 2 (Apr. 2017): 345–54. https:// doi.org/10.1007/s00779-016-0996-7.
5. Victor de Boer, "Semantic Technologies for Digital Humanities," Semantics Online, Mar. 29, 2019, https://2020-eu.semantics.cc/semantic-technologies-digital-humanities.
6. Discovery Center at Murfree Spring, https://explorethedc.org/.
7. "Quick Facts, Murfreesboro City," Census.gov, Jul. 1, 2019, https://www.census.gov/quickfacts/mur freesborocitytennessee.
8. John H. Falk, *Identity and the Museum Visitor Experience* (Oxfordshire, UK: Routledge, 2009); John H. Falk and Lynn D. Dierking, *The Museum Experience Revisited* (Walnut Creek, CA: Left Coast Press, 2013).
9. "Information and Technical Assistance on the Americans with Disabilities Act," accessed Feb. 27, 2021, https://www.ada.gov/ada_intro.htm.

10. Bettye Rose Connell, Mike Jones, Ron Mace, Jim Mueller, Abir Mullick, Elaine Ostroff, Jon Sanford, Ed Steinfeld, Molly Story, and Gregg Vanderheiden, "The Principles of Universal Design," Jan. 4, 1997, https://projects.ncsu.edu/ncsu/design/cud/about_ud/udprinciplestext.htm.
11. Approximately 850 million visitors per year; see https://www.imls.gov/news/covid-19-research-partnership-inform-safe-handling-collections-reopening-practices-libraries.

5

Design Thinking and Emotional Design

Everyone designs who devises courses of action aimed at changing existing situations into preferred ones.

—Herbert A. Simon, *The Sciences of the Artificial*

In 1996, I was recruited to open the Discovery Science Center in Santa Ana, California. Before I left New York, my sister, with whom I am close, gave me a Tiffany money clip. I've had the clip ever since, and it has become something of a touchstone. I'll often reach into my pocket and rub my thumb over it. When I do so, the object becomes home. It reminds me of my sister, of New York, and of where I have come from. It is an important artifact of my experiences, background, and history, and it serves as a physical reminder of my story and its significance. At some level, it guides my behavior. That is a big part of design thinking: Until you understand the physical and emotional touchstones of your clients and visitors, you can't understand their motivations and determine how to best interact with them.

Achieving that understanding takes work and requires empathy. That is what design thinking is all about: walking in someone else's shoes until you can understand why they make the decisions that they do. From there, you can start to define the challenge you are facing or what it is that you are trying to achieve.

DESIGN THINKING

Design thinking is the process of creating customer experiences. It is a creative problem-solving approach to providing a service or building a product, and involves innovation. It asks questions in three important areas:

- Desirability. What do people want?
- Feasibility. What can be achieved?
- Viability. Does the idea make good business sense?

The phases of this process include developing empathy for the user, gathering inspiration, generating ideas, making the ideas tangible, and, finally, sharing the story. The process starts with understanding the problem that needs to be solved, which necessitates familiarity with the people and environment involved.

In a museum environment, it's important to interact with the customers (visitors), which means getting away from the desk. This is the only way to design the best possible service or product. Design thinking should be based on the needs of the visitors, not on the needs of the museum. It is essential to comprehend the purpose of the service, the demand for it, and the best way to deliver it, and this can only be achieved by interacting with visitors to gain insights regarding their wants and needs.

Designing a new product or service also means questioning your assumptions before you implement an idea or a change. Organizations often start the design process by presupposing possible solutions, which is a mistake. Identifying problems and clearly defining them as challenge statements with a human focus opens doors to better understanding. Thinking creatively and identifying new possibilities are key when generating ideas.

Last but not least, when design thinking is involved, it is more important to *do* than to *talk*. Too many meetings and discussions will, in the end, become hurdles for the project to overcome.

The design thinking process can be applied to any issue within a museum: "How do we increase attendance?" "How do we raise more money?" "How do we create better museum programming?" Those who follow a design thinking process sometimes realize that their initial question was actually part of the issue. For example, instead of asking "How do we raise more money?" the question might become "How do we impact our intended audience for the lowest cost?" This ability to change perspectives is perhaps the greatest advantage of design thinking. Learn to visualize issues as challenges to be addressed instead of problems to be solved. Note that public programming, fundraising, museum operations, websites, exhibitions, graphics, and interior designs are all examples of design.

THE MUSEUM CX PROCESS

Over nearly ten years of working with students and museum clients, I have developed a process for creating customer experiences. The museum CX process is fluid and iterative, involving more lateral thinking (a method for solving problems by making unusual or unexpected connections between ideas) than linear thinking (a step-by-step approach to solving a problem or completing a task). When engaging in lateral thinking, if something doesn't work you move to your left, move to your right, try something different, or ask someone for input. Much of the process involves breaking or rethinking previous patterns.

Progressing through the steps in the museum CX process involves looking and listening for "aha!" moments, when you may discover unintended results. I have found the following helpful to remember during the process:

- The creators of the customer experience are not users.
- (Almost) anything is possible.
- All members of the CX team must be positive and well intentioned.
- If you assume that the process will yield positive results, it usually will.

The first assumption is the most important. During the entire process, you need to remember that your personal thoughts have no value. Everything is based on empathy with the user (see chapter 2).

THE DESIGNER IS NOT THE USER

At the start of workshops, I often introduce participants to the mantra, "The designer is not the user," and have them repeat it several times. Although it might seem a bit blunt, when working with students or clients I often add, "We don't care what you think. We care about what the user (visitor) thinks."

Once you get the hang of taking your own preferences out of the decision-making process, it becomes easier. Why? It removes the influence of the ego.

If you are unsure of a response or direction, go out and ask your visitors. During workshops, I often ask participants to get up from their seats in the room where we are gathered and go out to ask museum visitors what they think about an issue. (For more on conducting visitor interviews, see chapter 11.)

Design thinking is results driven. If you can't test the results with your user, change your methods. The process is fast and low fidelity; you are looking for direction, not exact answers. This is often difficult for museum evaluators because museum evaluation is typically a lengthy and detailed process.

Lean design—making sure that you are only doing the things to effect the change that you are trying to achieve—is an important aspect of design thinking. Lean design is based on the idea that it is more effective to develop ideas rapidly and with low fidelity until you know your general direction than to waste time with lengthy high-fidelity development that might not yield the desired results. We will learn more about lean design methodology in chapter 6.

THE IDEO DESIGN THINKING PROCESS

Once you have removed your own bias from the process, it is easier for everything to become results driven, with the user in mind. There are many methods of design thinking methodology, but I have found the IDEO process to be the most effective in museum design. According to IDEO's *Field Guide*, "When you understand the people you're trying to reach—and then design from their perspective—not only will you arrive at unexpected answers, but you'll come up with ideas that they'll embrace."[1] The five steps in the IDEO design thinking process are identified in figure 5.1.[2]

IDEO DESIGN THINKING PROCESS

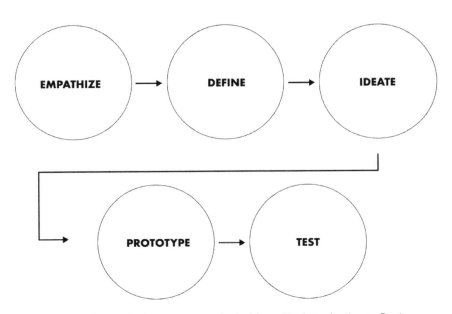

Figure 5.1. IDEO design thinking process, adapted from "An Introduction to Design Thinking," https://web.stanford.edu/~mshanks/MichaelShanks/files/509554.pdf.

Empathize

At the empathize stage of the IDEO design thinking process, you identify your user. What are their thoughts? Their emotions? How do they make decisions? I often begin workshops or classes with a quick exercise: Imagine a visitor named Caleb. He is twenty-five years old and lives at home with his parents. At twenty-two, Caleb was in a motorcycle accident and lost his right arm. I project a picture of Caleb on the wall to provide a visual to the workshop participants.

I ask everyone in the workshop to take off their right shoe. Then I tell them, "Now, pretend you are Caleb and don't have a right arm. Try to put your shoe back on your foot." I watch as people fumble around trying to put on their shoes. During the exercise, I ask, "How do you feel?" Typical responses include "incompetent," "silly," "self-conscious," and "frustrated." I allow the participants to put their shoe back on using both hands, then say, "You have begun the design thinking process, with empathy."

Be careful in implementing this exercise. As I mentioned in chapter 2, ensure you are not reinforcing stereotypes about race, culture, or gender. Be sure to explain to participants that we don't know how Caleb or the other users really feel. If this exercise were real, we would be speaking to real people and allowing them to express their feelings. Part of the IDEO design thinking process is working with, having empathy for, and understanding identified users. In the example above, the intention is to help the designers to begin to empathize with a user who has a disability.

Define

Defining the challenge to be addressed is often the most difficult step in the IDEO design thinking process. I often use the example of creating a device to assist Caleb for this part of the exercise. I ask the group, "What result would you like create for Caleb?" As members of the group answer, I write their answers on Post-its and stick them on the wall.

Once there are ten or fifteen ideas on the wall, I give each participant a Post-it and ask them to vote on only one result, with the stipulation that they cannot vote for their own answers. Once participants have placed their Post-its, we count them. The result with the most votes is selected. I then write the description of the result for Caleb and the winning result on a larger Post-it note, which I stick to the wall. To this point, the exercise has taken about fifteen minutes. We now move on to the next step: Ideate.

Ideate

Ideate means to "form an idea or conception of."[3] As you ideate, try to think without restrictions and create solutions called "what ifs." For example:

- "What if the museum were free? Would we have more visitors?"
- "What if every visitor were a potential donor?"
- "What if we could crowdsource all of our museum programming?"

As the next step in our exercise, I give each participant three Post-its and ask them to write one idea on each Post-it about how to create the desired result: an assistive device for Caleb. During the approximately five minutes allotted to come up with ideas, I walk around the room looking over participants' shoulders. If I see a particularly interesting response, I offer encouragement, such as "Great idea!" Once everyone has finished, I ask them to stick the three Post-its on the wall. I then begin to group the ideas, reading each Post-it aloud as I go. Once I have created a few groups, I ask the participants for help with classifying the responses, so creating the groups becomes a collaboration. At this point, I usually ask participants to stay seated so that we don't bump into each other as we group the Post-its.

Depending on the size of the workshop or class, we create ten or fewer idea groupings. If an idea doesn't fit in any of the groups, we set it to the side. I then ask participants to review each group of Post-its and come up with a way to create the desired result. During this review, if the group feels that an idea is missing or misclassified, or if they come up with a new idea, we adjust and rearrange the groupings.

I then give each participant two more Post-its and again ask them to vote for their favorite ideas. As in the previous round, they cannot vote for their own idea. Once all of the Post-its are up and counted, we review the results as a group. I ask for any feedback or if we missed anything. The define and ideate steps take about thirty minutes to complete.

Prototype

Prototyping involves re-creating the results of the ideate step for testing. It is important to develop low-fidelity prototypes early. A minimally viable service or product can be tested with consumers, then improved based on their feedback. By the end of this step, the designer will be in a better position to understand the inherent limitations of their design. One of my favorite results of this exercise was the development of a combination living community and outreach program in Mexico. Instead of concentrating on an assistive device to help the person, this group thought of a living community and outreach program to change other people's view of the person as "lesser than" to one of equality and empowerment.[4]

Test

At this stage of the process, you test and retest your ideas until the challenge has "actionable" items. An important part of design thinking is to get out of the mindset of "solutions." Instead, think of the challenge as iterative steps. In the example of the living community and outreach program mentioned above, a student went into a community of people with disabilities and found that a sense of humor was missing from the solution. Humor was used in this community as a way to "level issues" of disabilities to keep them from being perceived as "lesser than." This sense of humor, which is important in Mexican culture, had been missing from my thinking as an outsider.

Benefits of Design Thinking

Starting off a workshop or class with something like the Caleb exercise accomplishes a few things:

- Creates empathy. You may understand a certain condition intellectually (like Caleb's lack of a right arm), but having to physically perform under those conditions gives you new insight into your user.
- Introduces design thinking. This exercise introduces the group to the methodology of design thinking; this rapid process should be inclusive and empathetic to the user.
- Encourages user-centered collaboration. The exercise builds collaboration among participants that is centered on the user.

I find that participants will refer to Caleb by name throughout the workshop. They have obviously established a connection with the user/visitor embodied in Caleb. During the exercise, Caleb has become a persona, a representative user, for the purpose of your project (or, in this case, warm-up exercise). You should endeavor to come up with personas that the museum is likely to encounter. Examples might include a thirteen-year-old girl on the autism spectrum, a twenty-year-old woman who uses a wheelchair because of a limited ability to walk, and a seventy-year-old man with limited vision.

The design process steps by IDEO follow.

1. Define the client. This is often harder than you think. If you are an internal designer working at a museum, the easy answer is that the museum visitor is the client. In reality, the answer is more complex. Ask yourself, "Why is this project being created?" Often the reasons have to do with internal objectives held by one or more stakeholders; in this case the stakeholder—the person who influences and determines the success of the project—is the client.

2. Empathize with the client. Ask yourself, "Why is the client doing the project?" Success is often based on understanding the reasons a client decides to move forward. Put yourself in the client's shoes.

3. Define the client's goal. Ask yourself, "What is the client hoping to achieve with the project?"

4. Define the challenge. All design involves challenges to be addressed or problems to be solved. Make sure you know what they are.

5. Define the user. Remember, the designer is not the user, and the user is not the client (see number 1). Who will use your product or service?

6. Research the challenge. How have others addressed the challenge or solved the problem? Research other solutions and identify why they succeeded or failed.

7. Empathize with the user. Now it's time to put yourself in the museum visitor's shoes.

8. Create a project brief. This document will be reviewed by both client and user and should include price points. For more on creating project briefs, see the Museum Visitor Experience Toolbox on the website.

9. Stop! This important step is often overlooked during the rush of completing a design project. Learn to pause once all of the research is complete and the project is well understood, to allow inspiration (the next step) to occur. Give yourself and your team time to understand and reflect on the steps taken so far.

10. Allow inspiration. Now that you understand the project intellectually and emotionally, allow yourself to react so that inspirations emerge—objects, ideas, or forms that will guide your design thinking.

11. Create solutions. Using your inspirations as a guide and benchmark, create several solutions to the design challenge.

12. Sketch. Provide at least three options by sketching them in 2D (two dimensions) or 3D (three dimensions). Don't be too quick to reject options; less successful options often inform and influence more successful options.

13. Listen to client and user reviews carefully. Learn to "half listen." Make sure to listen to comments by the client and the user, but don't let your project become too watered down. Projects often lose their "sexiness" by making too many compromises in response to client and user feedback. Let the project have a life of its own.

14. Refine your design. Without losing sight of the client, goal, problem, user, and inspiration, refine your product or service.

15. Test. Test your product or service with your identified user and in the marketplace. Answer the following questions: Is the user interested? Is the marketplace interested?

16. Iterate. Iterations should be continual. Life is too short to create products that nobody wants. If there's not a market for what you are creating, keep iterating.

17. Production, marketing, sales. Only after the previous steps have been undertaken and your product has been refined can production, marketing, and sales begin.

EMOTIONAL DESIGN

Creating emotional connections with the visitor during the museum visitor experience is a powerful and important goal. While many museums focus on developing their visitor experiences, few understand the importance of developing an emotional relationship with the visitor. A successful museum visit involves the establishment of an emotional connection that leads to a sense of belonging and a feeling of security.

In general terms, emotional design is emotionally connecting with visitors to change behavior. It aims to create products that produce those emotions in users, resulting in positive experiences. I often tell my students that all design is problem solving and all worthwhile public experiences are about emotionally connecting with visitors and changing their behavior. Contrary to popular belief, it has been shown that emotions help in making decisions. Their evolutionary purpose was to allow us to survive environmental challenges. Positive experiences and emotions make us curious, while negative ones make us repeat past mistakes. It can be said that emotions are a necessary part of cognition; they are involved in everything that we think about, on a conscious level or even on a subconscious level. More importantly, emotions can change how we think and behave. Given that some experiences can evoke strong both positive and negative emotions, emotional design of products and services is important for guiding user behavior and affecting user experiences.

We relate emotionally to objects on three main levels: visceral, behavioral, and reflective. These are also the three levels of product design. The simplest, visceral design, is similar to what happens in nature, and is based on our initial reactions to certain environments and contexts. This level can be tested by putting users in front of a product and looking for their reactions. A great deal of traditional market research takes place at the visceral level. After looking at a product, people think they want it, and ask what it does and how much it costs. The main characteristic of visceral design is product appearance.

The next level, behavioral design, is concerned with product performance and use. On this level, the emotional relationship between user and product is based on the pleasure or effectiveness of product use. Today's advertising seems to involve little behavioral design. Most commercials convey happy people using a product; little, if any, information is shared about what exactly the product is supposed to do. Scenes connect positive user experiences with the product, without sharing much about the product itself. However, using a product without understanding it can lead to negative emotions such as uneasiness and frustration, caused by a lack of control over product usage. To truly use the product requires an understanding over and above the information on how the product works. A list of instructions is hard to memorize or keep in front of you all the time.

The next level, reflective design, is the most important and most complex design process. It is meant to offer a deeper emotional relationship between user and product. Reflective design is related to self-image, memories, and personal satisfaction. Unlike the other two levels, which are strongly related to the here and now, reflective design extends for a much longer period. The process of reflection can involve the past, the future, or both. Reflective design can override the influence of other levels of emotional design, but it is also the level that is the most vulnerable to differences in culture, experience, and education. Self-identity as it relates to the product is an important component of reflective design. Experience with the product can bring either pride or shame related to product ownership and usage. On this level, the message that the product brings is the meaning it evokes. Memories of how it felt and what it meant to use the product are also important. At the end of the day, reflective design should bring a full picture, or story, about the product and what it means to the user. It should create a desire to purchase—a desire that relates to a better future for the user. Products become symbols of what a user wants to be. The challenge of reflective design is to present a product in such a way that it can relate to different people with different backgrounds.

In the end, creating impactful emotional connections and behavioral changes is more important than metrics. Emotional design is often driven by seeking answers to the questions "What behavioral change is the intention of the project?" and "Does the project team believe that the solution will create the behavioral change with the identified user?" According to authors Alan Zorfas and Daniel Leemon, "the most effective way to maximize customer value is to move beyond mere customer satisfaction and connect with customers at an emotional level—tapping into their fundamental motivations and fulfilling their deep, often unspoken emotional needs."[5]

CONCLUSION

Before I let my industrial design students leave the classroom, I often ask, "What is the most important thing to remember about design thinking?" The answer that I am hoping for is, "The designer is not the user." If I don't get that response, I ask them to repeat that phrase after me. No matter the tool or the methodology, the most important aspect of creating user-centered experiences is understanding and having empathy for the user. The next chapter introduces the methodology that can be used to develop the museum customer experience, and chapter 7 covers the application of its tools.

NEXT STEPS

1. Find someone you know but are not close to. This should not be a family member. Tell them that you need to ask them some questions for an assignment. Ask whether they have an object (a touchstone) that becomes home to them, and elaborate on the idea if necessary. Their touch-stone might be an object that they carry with them every day, or it might be something that they keep in a box in a safe place. Then listen—really listen—to their answers. Listen at a level where you understand why they are saying what they are saying to achieve empathy.
2. Either alone or (preferably) in a group, frame a current museum challenge using the IDEO design thinking process (empathize, define, ideate, prototype, test). Which step did you find the most difficult? Were you surprised by the results?

KEY CONCEPTS INTRODUCED IN THIS CHAPTER THAT ARE DEFINED IN THE GLOSSARY

behavioral design
design thinking
emotional design
IDEO design thinking process
lateral thinking
linear thinking
persona
reflective design
visceral design

ADDITIONAL RESOURCES

Additional resources can be found in the Museum Visitor Experience Toolbox at https://www.museum
  -experiences.com/.
IDEO: https://www.ideo.com.
IDEO. *The Field Guide to Human-Centered Design*. Palo Alto, CA: IDEO.org, 2015.
Ries, Eric. *The Lean Startup: How Today's Entrepreneurs Use Continuous Innovation to Create Radically Successful Businesses*. New York: Currency, 2011.

NOTES

1. IDEO, *The Field Guide to Human-Centered Design* (Palo Alto, CA: IDEO.org, 2015).
2. Michael Shanks, *An Introduction to Design Thinking: Process Guide*, accessed Oct. 30, 2020, http://web.stanford.edu/~mshanks/MichaelShanks/files/509554.pdf; David Kelley is the founder of IDEO and Stanford University's Hasso Plattner Institute of Design, known as the d. school. The IDEO / d. school design thinking process is based on the work of Herbert Simon and his 1969 text *The Sciences of the Artificial* (Cambridge, MA: MIT Press).
3. See https://www.merriam-webster.com/dictionary/ideate.
4. As an example of this type of thinking put into action, see "Conanp impulsa el diseño para la artesanía hecha en áreas naturales protegidas," https://www.gob.mx/conanp/prensa/conanp-impulsa-el-diseno-para-la-artesania-hecha-en-areas-naturales-protegidas.
5. Alan Zorfas and Daniel Leemon, "An Emotional Connection Matters More Than Customer Satisfaction," *Harvard Business Review*, Aug. 29, 2016, https://hbr.org/2016/08/an-emotional-connection-matters-more-than-customer-satisfaction.

6

Customer-Experience Methodologies

You've got to start with the customer experience and work back toward the technology—
not the other way around.

—Steve Jobs[1]

Traditionally, museums have given little thought to their brand or to the customer experience. However, museums can offer a tremendous amount of insight into creating authentic visitor experiences. In fact, for-profit businesses wanting to provide immersive experiences for their consumers might consider looking to museums as experts. In this chapter, we'll take a look at the methodologies behind customer design and user design.

CX METHODOLOGY

As shown in figure 6.1, the framework for CX methodology[2] is human-centered design. The nested components of CX methodology include user interface, user experience (UX), customer experience (CX), experience design, and service design. Approaches to CX methodology include design thinking, which we looked at in chapter 5, and systems thinking, which is described later in this chapter.

User Interface

The user interface involves everything designed into an information device with which a person may interact. This can include a text panel, a display screen, a keyboard, a mouse, and the design of a digital desktop. The user interface is the first thing a customer encounters. The designer is responsible for such things as the right size of buttons, removing errors, and making sure that the visual feedback received is being implemented.

User Experience (UX)

The UX is the emotional impact of the product, experience, or service on a person. As indicated in figure 6.1, the UX is one step higher than the user interface and is responsible for the final satisfaction of users. It creates customer satisfaction by improving product features such as usability, desirability, and

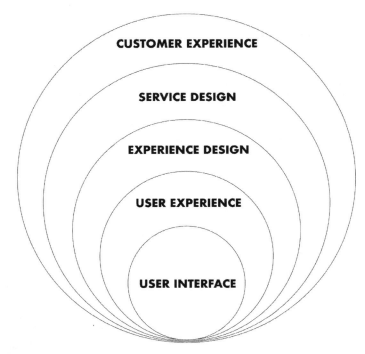

Figure 6.1. Range of influence: customer experience (CX), service design, experience design (XD), user experience (UX), and user interface (UI).

accessibility. In today's world, the UX ensures that the product delivers what it was built for. While ease of use is of utmost importance, it is not the only thing considered. A designer seeking to create a good UX must address relevance to the brand as well as the emotional responses to the product or service.

Customer Experience (CX)

The CX is the overall impact of the interactions between a person and company (in this case, the museum) at all touchpoints. As implied by figure 6.1, CX is a larger concept than the UX. In a sense, the UX is a subcategory of CX, because CX includes *all* individual experiences with the product or the service. CX includes the whole customer lifecycle, from finding information about the product, to paying for it, to using it—always keeping in mind the customer and their journey through the service or usage of the product. In simple terms, CX is the overall impression the museum makes on the visitor and UX is the usability of the interactions between museum and visitor.

The interaction between UX and CX is very important. For example, if you have state-of-the-art touchscreens (UX) but they are filthy (CX), the overall experience will not be optimal. On the other hand, you may have friendly staff members at the front desk (CX) but a confusing map (UX). Data regarding customer behavior are not enough to evaluate the customer experience. A number of questions need to be answered: Who are the customers as individuals? What is motivating them? What do they want and need? Answering these questions can be tricky, but without them the CX is difficult to design.

Examples of Museum CX

- Customer service of museum floor staff
- Museum navigation using museum signage

Examples of Museum UX

- Museum website interface
- Admission ticket sales kiosk interface
- Interactive exhibit interface

In summary, the museum CX is the overall impact of all the touchpoints between the museum and the customer, and the museum UX is how usable the interaction between museum and visitor is.

EXPERIENCE DESIGN

Experience design is a facet of user interface methodology that surrounds CX. In the context of museums, experience design includes all efforts to shape the CX; these can be anything from touchpads accompanying an object to the movements of the visitors. Museums rarely dedicate single staff members to experience design. Instead, they rely on participation by a range of specialists, including curators, exhibition designers, multimedia and web producers, and educators.

In an article on museum UX, communications specialist Cath Styles writes: "I believe it is important to regard visitor experience as a coherent opportunity space, whether that space is deliberately, explicitly designed or emerges as an aggregate of distributed effort."[3] She suggests that museums must broaden their focus from things and the stories they can tell to the relationships between those things and people, and among museum visitors: "However valuable their collections are, their highest value is in the relationships they create around them."[4] Experience design is evolving from a linear process in which a design is presented to the user as a fait accompli, to a dynamic, cyclical process in which the design is adjusted during production and possibly after release in response to the CX (see figure 6.2). As Styles says, "Design that develops through a participatory process can yield better results for the people that use it."[5]

STATIC, LINEAR DESIGN

Designer   User

DYNAMIC, CYCLICAL DESIGN

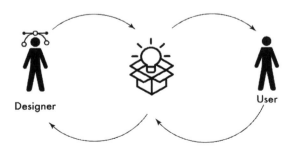

Designer   User

Figure 6.2. Linear design versus cyclical design.

Effective UX design produces results. To design a good experience, a number of factors need to be taken into account. Absorption and immersion of the customer (or visitor) are important. Absorption and immersion work together and involve both passive and active participation. A single museum experience might go from educational to escapist to aesthetic to entertaining in a seamless journey. Memorable experiences can be designed by eliminating any negative elements while harmonizing the design with the positive ones, keeping in mind the overall theme of the experience and engaging all five senses of the users. The important things to keep in mind with experience design are the connection between the user and the products, the existing environmental relationship, and how that relationship can be transformed.

SERVICE DESIGN

The "big picture" in CX methodology is service design. Service design is a holistic view of all related actors, their interactions, and supporting materials and infrastructures. It should include the creation and review of journey maps, to better understand the interaction of museum visitor from their pre-visit activities to their walk through the museum doors to what they do and how they feel after the visit is over. We'll take a closer look at journey maps in chapter 8.

Service design, like all aspects of CX methodology, should be user centered. The ultimate goal is to serve the visitors, not fulfill the needs of the museum. Creating value and efficiency for customers should always be the main concerns. This extends from permanent exhibits to special events. Service design should include all relevant stakeholders—both internal and external—in the design process.

This process includes *sequencing* and *evidencing*. Sequencing involves partitioning a complex service into separate processes, while ensuring the overall service design is unified and efficient. Evidencing is the process of visualizing service experiences and making them tangible. Service design involves a holistic approach, meaning that the interactions among objects and users need to be recognized and understood. It involves first presenting a minimum viable service to users, then adding additional value through customer feedback.

The goal of service design is to offer a systematic and creative approach so that the organization is competitive, customers' needs and expectations are met, and technology is used to its best advantage. Good service design should also address pressing environmental, economic, and social sustainability challenges, and foster and advance innovative models and behavior by the sharing of knowledge.

FEATURES AND GOALS OF CX METHODOLOGIES

There are a number of CX methodologies, but they all have the same overall objective: helping develop a product or a service. Effective CX methodologies are user-centric, and they lead to action. A good methodology must be flexible, allowing freedom and support for innovation. Methodologies should not be thought of as a goal, but as a means to an end.

Design thinking, which we looked at in chapter 5, can be of help in the initial part of a project, but methodologies such as "agile" are useful for transforming good ideas into a business model that actually works.[6] Agile is a product-management methodology that uses short development cycles called "sprints" to focus on continuous improvement in the development of a product or service.[7] At the end of the cycle shown in figure 6.3, incorporating agile methodology into the lean startup approach provides feedback that helps to adapt and make changes to the final product to ensure that customers—or museum visitors—get what they want.

Combine Design Thinking, Lean Startup and Agile

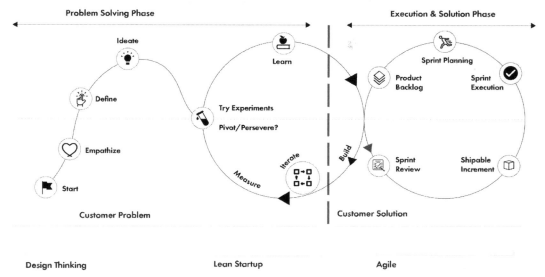

Figure 6.3. Combining design thinking, lean startup, and agile, adapted from "Enterprise Architects Combine Design Thinking, Lean Startup and Agile to Drive Digital Innovation," 2019, Gartner, https://www.gartner.com/en/documents/3941917/enterprise-architects-combine-design-thinking-lean-start.

LEAN DESIGN

One important component of the agile methodology is lean design. Lean design is making sure that you are only doing the things to effect the change that you are trying to achieve. It needs to start with good planning, before any process is started, so you don't waste time heading in the wrong direction. Failure to take this seriously can lead to post-process rationalization and suboptimal results. To avoid cognitive biases, put in place clear procedures and safeguards similar to those used in the empirical sciences. It is best not to eliminate gut feelings (intuition is a key part of the process), but it is important to have a way to balance and support them with rationally developed, carefully tested designs.

A number of habits have been proven to work well with lean-design teams:

1. Declare goals up front. Just trying things and seeing what will happen is a waste of time. Like a scientific experiment, the lean thinking process needs to start with a hypothesis or set of assumptions. Team members might be reluctant to make assumptions for fear of being proven wrong, so construct the assumptions as a team. To avoid groupthink (conformity to group values and ethics), have all members write down their assumptions individually, then share and discuss them. Team members might also be afraid to share their opinions because of a lack of information about possible results. Focus on estimation, and push perfection aside for the time being.
2. Make your set of assumptions specific. A vague assumption is hard to disprove but also hard to follow, which can lead to a number of problems and increase the possibility of suboptimal results. Assumptions should not be leaps of faith but clear, specific statements that can be adjusted over time.
3. Include a time frame for achieving the desired outcomes. Excessive optimism often causes a team to continue doing something even though the desired results are nowhere in sight. Utilizing a time-box[8]—an agreed-upon period during which a person or a team works steadily toward the

completion of a goal—helps teams avoid losing too much time on a project that is not running the way it should.

4. Use a control group as in scientific experiments. This can help increase understanding of the effect of the project compared to the previous state, and allows teams to see whether progress has been made.

Lean design principles can be understood through a value approach, a four-step process.

1. Identify values. What values are indicated by the customers' needs? Information such as customer expectations, timeline for delivery, and price are all vital to this step.
2. Map the value stream. To help understand the entire business operation, the value stream should identify all of the actions that take a product or a service through the process. Creating a value stream helps remove unnecessary steps and provides a better flow, allowing the necessary steps to be carried out with fewer delays.
3. Pull. The product should be ready to go. The customer should not have to go through extra steps to get to the product.
4. Aim for perfection. The final product, whether it is a tangible item or a visitor's path through a museum, should be of the highest quality you can achieve.

The value approach is by no means static. Suggestions for improvements should always be welcomed. If every member of the team implements lean design thinking in their work, over time it is likely that just a number of small changes will need to be made for the whole system to function in the best possible way. Do not lose sight of a core concept in lean design: the minimum viable product, which is essentially a working version of what you're trying to achieve. Without a basic version of the product, it is impossible to conduct testing and receive feedback.

SYSTEMS THINKING

In chapter 5, we looked at one approach to CX methodology: design thinking. Another valuable approach is systems thinking. Systems thinking was developed by American systems scientist Peter Senge as a method for solving complex problems.[9] It helps you make informed decisions by increasing your understanding of how systems work. Systems are not just collections of parts; when those individual parts are put together, they must function in harmony, making them much more than an aggregation. Thus, systems thinking involves far more than information about individual constructs.

Engagement in systems thinking requires awareness of a number of important features of systems:

- Interconnectedness. Systems are organized circularly rather than linearly. Each part is connected to many others.
- Synthesis. Because systems are complex and dynamic, the goal of systems thinking is *synthesis*, a more holistic approach than *analysis* (making complexity understandable by transforming it into manageable parts).
- Emergence. This nonlinear and self-organizing way that things interact is the outcome of the synergy of parts.
- Feedback loops. All systems have feedback loops. There are two main types: reinforcing and balancing. Reinforcing, a multiplication of the same effect, is usually understood as negative, but it can be beneficial if the element in the loop is continually refining itself.
- Causality. Causality explains how one event results in another. Because a dynamic system is always evolving, it is important to understand cause–effect relationships.

- Systems mapping. This is a representation of how elements interconnect and relate to one another and is one of the most important tools of systems thinking. A good map can offer unique insights that can help in developing effective interventions.

One useful tool for systems thinking is the iceberg model.[10] Like the iceberg, which is 90 percent underwater, there are many structures that are hidden from view. The iceberg model starts with visible *events* that are happening. Then it proceeds to *patterns of behavior* (understanding trends), *system structure* (the framework influencing the patterns), and *mental model* (the assumptions and models that shape the framework), all of which are "underwater." The underwater components are much more important and have a higher leverage than the individual event, and help us understand it. Making changes on the hidden levels may help avoid overreaction to short-term events and allow creation of lasting solutions.

CONCLUSION

Despite conventional resistance to the idea of museum visitor as customer, an understanding of CX methodologies can enhance the museum visitor experience by allowing you to separate and analyze the various methodology components and decide on an approach. In chapter 7, we'll apply the tools of CX methodology to the museum visitor experience.

NEXT STEPS

Select a museum challenge (such as low attendance, financial viability, or crumbling infrastructure) and apply systems thinking to it using the iceberg model.

KEY CONCEPTS INTRODUCED IN THIS CHAPTER THAT ARE DEFINED IN THE GLOSSARY

experience design
lean startup
service design
time-box
user experience (UX)
user interface

ADDITIONAL RESOURCES

"Five Design Tricks Starbucks Uses to Seduce You." *Bloomberg*, May 2014. https://www.youtube.com /watch?v=EBZ9mcJuNy4.
Guidance on Building Better Digital Services in Government: https://digital.gov/.
Gallo, C. "Starbucks' Secret Ingredient." *Bloomberg Business*, May 14, 2006. https://www.bloomberg .com/news/articles/2006-05-04/starbucks-secret-ingredient.
Gallo, C. "What Apple Store's Biggest Fan Taught Us about the Customer Experience." *Forbes*, Oct. 17, 2015. https://www.forbes.com/sites/carminegallo/2015/10/17/what-apple-stores-biggest-fan -taught-us-about-the-customer-experience/#284654d438a0.
MacDonald, C. "Assessing the User Experience (UX) of Online Museum Collections: Perspectives from Design and Museum Professionals." Apr. 8–11, 2015. Chicago: MW2015. https://mw2015 .museumsandtheweb.com/paper/assessing-the-user-experience-ux-of-online-museum-collec tions-perspectives-from-design-and-museum-professionals/.

McGonigal, J. "Gaming the Future of Museums." Lecture at the Center for the Future of Museums, 2008.

Rawson, A., E. Duncan, and C. Jones. "The Truth About Customer Experience." *Harvard Business Review*, Sep. 2013. https://hbr.org/2013/09/the-truth-about-customer-experience.

Rockwell, T. "Design for Museum Visitor Experience and Hands-On Learning." UX Week, 2013. https://www.youtube.com/watch?v=0E46rBapyW8.

Simon, Nina. *The Participatory Museum*. Santa Cruz: Museum 2.0, 2008.

User Experience Basics: https://www.usability.gov/what-and-why/user-experience.html.

UXmatters: https://www.uxmatters.com/.

NOTES

1. Micah Solomon, "How to Think Like Apple about the Customer Service Experience," *Forbes*, Nov. 11, 2014, https://www.forbes.com/sites/micahsolomon/2014/11/21/how-apple-thinks-differently-about-the-customer-service-experience-and-how-it-can-help-you/.

2. Franki Lake, "Human Centered Design vs Design Thinking vs Service Design vs UX . . . What Do They All Mean?" LinkedIn, Jun. 8, 2016, https://www.linkedin.com/pulse/human-centred-design-vs-thinking-service-ux-what-do-all-simonds/.

3. Cath Styles, "Museum Experience Design: Lessons from across the Field," *Semantics Scholar*, 2010, https://pdfs.semanticscholar.org/d8ed/a250ecad163538cc41ecce39a41cdf29c747.pdf.

4. Ibid.

5. Ibid.

6. Ash Maurya, *Running Lean* (Sebastopol, CA: O'Reilly, 2012).

7. Moira Alexander, "Agile Project Management: 12 Key Principles, 4 Big Hurdles," *CIO*, Jun. 19, 2018, https://www.cio.com/article/3156998/agile-project-management-a-beginners-guide.html.

8. Ash Maurya, "The LEAN Sprint," Oct. 1, 2015, https://blog.leanstack.com/the-lean-sprint-bc3f9f8caafd.

9. Peter M. Senge, *The Fifth Discipline* (New York: Doubleday, 1990).

7

Applying Customer-Experience Tools to the Museum

The first step in exceeding your customer's expectations is to know those expectations.

—Roy H. Williams[1]

In order to craft a quality visitor experience, solid groundwork is key. If you leave ample time for preparation and ensure you have all stakeholders on board, the process of creating the museum visitor experience will go more smoothly. In this chapter, we'll look at the essential CX tools used in developing most museum projects. These tools allow you to do much of the messy thinking and experimentation before you go hands on. Additional tools can be found in the Visitor Experience Toolbox at https://www.museum-experiences.com/. There, you can also see examples of student and professional projects.

Museum projects that might use the CX tools presented here include capital campaigns, board-of-directors retreats, building renovations, and new exhibitions. Note that there is some overlap among the tools. For example, the information from a persona diagram would be used in a journey map.

ESSENTIAL CX TOOLS

Mood Board
Empathy Map
Persona Diagram
Theory of Change Canvas
Stakeholder Analysis
Lean Canvas
Positionality
Journey Map
Bubble Diagram
Content Map
System Map

Mood Board

The goal of a mood board is to create a visual statement that matches intended users with the project's visual aesthetic. It is a visual tool in poster form that includes colors, images, shapes, light, and visual effects to capture the emotional intent of a project. The goal is to evoke or project a particular style, and to share the essence of the museum visitor experience. Images of intended users are often included. A common question asked during the presentation of a mood board is: "Do you see that user being attracted to this museum visitor experience?" The mood board establishes the overall feel of the project (see figure 7.1).

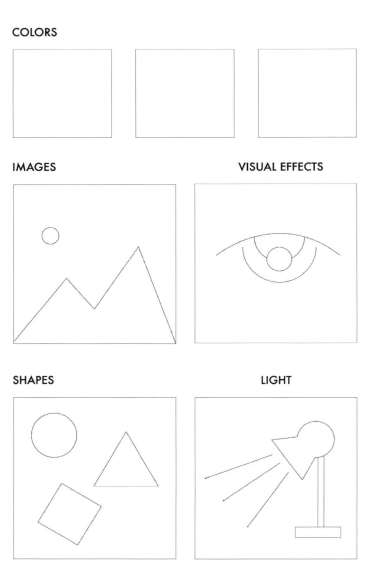

Figure 7.1. Mood board.

Empathy Map

As we learned in chapter 2, an empathy map is designed to start with the observable phenomena of things the user sees, says, does, and hears, and end at the center with what it feels like to actually *be* them. Refer back to figure 2.5 if you need to.

Positionality

Positionality involves repeating the mood board and empathy map processes as a group exercise, to uncover implicit bias. Do this in a classroom setting, and ensure you leave enough time for discussion.

Persona Diagram

As we learned in chapter 4, a *persona* is a representation of a type of user, based on clusters of behaviors and needs.[2] A persona is constructed by building a persona diagram (see figure 7.2). Such archetypes result in better understanding of your stakeholders and potential museum visitors. Each persona is based on conversations with an existing social group, identifications of its features, and better understanding of members' needs, habits, and backgrounds.

Figure 7.2. Sample persona diagram.

Theory of Change Canvas

Now that you have an understanding of the personas you are targeting, what are the behavioral changes necessary for individuals and the community to reach your target personas? The theory of change canvas can help you fill this out (see figure 7.3).

Stakeholder Analysis

With the empathy map and persona diagrams completed, you should now start to think about the people who will make the identified change for the identified user (the museum visitor). List stakeholders, including the director of the museum, a donor, and people who influence the identified user (see figure 7.4).

The next step is to complete a stakeholder analysis, which lists the people in the process with disproportionate influence as well as those who have little influence. For example, Malia, an eight-year-old Black girl, is included in the stakeholder analysis in figure 7.4. She has little influence on the process, but is of the highest importance to the success of the project. The mayor of the city where the museum is located may have great influence, but in terms of the objective he or she has low importance. Remember our mantra: "The designer is not the user." What a museum designer thinks about a solution should have little impact. It is the user who has the greatest influence on the success of a project. In this case, what eight-year-old Malia thinks about the project is of paramount importance.

Lean Canvas

Developed by Ash Maurya in the world of business start-ups with limited capital, the lean canvas is a one-page planning document that helps define problems and connect to solutions, including revenue structure, costs, and value proposition (see figure 7.5). It also includes a strategic understanding of why a project is being pursued and describes the tools needed to accomplish it. Such a plan should only take about half an hour to create, and should answer the following questions: "Why are we doing this?" "What is the fastest and least expensive way to achieve our objectives?" and "Who are the stakeholders to achieve our objective?"

The lean canvas is divided into nine categories:

- Problems. List your top one to three problems, along with ways in which those problems are currently addressed.
- Solutions. Outline a way to solve each of the identified problems.
- Key Metrics. Identify the data that explain the status of the business.
- Unique Value Proposition. Create a clear message about how your concept is different from (and better than) others, including high-level comparisons to other concepts.
- Unfair Advantage. Identify something unique about your concept that makes it stand out from the crowd.
- Channels. Explain the channels through which you will deliver your concept to customers, and how they can connect to you.
- Customer Segments. Identify target customers or users, and characteristics of your ideal customer.
- Cost Structure. List fixed and variable costs.
- Revenue Streams. Identify sources of revenue.

I want to clarify my priorities

by defining my goals and the path to reach them

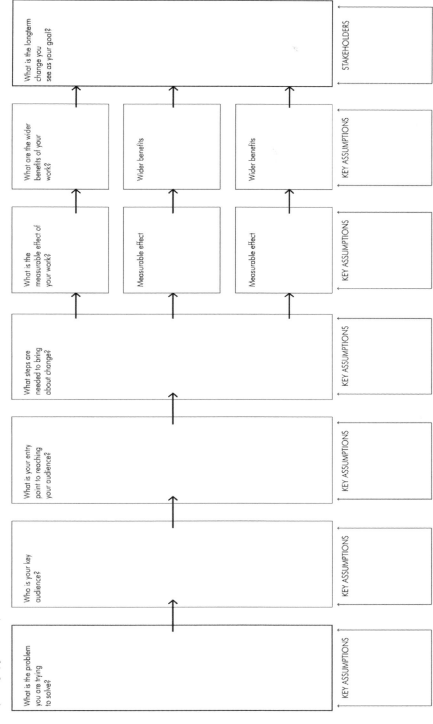

Figure 7.3. Theory of change canvas, adapted from "The Development Impact and You" by Nesta, https://diytoolkit.org/tools/theory-of-change.

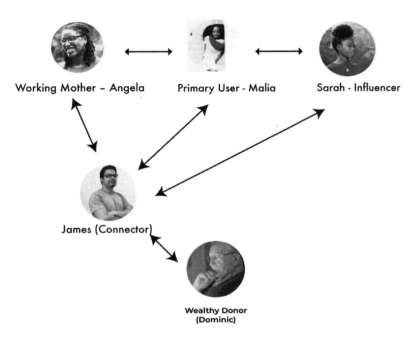

Figure 7.4. Stakeholder diagram.

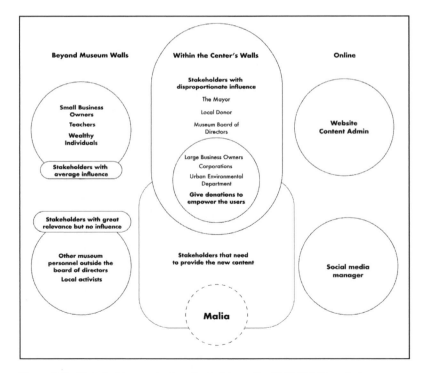

Figure 7.5. Stakeholder analysis, adapted from the "APMAS Knowledge Network Importance/Influence Matrix," http://www.mspguide.org/tool /stakeholder-analysis-importanceinfluence-matrix.

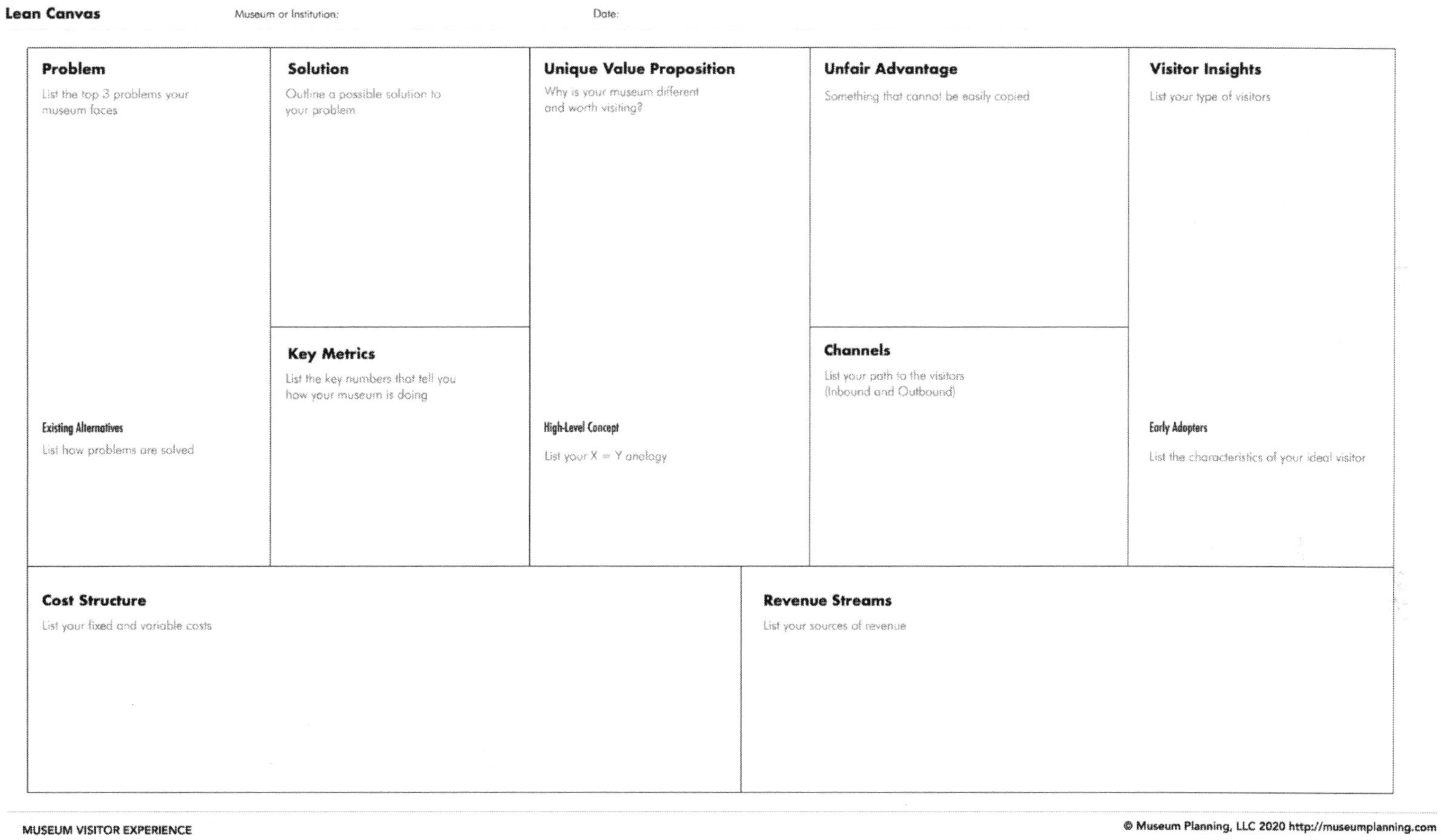
Lean Canvas
Museum or Institution:
Date:
Problem
List the top 3 problems your museum faces
Existing Alternatives
List how problems are solved
Solution
Outline a possible solution to your problem
Key Metrics
List the key numbers that tell you how your museum is doing
Unique Value Proposition
Why is your museum different and worth visiting?
High-Level Concept
List your X = Y analogy
Unfair Advantage
Something that cannot be easily copied
Channels
List your path to the visitors (Inbound and Outbound)
Visitor Insights
List your type of visitors
Early Adopters
List the characteristics of your ideal visitor
Cost Structure
List your fixed and variable costs
Revenue Streams
List your sources of revenue
MUSEUM VISITOR EXPERIENCE
© Museum Planning, LLC 2020 http://museumplanning.com

Figure 7.6. Lean canvas, adapted from *Running Lean: Iterate from Plan A to a Plan That Works* by Ash Maurya.

Journey Map

A journey map is a map created from a process called journey mapping, which divides the customer journey into three periods: pre-service period (expectations), service period (experiences), and post-service period (satisfaction/dissatisfaction). It represents different customer *touchpoints*—the interactions of a customer with the product or service. An example of a museum journey map is shown in figure 7.7.

Journey mapping is iterative and involves understanding the "pain points" for the visitor in their journey to your museum (both digital and in person). As an example, pick any museum website and try to find out how to visit the museum by bus. More often than not, the information for bus travel to the museum is not included in a museum's website and is causing a pain point for visitors coming to the museum by bus.

A journey map is also a way to orchestrate the visitor's experience by answering the question "Where do you want the crescendo (or crescendos) for the experience?" Identifying the points in the journey that are difficult for the visitor to navigate can help determine how those points might be addressed. As an example, during the current COVID-19 pandemic, many museums are using timed online ticketing and creating outdoor areas separate from the museum entrance in order to mitigate the spread of coronavirus and lower visitor anxiety caused by close proximity.

Journey mapping can be particularly useful in the process of fundraising. It changes the perspective from the museum to the potential donors by answering the question "What is the donor hoping to achieve with a gift to the museum?" During the process of working with clients, I create empathy maps, persona diagrams, and journey maps to help them recognize the impact the museum will have on the visitor.

Creating a journey map can help you understand a particular visitor's journey or assist in planning one. If you want to expand visitorship into a geographic area with a lower level of museum attendance, ask the question "How does the visit from one community differ from the visitor from a different community?" The process offers the perspective of the user (visitor, donor, or other stakeholder).

Bubble Diagram

You'll recall from chapter 5 that the prototype stage of the IDEO design thinking process involves re-creating the results of the ideate step for testing. Bubble diagrams—visual representations of the visitor's literal path through a museum and the associated content along the way—are the most essential CX tool for prototyping. In addition to visitors, they include other stakeholders, such as staff, volunteers, board members, and vendors. Another use of bubble diagrams is to describe the safe and secure handling of art and artifacts. See figure 7.8 for a sample bubble diagram.

Content Map

If a group that is highly specialized in a particular content area (such as art, science, or history) starts designing content without a layperson's understanding, the content is likely to be lost on a majority of visitors. I often encounter this in art museums, where curators organize exhibitions according to their own understanding of art history, and the meaning of an artwork is inaccessible to the typical visitor.

A content map (see figure 7.9) can help design content based on where you are and where you want to be. It begins with your *audience*, identifying who your target is and why they have come to visit. The *audit* category helps you understand what has already been done and how good it is. *Brand* takes into account existing guidelines for the brand and what you can't do with your content. *Production* should include the members of the team and a prepublication checklist. *Formats* identifies how content will be delivered. The *workflow* should include the tools to be used and a calendar with specific dead-

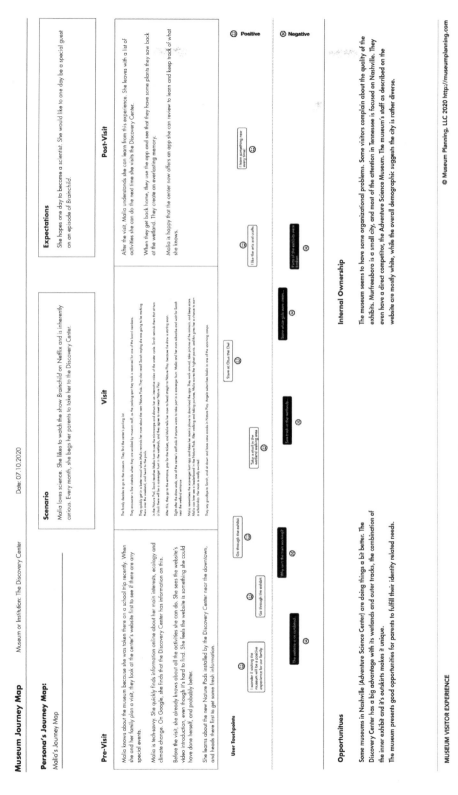

Figure 7.7. Museum visitor journey map, adapted from "Customer Journey Canvas" by Marc Stickdorn and Jakob Schneider.

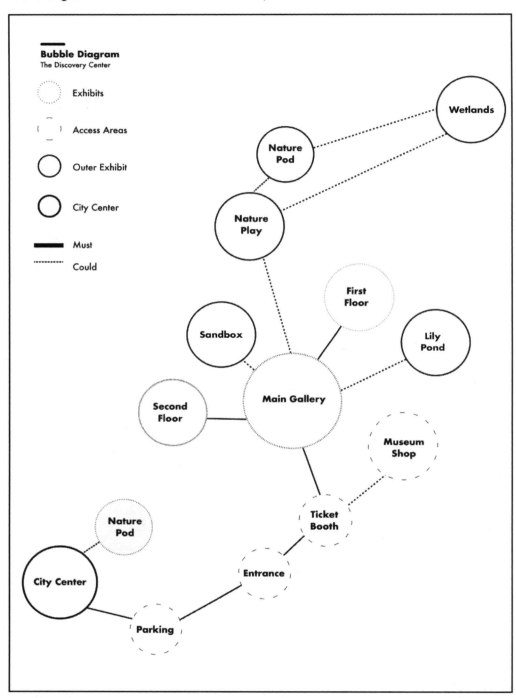

Figure 7.8. Museum bubble diagram.

Museum Content Map Canvas   Museum or Institution: The Discovery Center   Date: 19.10.2020

	Overall Scheduling		Content Creation		Channel	
	Current Exhibition Content	**Desired Content**	**Current Exhibition Content**	**Desired Content**	**Current Exhibition Content**	**Desired Content**
Offline	Traditional approaches are met, guided tours, shows The center has camps year round, traveling exhibits and performances Exhibits organized into categories that fit STEAM guidelines	Generate an experience that invites Malia to feel part of the Discovery Center Schedule events that involve successful members of Malia's community Use the wetland as a place to experiment, the Discovery Center as a place to reinforce knowledge and the sense of inclusion	Content created by board members, fundraising events sponsored by liquor companies Content creation is not aligned to the museum's purpose or its visitors; why would I use the site? Need to define the website's goal. If it's to inform, then the current design lacks the ability to do so.	The content is tailored for members of Murfreesboro's community and its surroundings The focus is on ecology, climate change and the science of the wetland Through a curator, the Discovery Center understands how to expand science topics to include issues affecting the community.	Museum staff guides users The staff, through its day to day activities, offers direct information Nature Pod App. The role is to involve the user in generating content and then advocacy. Nature Pod, Knowledge Bank, Wiki Membership card: events on ecology, climate change	The Discovery Center's staff, the city's Wetland Environmental department Kids are taught how to build water calculators, carbon footprint calculators. They learn about the cost of adding solar cells to their homes. They are encouraged to make an appointment to clean the wetland and get rewarded with a badge. Special events are key to open ways of discussing subjects ranging from conservation to brainstorming ways to improve society as a whole
Online	Website and presence in social media such as Facebook.	Scheduling in the wake of pandemics means museums in general will have to be more flexible. Guided virtual tours of streaming events are tools that should allow a deeper reach. View scheduled sessions to create mini-apps with the help of the Discovery Center's Staff	Content not updated, discontinuity leads to lack of use or interest	Influencers are part of our new digital society. Empowering some staff members like Sarah can inspire a new generation of museum visitors like Malia to explore science and develop their careers in STEM fields. Work with nature play app and learn to code	Facebook page and website not generating content at the moment	Channels such as messenger apps, YouTube, Twitch. Some kids help make the strategy, others find plants using nature play's app. Some are encouraged to write their own wiki entry based on their research. They become citizen scientists.

Figure 7.9. Museum content map canvas, adapted from "Content Strategy Canvas" by Chris Lake.

lines. In the *distribution* section, clearly identify how the content will be distributed. In the *stakeholders* section, include expectations of all stakeholders regarding the content. All goals should be recorded in the *goals* section, along with the metrics of success.

System Map

A system map is a way to understand and visualize the ecosystem of the museum (see figure 7.10). The museum ecosystem includes galleries, libraries, archives, and museums, as well as for-profit art galleries, art service and art storage firms, and other area nonprofits. Too often, museum staff members think of themselves as separate from their ecosystem. The process of system mapping provides an understanding of community stakeholders and potential project partners. System mapping is especially important for the process of creating digital content. Ask yourself the following questions: "Who are the people reposting our information online?" and "Who are the potential sources that might drive traffic to our brick-and-mortar location?" As with empathy mapping, if you don't understand your visitors on both an emotional and an intellectual level, you cannot understand their needs. Without an understanding of the context and ecosystem of the museum (both online and in person), you will be unable to find or create areas of commonality and digital partnerships.

CONCLUSION

This chapter has presented a number of customer experience tools that you can use to enhance the museum visitor experience. One essential feature of most of these tools is the museum visitor, without whom your project will not succeed. In the next two chapters, we'll look more closely at who museum visitors are, and what they expect and need when they come through your doors.

NEXT STEPS

Identify a problem or challenge and apply one of the tools included in this chapter. Did you find the tool helpful in solving the problem or addressing the challenge? Why or why not? Would another tool have worked better?

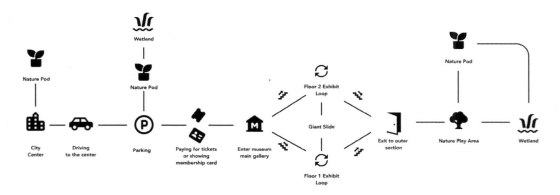

Figure 7.10. Museum system map, adapted from "System Map" by Nicola Morelli.

KEY CONCEPTS INTRODUCED IN THIS CHAPTER THAT ARE DEFINED IN THE GLOSSARY

bubble diagram
content map
journey map
lean canvas
persona diagram
positionality
mood board
stakeholder analysis
stakeholder canvas

ADDITIONAL RESOURCES

Lean Canvas: https://leanstack.com/leancanvas.
Empathy Map: https://medium.com/the-xplane-collection/updated-empathy-map-canvas-46df22d
    f3c8av.
Personas: https://www.interaction-design.org/literature/topics/personas; https://www.thisisservice
    designdoing.com/methods/creating-personas.
Stakeholder Canvas: https://www.interaction-design.org/literature/article/map-the-stakeholders.
Journey Map: https://www.nngroup.com/articles/journey-mapping-101/.
Bubble Diagram: https://uxdesign.cc/uxa-before-ia-there-was-4b9356434252.
Content Map: https://blog.alexa.com/content-mapping/.
System Map: https://www.thisisservicedesigndoing.com/methods/system-mapping.
Nielsen Norman Group: https://www.nngroup.com/articles/service-blueprints-definition/.
Service Design Thinking: http://thisisservicedesignthinking.com/.
Service Design Tools: https://servicedesigntools.org/.
Interaction Design Foundation: https://www.interaction-design.org/.
Don Norman: https://jnd.org/.
Community Canvas: https://community-canvas.org.
Cool Hunting: https://coolhunting.com.

NOTES

1. Roy Hollister Williams, author of the *Wizard of Ads* trilogy.
2. "Personas," Service Design Tools, accessed Nov. 10, 2020, https://servicedesigntools.org/tools/personas.

8

The Museum Visitor's Journey

You can only understand people if you feel them in yourself.[1]

—John Steinbeck

The museum visitor's journey involves much more than walking through the doors and looking at exhibits. An effective way to visualize and understand the journey is to create a Museum Journey Map like the one we learned about in chapter 7. American market research company Forrester Research defines journey maps as "documents that visually illustrate customers' processes, needs, and perceptions throughout their relationships with an organization."[2] I used the Museum Journey Map to describe the stages in the museum visitor experience from pre-visit to visit to post-visit activities (see figure 8.1). Each segment of the visitor journey involves feelings, touchpoints, pain points, and opportunities, as well as what visitors are actually doing.

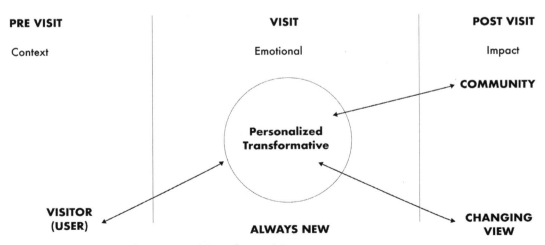

Figure 8.1. Museum cycle: pre-visit, visit, and post-visit.

In my classes, I sometimes offer the metaphor of visiting a friend's house for dinner. Think about what you did before arriving at the house, when the host welcomed you over their threshold and shook your hand (or offered a kiss or a bow). Even before a visitor arrives at the museum's front door, they have gotten themselves dressed, found the address to the museum, driven or taken the bus to the museum location, and found the front door. As anyone who has been part of a museum field trip can tell you, this is often not an easy experience. It is important to recognize the effort visitors must make simply to arrive at the museum's front door.

Extending the dinner-guest analogy, once a museum visitor has crossed the threshold (passed through the museum's front door) and you have greeted them (given them a handshake), they have entered a new world. It is now the responsibility of the museum host (staff and stakeholders) to care for the visitor as their guest. This important transition should not be taken lightly. Legally[3] and figuratively, the visitor is now the responsibility of the museum.

I love photographing door handles at the thresholds of experiences. One of my favorites is the trademark door handle of national retailer REI, which is shaped like an ice pick (see figure 8.2). REI's pickax door handles set a tone and literally act as a connection between visitor and store, providing a "handshake" signaling that you are welcomed as an adventurer.

Figure 8.2. Ice-pick door handles welcome customers at an REI store. *Adam Cairns/USA TODAY NETWORK.*

Another favorite of mine is the entrance to the Denver Children's Museum (see figure 8.3). This museum has a separate entrance only for children that is before the entrance for adults. This sets a tone for the experience, indicating that, here, children come first.

Figure 8.3. A door for children at the Denver Children's Museum.
Photo by the author.

This chapter is organized according to the components of the museum visitor's journey. These are identified as pre-visit, visit, and post-visit. Throughout the chapter, we'll be using the example of a school group's visit to a museum. Let's begin with pre-visit activities and resources.

PRE-VISIT

To begin their journey, visitors must first become aware that a museum exists. The museum journey map includes two pre-visit components: awareness and online. Two other possible pre-visit components are word of mouth and printed materials.

Awareness

Say that plans are being made for a local school group to visit a museum. Decision makers in this process include parents, teachers, and administrators. Pain points in creating awareness might include searching for an appropriate venue, struggling to find a suitable date and time that minimize conflicts with academic requirements and other school activities, and the hassle of arranging transportation for a large group. Opportunities might include improving relationships among students and teachers and enhancing interest in related school curriculum.

Touchpoints between museum and visitor, which are primarily directed at the decision makers (stakeholders), include print and online advertising, news coverage, and online articles. At this point, the museum visitors (students) are hopefully doing their schoolwork or homework. In addition to addressing the logistical challenges of date, time, and transportation, the actions by the decision makers involve finding a museum to visit. They might see an online article or print ad and recognize a museum logo, icon, or exhibit. The primary feelings at this stage include connection—that "aha!" moment that occurs when an appropriate field trip destination is identified. Important in this process is effective frequency,[4] or how many times a potential visitor needs to see a notice (print ad, online article, word of mouth) to reach awareness.

Online

The next component is essential to museums today: the online experience. Pain points include user challenges in accessing online content and struggles to use online tools. An important, not-to-be-missed opportunity here is to increase positive feelings in anticipation of the museum visit. Touchpoints include online reviews, social media, website games, and blog posts. Note that internet access is not a given, and can be a pain point for some users.

Going back to the school field trip example, the use of the touchpoints depends somewhat on the age of the students. A teacher might ask older students to read online reviews and blog posts or follow the museum on social media prior to the visit. Younger students might be assigned a website game as a pre-visit activity.

VISIT

As many museum educators can attest, it is best to establish expectations and rules while students are still in their seats on the bus. This often becomes a point of negotiation: "If you would like to visit the museum, these are the rules and expectations for the museum visit." Considerable logistical issues must also be addressed for a large group visit. These include securing student backpacks and coats in a rolling bin, placing lunches in a separate rolling bin for access during the lunch break, orienting students to the museum, navigating the facility (including bathroom locations), distributing educational materials to be used during the visit, and counting students to ensure their safety (so that the same number of students—no more, no fewer—return to the bus).

As shown on the map, the visit stage involves the most actions. Touchpoints include exhibitions, programs, lectures, smartphone apps, the museum restaurant, and the museum store, as well as the inevitably chaotic group restroom breaks. One example of a touchpoint was the smartphone app created by the American Museum of Natural History (AMNH) that featured a game called "The Power of Poison"[5] to augment the information included in a special exhibition. The primary feelings at this stage hopefully include engagement and enjoyment, but some members of large groups may experience boredom or frustration (caused, for example, by not understanding what is being presented or being unable to see over the shoulders of other group members).

Let's return to the analogy of a dinner at a friend's house. Before leaving for the evening, the host retrieves the guests' coats, you again shake hands (or kiss or bow), and then you make plans for the next get-together, which is often a reciprocated dinner at a guest's home. The host will sometimes offer a token gift as a remembrance of the evening. All of the same steps exist for the exit from the museum. Staff should say "goodbye" and "thank you" to visitors for their visit to your museum, and possibly distribute a remembrance such as a brochure of upcoming events that includes a link to on-line information about the museum experience. Making plans for the next visit might involve sharing information about a museum event or a new museum exhibition or program. An excellent example of a remembrance is offered by the Cooper Hewitt Design Museum in New York City: every visitor receives a digital pen to be used during their visit that has an individual website URL associated with the visitor's admission ticket. When visitors return home, they can visit the website URL on their admission ticket to review information about their museum visit as an element of their post-visit experience.

POST-VISIT

Ideally, the visit has left students energized and excited to return to the museum. They probably do not yet understand the full meaning and significance of the visit, and the debriefing as they share their experiences with fellow students on the bus trip back to school, and then with teachers and with parents, is an important part of the process. Post-visit pain points for students may include difficulty retaining what they saw and learned. Teacher pain points may include difficulties applying the experience to the school curriculum, getting students back on track in the classroom, and having to send notes home to parents about the need to improve field trip behavior. Opportunities include renewed engagement with curriculum and a desire to learn more about what they saw.

Post-visit touchpoints revisit some of the same resources used pre-visit. This time, instead of reading museum reviews, students might be encouraged to write their own reviews or create blog posts related to their experiences. An interesting activity might be to compare the individual reviews or posts to discover how the experiences differed from student to student. The students might also be encouraged to follow the museum on social media and share their experiences with family and friends. If museums receive such feedback, they should pay attention to it so that they can highlight their successes and address any deficiencies.

CONCLUSION

The museum journey map can help you visualize how the museum visitor experience extends beyond the visit, both spatially and temporally. It shows how museums must focus not just on their collections, but on communicating them to the world both pre- and post-visit. In addition, they must pay attention to what visitors are communicating to them during the visit.

NEXT STEPS

1. Using the information you learned in chapter 4, create a persona. Then take this persona on a museum visit using the museum journey map. Envision their pain points, opportunities, actions, and feelings during the pre-visit, visit, and post-visit stages.
2. Select a local museum that you have not yet visited. View their website and make notes of what you might expect to happen during a visit. After visiting the museum, compare your expectations to the in-person experience. Did the in-person visit meet or exceed your expectations, or was it below your expectations?

KEY CONCEPTS INTRODUCED IN THIS CHAPTER THAT ARE DEFINED IN THE GLOSSARY

awareness
effective frequency
threshold

ADDITIONAL RESOURCES

American Museum of Natural History: https://www.amnh.org.

Paqua, M., and S. Stewart. "Visitor Journey Mapping in Museums." *Pratt*, May 15, 2018. https://muse umsdigitalculture.prattsi.org/visitor-journey-mapping-in-museums-f18442ee1d99.

Rodà, Conxa. "Visitor Journey Mapping: Walking in Our Visitors' Shoes." Museo Nacional d'Art de Catalunya. Jun. 22, 2017. https://blog.museunacional.cat/en/visitor-journey-mapping-walking-in -our-visitors-shoes/.

NOTES

1. John Steinbeck, *East of Eden* (New York: Viking, 1952).
2. Tony Costa and Joana de Quintanilha, "Mapping the Customer Journey: Four Approaches to Customer Journey Mapping; When and How to Use Them," *Forrester*, Nov. 16, 2015, https://www.forrester.com /report/Mapping+The+Customer+Journey/-/E-RES55987#.
3. "What Is Premises Liability?" NOLO, accessed Feb. 27, 2021, https://www.nolo.com/legal-encyclopedia /what-premises-liability.html.
4. Igor Makienko, "Effective Frequency Estimates in Local Media Planning Practice," *Journal of Targeting Measurement and Analysis for Marketing* 20, no. 1 (Feb. 2012): 57–65, https://link.springer.com/article /10.1057/jt.2012.1.
5. Edward Rothstein, "A Touch of the Toxic, for Good or Ill," *New York Times*, Nov. 14, 2013, https://www .nytimes.com/2013/11/15/arts/design/the-power-of-poison-at-american-museum-of-natural-history .html.

Part III
Supporting the Museum Visitor Experience (How)

9

Museums, Politics, and Culture

The nation's museums face a tall and challenging order, increasingly called upon to be civic anchors, community gathering places, and stewards of our most prized artistic and cultural heritage.

—National Endowment for the Arts[1]

I love the quote above. By describing museums as "civic anchors" and "community gathering places," it repositions the role of museums from artifact-containing warehouses to places for people to gather and engage in important conversations. In chapter 1, we learned about *placemaking*, a multifaceted approach to the planning, design, and management of public spaces that utilizes a local community's assets, inspiration, and potential. I think of placemaking as a camera's zoom lens. You zoom in to understand the emotional needs of each visitor, and zoom out to understand the needs of the surrounding community. Political and cultural issues are deeply entwined in the lives of people and the communities in which they live. Museums should not abstain from politics or hot-button issues; however, there are some legal restrictions on their activities, which we will look at later in this chapter.

HOW MUSEUM EXHIBITIONS CAN CHANGE LIVES

Perhaps more than any other medium, museum exhibitions have the opportunity to change the way people think and feel. I recently visited the United States Holocaust Memorial Museum. The building is brutalist steel and concrete, with a stark, almost bunker-like presence. I started my visit on the lower level at the exhibition "State of Deception: The Power of Nazi Propaganda." I was struck by the similarities between exhibition design and content. Both used simple messages, theatrical tools, and strong visuals. The same message was communicated using different methods, repeating them, and using crowds to build energy. The exhibition design intentionally incorporated some of the tools of propaganda to strengthen the message.

Next I visited "Daniel's Story," which initially struck me as overly simplistic. Later in my visit I began to understand the reason for including it. Some of the museum visitors are children as young as seven. It is important to share the Holocaust history, and "Daniel's Story" presents the content in a way that kids can digest. It does so early in the journey through the museum so parents can keep their children from experiencing potentially traumatic images elsewhere in the museum.

I headed upstairs to the second floor and visited "From Memory to Action: Meeting the Challenge of Genocide." Here I was impressed by the call to action and the use of the Pen Scribe, an interactive pledge wall. Instead of having visitors key in their pledges, they write their promises on special digital paper. Visitors then drop the signed paper stubs into clear, beautifully lit plexiglass cases. The digital paper "remembers" the location of the pen marks, so the handwritten pledges are magically projected on a digital projection wall.[2]

Though I was stirred by these moments, I felt as if I was missing part of the museum. I had heard about it for years and knew there was more to it than what I had seen so far. After asking about the location of the main gallery at the information desk, I was given a map and directed to an elevator in an imposing wall clad in weathered steel. Before I got on the elevator, a staff member provided an overview of the permanent exhibition, "The Holocaust," which is divided among three floors: "Nazi Assault" on the fourth floor, "Final Solution" on the third floor, and "Last Chapter" on the second floor.

As I started my tour of the fourth floor, I thought, "Okay, this is a typical theatrical exhibition." But moving through the exhibits, I smelled the odor of the interior of the railcar similar to those used to transport thousands of victims on the third floor, and smelled the leather of thousands of shoes of Holocaust victims in the "Last Chapter" on the second floor (see figure 9.1). By the end, I was immersed. I had been changed.

Figure 9.1. Shoes at the Holocaust Memorial Museum in New York City. *Giuseppe Crimeni/Alamy Stock Photo.*

Yes, the sights, sounds, and smells had been used to manipulate me, but as I went through the exhibits I began to trust the authority of the museum and allow myself to be transported. Although I am a strong believer in the democratization of content—a transparent, "open source" method that involves the visitor—there is no way that this story can be told by anyone other than those who lived through it. In this case, I did not want to hear the thoughts of others. I wanted exactly what the museum provided: an experience that was clear, concise, well edited, factual, theatrical, and life changing.

Chapter 9

The Holocaust Museum uses the museum visitor's journey to emotionally attach the visitor to the content. When I worked as an exhibit developer at Liberty Science Center in the 1990s, we developed a simple tabletop activity. Visitors could move a tape head across a magnetic tape and hear the recorded sound. Changing the perspective from moving the tape to moving the tape head allowed visitors to understand how the tape head "reads" the information contained on the magnetic tape. The Holocaust Museum uses a similar approach, but instead of moving a tape head, the interactive activity is walking: the visitor is the tape head. As I walked across the three theater stages, I became an actor in the "show." I loved the white spaces between each floor, which allowed me to take a breath before going on to the next act. Artwork, including *Gravity* by Richard Serra, *Consequence* by Sol LeWitt, and *Memorial* by Ellsworth Kelly, is positioned at each "pause" between galleries.

By the time I reached the second floor of "The Holocaust," I could feel the burden of pent-up emotion within my chest and wanted to leave in order to gather my thoughts. But before I left, I paused at the theater and listened to a Holocaust survivor describing one of his experiences at the end of the war. A soldier was approaching, and the Jewish man took off his wooden shoe, intending to hit him in the head. The soldier, an American, said, "I am here to save you, not kill you." I stood at the back of the theater and wept.

CURATORIAL ACTIVISM

Curatorial activism, which is the active participation of the curator in creating impactful experiences between museum and visitor and creating dialogues[3] among visitors, is a subject of passionate debate. Although prohibited by law from participating in political activities,[4] museums are, of course, not neutral. Nor should they be. We do not have a single history. Rather, we have many histories, with many people involved. And with different viewpoints come different stories. In addition to being cultural archives, museums should be safe spaces for activism.

I love the Brooklyn Museum, but many dislike it because they feel its solicitation of attention through provocative exhibitions is self-serving. However, this is exactly what museums can and should do—shake up and provoke people. Museums should embrace their ability to inspire. The word *inspiration* is from the Latin *inspirare*, meaning "to breathe into." Museums should breathe new life into the minds of their visitors.

MUSEUMS AND POLITICS

More recently, debate has arisen about how cultural institutions should react to current events, primarily political ones. In 2017, as Inauguration Day was approaching, a number of artists and other cultural workers were asking museums and galleries to close their doors to protest Donald Trump's election as president of the United States. The Davis Museum at Wellesley College organized a protest against Trump's immigration policies by covering art pieces made by immigrants.[5] The New York Historical Society, in partnership with the City University of New York's Citizenship Now!,[6] created the Citizenship Project, a major initiative to help the more than one million immigrants in the New York region who are eligible for US citizenship.[7] Other initiatives, like the "Day of Facts,"[8] included subjects such as global warming and evolution. Most of these initiatives had an educational purpose, yet their motivation and presentation clearly carried a political message as well.

However, some balked at incorporating biased political content so blatantly. For example, Richard Armstrong, director of the Guggenheim Museum, abstained from the anti-Trump rhetoric and called for caution in reacting to recent events.[9]

Controversial political and social topics need to be treated thoughtfully. While artists have complete freedom to react to everyday events, institutions have an obligation to take a longer-range view.

Some kind of balance must be achieved so that politically involved artists do not lose their place in the exhibition spectrum.

How Museums Should Handle Political Issues

Museums are currently active participants in discussions about highly political issues, including global warming, decolonization, reparations for Native American groups, and discrimination. Museums are categorized as 501(c)(3) by the IRS, and as nonprofits they are prohibited from participating directly or indirectly with political campaigns.[10] The IRS restricts museums and other 501(c)(3) organizations from becoming involved in partisan politics (i.e., favoring one candidate or party over another). However, they are allowed to "engage in public advocacy not related to legislation or election of candidates."[11] So the idea that museums cannot be political is a fallacy. Museums can be involved in political issues as long as the presentation is nonpartisan.

The IRS also restricts the legislative work of museums:

> In general, no organization may qualify for section 501(c)(3) status if a substantial part of its activities is attempting to influence legislation (commonly known as lobbying). A 501(c)(3) organization may engage in some lobbying, but too much lobbying activity risks loss of tax-exempt status.[12]

Museum collections can give substance to political issues and have the interpretive skills to present them in a well-researched and engaging manner. Museums are exactly where political issues *should* be discussed. Museums are inevitably affected by politics and are entitled to express their engagement in the issues of the day.[13] Some examples of right and wrong ways in which a museum can express itself in the public arena follow.

- Right: "XYZ Museum joins in congratulating Jane Doe, Springfield's new county executive."
- Wrong: "XYZ Museum is proud that our ecology-minded voters helped elect Jane Doe."
- Right: "XYZ Museum is putting on an exhibit detailing the effects of climate change."
- Wrong: "XYZ Museum mobilized ecology-minded voters to defeat corporate polluter Rick Roe."

Lobbying is political advocacy, such as meeting with members of Congress to encourage them to act in a certain way on legislative action. As noted previously, museums and other 501(c)(3) organizations are restricted from lobbying. The following examples compare lobbying to a museum making its position known.

- Lobbying: Visiting your local congressperson to influence him or her to vote yes on a bill requiring factory emissions to meet certain standards.
- Not Lobbying: Talking with members of Congress about the importance of legislative action on climate change.
- Not Lobbying: Urging the new administration to recognize climate change.

With certain restrictions, a public nonprofit organization designated 501(c)(3), such as a museum, may do the following.

- Engage in limited lobbying, including work on ballot measures.
- Continue to advocate for the organization's issues during an election year.
- Educate all candidates on public-interest issues within the purview of the organization.

- Criticize sitting elected officials, especially if the organization has a history of publishing legislative scorecards.
- Conduct nonpartisan public education and training sessions about participation in the political process.
- Rent mailing lists and facilities to other organizations, legislators, and candidates at fair market value, as long as it is for an ongoing activity and not arranged solely for a particular candidate or party.
- Conduct nonpartisan get-out-the-vote and voter-registration drives.
- Canvass the public on issues.
- Sponsor candidate debates.
- Work with all political parties to get its positions included on the party's platform.

However, 501(c)(3) organizations *cannot* do the following:

- Endorse candidates for public office.
- Make any campaign contributions (monetary or in kind).
- Make expenditures on behalf of candidates.
- Restrict rental of their mailing lists and facilities to certain candidates or engage in such business transactions for the first time with candidates.
- Ask candidates to sign pledges on any issue.
- Increase the volume or amount of criticism of sitting officials who are also candidates as election time approaches.
- Publish or communicate anything that explicitly or implicitly favors or opposes a candidate.
- Highlight the differences between the views of candidates for public office on a high-profile issue.
- Make a positive or critical reference to someone related to their status as a candidate.
- Engage in issue advocacy when your organization cannot articulate a clear nonelectoral purpose for the activity or communication.
- Criticize sitting legislators or other elected officials by attacking their personal characteristics or their status as a candidate, rather than focusing on the substance of a policy issue.

CONCLUSION

For a long time, I thought that museums performed a role similar to that of journalists, and should maintain an objective viewpoint. Over the last few years, my opinion has changed. Museums need to advocate actively for civil society to remind people of their importance.

Museums must protect and advocate for freedom of speech and freedom of individual vision for those who cannot protect themselves. This goes for both visitors and artists. Civil society will be compromised unless museums protect and advocate for artistic rights.

Museums must remain safe places for all. Within their walls, every visitor must be treated equally and with respect, and individual freedoms must be protected. Museums need to become evangelists for civil society and protect the freedoms of religion, speech, press, assembly, and petition guaranteed in the US Constitution's Bill of Rights.

NEXT STEPS

Think of a current controversial issue and explore how museums are reacting to it by conducting an internet search. How did the results match your expectations?

KEY CONCEPTS INTRODUCED IN THIS CHAPTER THAT ARE DEFINED IN THE GLOSSARY

curatorial activism
democratization of content
lobbying

ADDITIONAL RESOURCES

Association of Art Museum Curators. "Professional Practices for Art Museum Curators." 2007. https://c.ymcdn.com/sites/www.artcurators.org/resource/resmgr/Docs/aamc_professional _standards.pdf.

Bowley, G. "Museums Chart a Response to Political Upheaval." *New York Times*, Mar. 13, 2017. https://www.nytimes.com/2017/03/13/arts/design/museums-politics-protest-j20-art-strike.html.

Davis Museum at Wellesley College: https://www.wellesley.edu/DavisMuseum/.

Hannon, K. "New Message at Some Museums: Don't Just Look. Do." *New York Times*, Mar. 13, 2017. https://www.nytimes.com/2017/03/13/arts/design/museums-inspire-social-activism-politics .html.

Japanese American National Museum. "JANM Statement Regarding the 2016 Presidential Election." Press release. Nov. 10, 2016. http://www.janm.org/press/release/410/.

Liberty Science Center: https://www.lsc.org.

McLeod, K. "The Role Museums Play in Social Activism." *ArtsBlog*. Aug. 2, 2017. https://blog.ameri cansforthearts.org/2019/05/15/the-role-museums-play-in-social-activism.

Meier, A. "After the Election, US Museums Affirm Their Roles as Safe, Open Spaces." *Hyperallergic*. Nov. 18, 2016. https://hyperallergic.com/338854/museums-across-the-us-affirm-their-post -election-roles/.

Murawski, M. "Museums Are Not Neutral," *Art Museum Teaching*, Aug. 31, 2017. https://artmuseum teaching.com/2017/08/31/museums-are-not-neutral/.

Richardson, J. "Should Museums Be Activists?" *MuseumNext*, Apr. 24, 2017. https://www.museum next.com/article/should-museums-be-activists/.

Society of Professional Journalists. "SPJ Code of Ethics." Sep. 6, 2014. https://www.spj.org/ethicscode .asp.

United States Holocaust Memorial Museum: https://www.ushmm.org.

Walls, C. "Tools and Resources in the Wake of Charlottesville." *American Alliance of Museums*. Aug. 18, 2017. https://www.aam-us.org/2017/08/18/tools-and-resources-in-the-wake-of-charlottesville/.

NOTES

1. National Endowment for the Arts (NEA) website, 2015, https://web.archive.org/web/20150319151334 /http://arts.gov/grants-organizations/art-works/museums.
2. United States Holocaust Memorial Museum "Pledge Wall": a collaboration between Small Design Firm, C+G Partners, Potion Design, Upstatement, and CornerStone Exhibits, https://www.davidsmall .com/holocaust-museum, https://www.cgpartnersllc.com/projects/holocaust-museum-from-memory -to-action/.
3. David W. Angel, "The Four Types of Conversations: Debate, Dialogue, Discourse, and Diatribe," Dec. 31, 2016, https://medium.com/@DavidWAngel/the-four-types-of-conversations-debate-dialogue -discourse-and-diatribe-898d19eccc0a.
4. "The Restriction of Political Campaign Intervention by Section 501(c)(3) Tax-Exempt Organizations," Internal Revenue Service, accessed Feb. 28, 2021, https://www.irs.gov/charities-non-profits /charitable-organizations/the-restriction-of-political-campaign-intervention-by-section-501c3-tax -exempt-organizations.

5. R. Russeth, "Protesting Trump, Wellesley's Davis Museum Will Remove from View Works Made or Donated by Immigrants to the United States," *ARTnews*, Feb. 15, 2017, https://www.artnews.com/art-news/news/protesting-trump-wellesleys-davis-museum-will-remove-from-view-works-made-or-donated-by-immigrants-to-the-united-states-7781/#!

6. "Citizenship Now!" City University of New York, accessed Feb. 28, 2021, http://www1.cuny.edu/sites/citizenship-now.

7. "The Citizenship Project," New York History, accessed Feb. 28, 2021, https://www.nyhistory.org/education/citizenship-project.

8. Sarah Kaplan, "Museums and Libraries Fight 'Alternative Facts' with a #DayofFacts," Feb. 17, 2017, https://www.washingtonpost.com/news/speaking-of-science/wp/2017/02/17/museums-and-libraries-fight-alternative-facts-with-a-dayoffacts/.

9. G. Bowley, "Museums Chart a Response to Political Upheaval: In a Tumultuous Era, Some Museums Are Rushing to Embrace the Political Moment, While Others Deliberately Retreat," *New York Times*, Mar. 13, 2017, https://www.nytimes.com/2017/03/13/arts/design/museums-politics-protest-j20-art-strike.html.

10. "The Restriction of Political Campaign Intervention by Section 501(c)(3) Tax-Exempt Organizations," Internal Revenue Service, accessed Nov. 14, 2017, https://www.irs.gov/charities-non-profits/charitable-organizations/the-restriction-of-political-campaign-intervention-by-section-501c3-tax-exempt-organizations.

11. Internal Revenue Service, "Common Tax Law Restrictions on Activities of Exempt Organizations," Sept. 23, 2020, https://www.irs.gov/charities-non-profits/common-tax-law-restrictions-on-activities-of-exempt-organizations.

12. "Lobbying," Internal Revenue Service, accessed Nov. 14, 2017, https://www.irs.gov/charities-non-profits/lobbying.

13. "Can We Really Say That?" Bolder Advocacy, accessed Nov. 14, 2017, https://www.bolderadvocacy.org/wp-content/uploads/2017/01/Can-We-Really-Say-That.pdf.

10

Placemaking: Museums and the Community

All museums are local.

—paraphrase of Tip O'Neill's "All politics is local."[1]

Pendleton, South Carolina, is a small rural community with a population of approximately three thousand.[2] The town is on the National Register of Historic Places; however, like so many traditional towns, its character has eroded over the years as investment went elsewhere. Its historic town square has become poorly defined due to the development of surrounding properties, depriving the community of a strong focal point. The National Endowment for the Arts (NEA) is helping the town's Clemson Little Theater and five local organizations work with landscape architects and urban designers to create a master plan to renovate the town square, including public art, designs for the surrounding streetscape, and performance spaces to foster cultural activity. The changes will give context to the history of Pendleton and provide a plan for cultural organizations to collaborate and make their town stand out. The NEA-funded "Our Town" program assists Pendleton and other small cities in "creative placemaking" by strengthening "community identity and a sense of place, and help[ing] revitalizing local economies."[3]

WHAT IS PLACEMAKING?[4]

As we learned in chapter 1, placemaking is a multifaceted approach to the planning, design, and management of public spaces that utilizes a local community's assets, inspiration, and potential. The intent is to create public spaces that promote people's health, happiness, and well-being. Placemaking is both a process and a philosophy.[5]

As a process of reinventing public spaces, placemaking involves the community and is a collaborative effort to maximize the value of the public space a community shares. It is not just an urban design process; it is intended to break down the limits usually associated with the rigid planning undertaken during the twentieth century, as well as any narrow planning focus. Placemaking is an ongoing evolution that focuses on the social and cultural identities of the people. During the process of placemaking, you first observe the people who use that place, asking them questions and understanding their needs as a community. The next step is to create a common vision.

Placemaking is different from simply constructing a building, a shopping mall, or a park. It is a philosophy, with a focus on people and their interactions as well as on the landscape, architecture, and objects. Good public places need to serve the community. Because this goes beyond any physical attributes of the space, it is measured by the uses and activities provided, the access and linkages, and sociability (see figure 10.1). Great places must host activities that give people a reason to come and use them. They need to be inviting, comfortable, and accessible, and provide positive perceptions of safety and cleanliness. A good public place should be easy to enter and navigate, which makes the boundaries of the space important. Sociability is perhaps most difficult factor to achieve, but it is the most important. In the end, a public place is meant to attract people to be with other people, to be with their neighbors, and to feel comfortable doing so.

Figure 10.1. Placemaking, adapted from "What Makes a Great Place?" by Project for Public Spaces, https://www.pps.org/article/what-is-placemaking.

The Project for Public Spaces has expanded the details surrounding each of the core attributes of uses and activities, comfort and image, access and linkages, and sociability. For example, sociability is a key attribute associated with the intangibles *diverse, stewardship, cooperative, neighborly,* and *welcoming*. Its measurements include number of women, children, and elderly; volunteerism; evening use; and street life.

As we saw above, placemaking is community driven and visionary, focused on function rather than form. It is not driven by cost-benefit analysis, but is adaptable, inclusive, and dynamic, focused on the community and its future.

OF/BY/FOR ALL

The organization OF/BY/FOR ALL[6] is a global movement and set of tools to help an organization "become of, by, and for the community." The OF/BY/FOR ALL approach can be represented by a formula:

$$OF + BY \rightarrow ALL$$

What does this mean? It means that if you want to be FOR your whole community, you have to be representative OF them and cocreated BY them. If people don't see themselves as part of your work, they won't see your work as an essential part of their lives. Putting up a welcome sign is not enough. To involve people in meaningful, sustainable ways, you can't just make programs FOR them. You have to involve them in their creation. And that means becoming OF and BY them too.[7]

PRINCIPLES OF MUSEUM PLACEMAKING

According to the Project for Public Spaces—a nonprofit planning, design, and educational organization dedicated to helping people create and sustain public spaces that build stronger communities[8]—successful placemaking is based on eleven basic principles divided into four categories: underlying ideas, planning and outreach techniques, translating ideas into action, and implementation.

Underlying Ideas

1. The Community Knows Best

    An important aspect of placemaking is taking into account the input of the people who will be using the public space most frequently—the community for which that space is intended. This is important because members of the community are likely to have useful insights into how the space functions (or should function), as well as a historical perspective of the area and an understanding of what does and does not matter to other members of the community.

2. You're Building a Place, Not Executing a Design

    Placemaking is not just about designing a park or a plaza with efficient pedestrian circulation. It involves taking into account the relationships among surrounding retailers and vendors, the amenities provided, and the activities taking place in the space, and then fine-tuning the space with landscape changes, additional seating, and whatever else is necessary to allow those elements to mesh. Physical elements should be introduced not as a goal but as a means to the end of making the space comfortable and social. The result should be a cohesive unit that creates greater value for the community than just the sum of its parts.

3. Placemaking Is a Group Effort

    Partners for political, financial, and intellectual backing are crucial to getting a public space improvement project off the ground. These partners might be individuals, private or municipal institutions, museums, schools, or other entities. Successful placemaking should mobilize public will and attract interest from the private sector. Try to gain the support of artistic and cultural leaders and build partnerships with local government agencies.

4. Make and Act on Observations

    By observing how a public space is used, it is possible to gain an understanding of what the community does and does not like about it. As mentioned above, it is possible to create testable parameters such as use by women, use at night, and so on to judge how effective the space is. This understanding can be used to assess what activities and amenities may be missing from the space. Even after a public space has been built, observation is key to effectively managing it, and evolving it to better suit the community's needs. In addition, observe what others have done, both their successes and their failures. Analyzing the failures of others can help you avoid repeating the same mistakes.

Planning and Outreach Techniques

5. Have a Common Vision

    As with many other types of project, a placemaking project needs a vision to succeed. This vision should not be the grand design of a single person, but the aggregate conception of the entire community. Having a vision is important, but it must be a common vision, with as many stakeholders on board as possible. Ideally, changes to public spaces will first be vetted in a public forum, such as town council meetings or on a local online news site.

6. Have Patience

    A placemaking project does not happen overnight. Do not be discouraged if things do not go exactly as planned at first, or if progress seems slow. Design of a public space is never finished; it always develops and evolves. It's best to start with what is lighter, quicker, and cheaper. By starting small, you can see what works and what doesn't.

Translating Ideas into Action

7. Triangulate

    Triangulation is simply the strategic placement of amenities so that they encourage social interaction and are used more frequently. For example, if you're designing a new library, consider locating the children's reading room so it is adjacent to a playground. Children will be more likely to move into that space, and will associate it with enjoyable activity. Similarly, placing a food kiosk near the reading room will lead to greater engagement.[9]

8. Ignore Naysayers

    Just because it hasn't been done, that doesn't mean it can't be done. Placemaking almost always involves stepping out into the unknown, and that can be frightening for many people. For example, when Bilbao, Spain, decided to revitalize their crumbling port area, the planners settled on a Frank Gehry–designed Guggenheim Museum that would cost more than $200 million. Plenty of disgruntled pundits and public servants complained that the cost was too high; it would become a burden on the community. However, the museum proved a spectacular success, paying for itself within four years. It has spearheaded the revitalization of Bilbao and the Basque area of Spain.[10]

9. Form Supports Function

    A public space's form factor should be formulated with its intended function or functions in mind.

Implementation

10. Money Should Not Be an Issue

    If networking and team building have been executed correctly, public sentiment toward the project should be positive enough to outweigh the monetary cost. However, it is important to keep all stakeholders on board from the outset, to be honest about costs, and to factor in any associated costs, such as maintenance.

11. Placemaking Is an Ongoing Process

    Placemaking is never done. Minor tweaks can be made to improve the space's usefulness to its community over time, and regular maintenance of facilities and amenities is a fact of life.

Great public spaces will in the end help a community flourish culturally and creatively, which in turn will bring about many different developments. The neighborhood will attract both businesses and creative individuals. Creative places, after all, attract entrepreneurs, who bring even more opportunities.

COMMUNITY MATRIX

Creative placemaking encompasses all of the aspects of the CX process at both a micro level of individual users and visitors, and at the macro level of societal impact. Before going further into the range affected by placemaking, it is important to make a distinction between *civil* and *civic*.

Civic is an adjective that describes an entity as having to do with a city or town. It often describes the government of a city or the duties involved with running a city.

Civil is an adjective that describes an object or a person relating to citizenship or a citizen, as opposed to the military or religious leadership. Civil rights are things that every person in the community has the right to. Note that we are not referring to human rights, which are things each human on earth is entitled to, without requiring membership in a community.

Placemaking moves from the level of individual identity to context over time, incorporating various types of experiences. It ties together the cultural organizations of a community to build societal impact. Multiple cultural originations can collaborate to create greater impact by coordinating events, exhibitions, and community programming from pre-visit to visit to post-visit to return, creating a matrix of events and experiences for community members.

The small town of Green River, Utah, population 950, was revitalized through the work of a nonprofit called Epicenter, which is using art and architecture to bring new energy into the community. The Epicenter's executive director notes that "Architecture isn't just looking at a building. It's looking at how the city is shaped, and then thinking about, what can we do as citizens to make it a better place to live through architecture and design?"[11]

The reinvention of Green River included an exhibition at the Utah Museum of Fine Art, "Epicenter: Our Futures," which at one point asked community residents to vote on one of four possible futures: (1) helping Green River to become a tourist magnet, (2) luring a new industry such as waste recycling, (3) establishing a futuristic space-research colony, or (4) withdrawing further from the outside world.[12] Visitors voted by placing marbles into one of four containers. The exhibition was featured in the Utah Museum of Fine Art's ACME Lab (Art, Community, Museum, Education), an exhibition space for art experimentation and exploration (see figure 10.2).

Figure 10.2. Children vote with marbles in the "Our Futures" exhibit at Epicenter, Museum of Fine Arts, Green River, Utah. *Epicenter and the Utah Museum of Fine Arts.*

The Epicenter initiative has succeeded in revitalizing the small town, refurbishing spaces, putting up public signage and art, and celebrating Green River's desert landscape. It has led to increased visitor interest and renewed energy and bonding among the citizens. A sense of place has been achieved.

CONCLUSION

The benefit of placemaking is that no cultural institution exists in isolation. Instead, each supports a larger culture of "place" for the community. A secondary benefit is synergy of cultural organizations throughout a community, including coordinated events. These might include a lecture at the art museum on Tuesday, a film at the history center on Wednesday, and parents' night at the children's museum on Thursday. As cultural institutions, museums must participate in placemaking in their communities. Museums can become leaders or initiators of such efforts where placemaking doesn't already exist. One way to get to know your community is by conducting feasibility studies, which is the topic of the next chapter.

NEXT STEPS

Using the content in this chapter, develop five specific examples of ways in which a museum can participate in placemaking in the community.

KEY CONCEPTS INTRODUCED IN THIS CHAPTER THAT ARE DEFINED IN THE GLOSSARY

civil
civic
creative placemaking
triangulation

ADDITIONAL RESOURCES

City Lab: https://www.bloomberg.com/citylab.
Markusen, A., and A. Gadwa. "Creative Placemaking." White paper. National Endowment for the Arts. https://www.arts.gov/sites/default/files/CreativePlacemaking-Paper.pdf.
MIT Sensible City Lab: http://senseable.mit.edu/.
National Endowment for the Arts. "How to Do Creating Placemaking." Accessed Feb. 28, 2021. https://www.arts.gov/sites/default/files/How-to-do-Creative-Placemaking_Jan2017.pdf.
OF/BY/FOR ALL: https://www.ofbyforall.org/.
Project for Public Spaces. "Placemaking: What If We Built Our Cities around Places?" October 2016. https://dn60005mpuo2f.cloudfront.net/wp-content/uploads/2016/10/Oct-2016-placemaking-booklet.pdf.
Project for Public Spaces. "What Is Placemaking?" https://www.pps.org/article/what-is-placemaking.
Richard Florida: https://creativeclass.com/.

NOTES

1. Chris Matthews, *Hardball: How Politics Is Played, Told by One Who Knows the Game* (New York: Simon and Schuster, 1999), 53.
2. National Endowment for the Arts "Our Town" Creative Placemaking grants, 2012, Town of Pendleton: Pendleton, South Carolina $25,000, https://web.archive.org/web/20140821025244/https://www.arts.gov/national/our-town/grantee/2012/town-pendleton.

3. "Our Town," National Endowment for the Arts, accessed November 6, 2020, https://www.arts.gov /grants/our-town.

4. Material in this section is adapted from "What Makes a Successful Place?" by Project for Public Spaces, https://www.pps.org/article/grplacefeat.

5. "The Placemaking Process," Project for Public Spaces, Dec. 21, 2017, https://www.pps.org/article/5 -steps-to-making-places.

6. "Want to Make Your Organization Of, By, and For Your Diverse Community?" OF/BY/FOR ALL, accessed Feb. 28, 2021, https://www.ofbyforall.org/.

7. Ibid.

8. Resources, OF/BY/FOR ALL, accessed Feb. 28, 2021, https://www.ofbyforall.org/.

9. Project for Public Spaces, "Placemaking: What If We Built Our Cities around Places?" Oct. 2016, https:// dn60005mpuo2f.cloudfront.net/wp-content/uploads/2016/10/Oct-2016-placemaking-booklet.pdf.

10. Silke Wünsch, "The Museum That Changed a Whole City: Guggenheim Museum Bilbao Turns Twenty," Oct. 19, 2017, *Deutsche Welle*, https://www.dw.com/en/the-museum-that-changed-a-whole-city-gug genheim-museum-bilbao-turns-20/a-41013716.

11. Jeffrey Brown, "Can This Rural Town Go from a Youth Exodus to an Art Epicenter?" PBS, Apr. 17, 2018, https://www.pbs.org/newshour/show/can-this-rural-town-go-from-a-youth-exodus-to-an-art-epicenter.

12. "Epicenter: Our Futures," Utah Museum of Fine Arts, accessed Nov. 6, 2020, https://umfa.utah.edu /our-futures.

11

Using Data to Create a Unified Visitor Experience

Art is not predictable. Art is not golf, as great as that may be. There are 360 degrees of choice to make.

—Tina Weymouth

As museums move into a dynamic future that involves visitors in shifting, immersive experiences, the texture of the exhibit is changing. One term museum planners are starting to use more frequently is "interactive museum transmedia exhibit." This can be defined as "a narrative dispersed across multiple channels for the purpose of creating a unified experience, with each medium making a unique contribution to the unfolding of the story."[1]

I view interactive transmedia exhibits as tools that form part of a larger experience plan, which we can call an omni experience. In this chapter, we'll look at the elements involved in an omni experience, as well as how to create omni experiences by accessing and incorporating data such as visitor feedback.

CREATING MUSEUM OMNI EXPERIENCES

An omni experience refers to an integrated message (*omni* = all) communicated by multiple channels. In other words, it's a unified experience at all touchpoints between user and museum. A museum omni experience is multicultural, and involves the following:

- Cocreation across media channels (in person, online, smartphone, tablet, app, and so on) that includes pre-visit, visit, and post-visit experiences, creating a feedback loop that draws the visitor to return to the museum because of in-person cocreated content.
- Integration of institutional culture and community outreach (an outgrowth of institutional culture) to impact the surrounding community.
- Emotional impact on visitors that encourages growth of both visitor and community.
- A transformative experience that extends beyond a didactic encounter.

I find it helpful to think big to small, so here's the museum omni experience working from the larger picture to the details:

1. Museum Mission. A museum's mission statement should be written as a solution to a problem, such as this one from the Museum of Us: "Inspiring human connections by exploring the human experience."[2] This puts the museum in a position to solve the problem, which in this case is a lack of human connections.
2. Umbrella Concept. The umbrella concept is how the museum will accomplish its mission. For example, the Museum of Us's vision is "to be San Diego's dynamic place to go to learn about each other, reflect on our place in the world, and build a better community."[3]
3. Strategy. To determine the strategy needed to accomplish the mission and achieve the vision, you need to answer the following questions: Who is your audience? How will you attract and create behavioral change in your identified audience? What exhibits and programs will you offer? How can you engage in outreach to the surrounding community?
4. Tactics. Tactics are the tools you will use to accomplish items one to three above. A mobile interactive transmedia experience is one such tool. Others include community outreach, museum programming, and museum marketing. A museum dashboard, which is a concept adapted from the data dashboards used in information management, is an online snapshot of metrics to view the performance of museum strategy and tactics (see figure 11.1).

Figure 11.1. Sample museum dashboard.

Museum data can be visualized by stakeholders (staff, board members, visitors, volunteers, and partners) working together to create an omni experience. Current technology offers plenty of tools to collect and analyze data. Examples of data include social media analytics, number of museum app downloads, time spent on a website page, viewing time, tracking eyeball movement at an exhibit,[4] tracking visitor gallery movements, key performance indicators, and net promoter score data.[5] The last two are particularly useful tools in a museum setting.

Key Performance Indicators

Key performance indicators (KPIs) are the critical indicators of progress toward an intended result. A 2012 White Oak Institute bulletin found twenty-seven KPIs in five different categories: membership, attendance, revenue, expenses, and staffing. The top five indicators were gate admission visits by category; percentage of total expenses for selected expense categories; admissions revenue as a percentage of earned and total revenue; revenue by category (earned, private support, public support, and endowment/interest income); and personnel expenses as a percentage of total expenses. The purpose of collecting and sharing such data in a museum setting is to equip museum leaders, managers, board members, and others who participate in organizational assessment and planning.

Net Promoter Score (NPS)

The Net Promoter Score (NPS) measures customer satisfaction and predicts business growth. It is similar to the KPIs discussed above. KPIs are used more often, but Sprinklr, the industry standard, refers to NPS. NPS uses a scale from one to ten to determine, for example, whether a customer is satisfied enough to recommend a museum to a colleague:

- Promoters (9 or 10) are actively visiting the museum and will continue to do so.
- Passives (7 or 8) are satisfied but are open to other offerings by competitors.
- Detractors (0 to 6) are dissatisfied customers who share negative feedback.

Subtracting the percentage of detractors from the percentage of promoters yields the NPS, which can range from a low of -100 (if every customer is a detractor) to a high of 100 (if every customer is a promoter).

Where museums are concerned, the NPS score can be related to the museum content, its brand, or other aspects of the museum visitor experience.

COMMUNICATION AMONG STAKEHOLDERS: THE VISITOR INTERVIEW

To accomplish a museum omni experience, there must be effective communication among stakeholders. One type of communication that can provide valuable feedback about the impact of a museum visitor experience is the visitor interview. My father, a real estate developer and salesperson, used to say, "Buyers are liars." If a person came into his office asking for a two-bedroom house on a quiet street, he was quite sure that if they bought a house, it would most likely *not* be a two-bedroom house on a quiet street. People often tell you what they think you want to hear. While interviewing people, you should pay attention to their body movements, facial expressions, and use of words, as well as listening to what they are saying. *How* they are saying it is at least as important as *what* they are saying.

The most important advice is to frame the interview as a dialogue. The following is some practical advice for conducting five- to ten-minute visitor interviews.

- Before you speak with visitors, ensure you are nicely dressed in a professional yet approachable style.
- When you first approach someone, wear your name badge and museum attire, and have a clipboard and pen in hand.
- If you are approaching a child, make sure to speak to the guardian before speaking to the child.
- Begin by saying, "I am a staff member at XYZ Museum, and we are speaking with people about a new exhibit. Would you mind if I asked you (or your child) a few questions?"
- If you get a less-than-interested response, thank them and walk away.
- Do not take photos of someone without their permission.
- Start with a short introduction about the objective of your project.
- Consider working from a script on your clipboard (a sample script and questionnaire can be found on the companion website, https://www.museum-experiences.com/).
- Ask the easiest (least intrusive) questions first, working your way up to the most difficult (most intrusive) ones.
- If at any time during the interview you sense the person is becoming uncomfortable, say, "Thank you so much for taking the time to speak with me," and walk away.
- Consider working in pairs, with one person approaching the potential interviewee and the second one standing back with clipboard in hand, but close enough so it is clear that you are both conducting the interview. Working in pairs makes the interaction appear more professional. Be sure to maintain appropriate eye contact while you are asking the questions.
- Write down the person's answers on the clipboard as you ask the questions; don't wait until the end of the interview. When you are finished, ask the user, "Do you have any other thoughts or comments?" Write those down as well.
- Thank them for their time and offer any additional information you have about the project. For example, you might say, "The new XYZ Museum exhibit will open in January of 2022. I hope you'll return to see it."

The purpose of this type of five- to ten-minute initial interview is to improve your personas (see chapter 4). After you have conducted the interview, take a couple of minutes to write your impressions on the questionnaire. For example, you might write something like "Although they answered all of the questions, they seemed uninterested in science or the topic of the exhibition." This type of apathetic respondent is precisely who you are looking for. As I tell my students, there is no reason to "sell to the sold." You are looking for uninterested people to discover how you can create interest. That is why empathy for the user, which we learned about in chapter 2, is so important.

EXHIBITION EVALUATION

Museum exhibition (experience) evaluation is a balancing act between visitor comprehension on the one hand and the museum's mission and revenue on the other. You are evaluating not just the exhibition, but the museum visitor experience. This process should answer the question, "What is the visitor gaining from the exhibition?" Because museum exhibitions are a form of communication with the visitor, exhibit evaluation analyzes that communication, and should also answer another question: "What is the exhibition communicating to visitors?" The website for the Institute of Museum and Library Services includes information on evaluation resources (see the Additional Resources at the end of the chapter). Exhibition evaluation can be divided into four phases: front-end evaluation, formative evaluation, remedial evaluation, and summative evaluation.

Front-End Evaluation

The *front-end evaluation* provides background about visitors' prior knowledge and experience, and gathers data on their expectations regarding a proposed exhibition. The primary goal of front-end evaluation is to learn about the audience before an exhibition has been designed to better understand how visitors will respond to it. This information can help ensure that the final product will meet visitor needs and project goals.

The aims are to

- define the exhibition objectives for use in the *project charter*, a formal document that describes an entire project, including its objectives, how the project will be completed, and its stakeholders (see the companion website for a sample project charter);
- gain an understanding of visitors' prior knowledge and interests related to the exhibition concept;
- test theories about visitor behavior and learning;
- identify visitor needs and how they can be met; and
- collect relevant information about audiences and any proposed ideas to help decision making.

The methods used include focus groups, interviews and surveys, questionnaires, informal conversations and feedback, community days and workshops, and reviews of market research.

Formative Evaluation

A *formative evaluation* provides information about how well a proposed exhibition communicates its intended messages. Formative evaluation occurs while a project is under development. The evaluator measures visitor responses to program or exhibit models, plans, and prototypes. Although it may be more roughly constructed, a *prototype* (a working version of an interactive exhibit) should resemble the final product as closely as possible in form and labeling. The more developed the model or prototype, the more likely it is that visitor reactions in the formative stage will anticipate their reactions to the final product.

The aims are to

- seek feedback related to how well the proposed exhibition communicates the messages,
- produce the optimal exhibition program within the limits of what is possible, and
- provide insight into learning and the communication processes.

Information from a formative evaluation is used to make changes to improve the design of a program or exhibit before it is implemented. The formative evaluation process is repeated until exhibition developers are satisfied with responses to the items being tested.

Remedial Evaluation

A *remedial evaluation*, which takes place once an exhibition is open to the public, is useful in troubleshooting problems, and informs museum staff and designers about improvements that can be made to maximize the visitor experience. Remedial evaluation addresses problems that could not be foreseen during the development of a program or exhibit, such as lighting, crowd flow, and signage issues.

The aims are to

- check that the program works in a practical sense,
- determine what maintenance and resources are needed,

- improve the short- or long-term effectiveness of the program for visitors, and
- provide some early insights into how visitors use the program.

The methods used include observations, informal visitor feedback, surveys and interviews, comment books, and staff feedback, especially from "front-of-house" and floor staff.

Summative Evaluation

A *summative evaluation* explains the impact of a project after it has been completed. Conducted after an exhibit has opened to the public or following presentation of a program, a summative evaluation can be as simple as documenting who visits an exhibit or participates in a program, or as complex as formal testing of what visitors have learned. Generally, the understanding of existing programs resulting from a summative evaluation is used to improve future activities. Through a variety of methods, it checks whether the intended messages were delivered; determines what learning occurred and how satisfied people were with the program; and analyzes marketing strategy performance. It is conducted using a combination of internal sources (the project team and other staff members) and external feedback (from visitors, special interest groups, and others).

The aims are to

- give feedback about the achievement of objectives;
- provide information on how a program is working overall, how people use it, what they learn from it, and how they are changed;
- provide reports; plan for future projects; suggest research; identify problems with visitor usage, interest, and learning; and identify successful strategies and layouts; and
- identify the relationship between the program costs and outcomes through a cost-benefit analysis.

Museum Theory

Museum theory can also be applied to help meet museum visitor needs. Visual Thinking Strategies (VTS)[6] is a process through which students and professionals in other fields can use art as a conduit to learn observation and analysis skills. For example, some museums take students in the medical field on specially planned tours meant to teach them to read and analyze nonverbal cues based on deep thinking and understanding multiple perspectives.

Another application of VTS is increased understanding of the societal significance of museum exhibits. For example, VTS can help visitors formulate opinions on where museum artifacts and exhibits should be located. Recently, there has been much discussion about the decolonization of museums. A significant portion of the holdings of Western museums involves art and artifacts that were essentially looted from colonized lands and peoples. The decolonization movement has three aims.

1. Return art and artifacts that were illegally or unethically removed from their source cultures or countries. This first step is the most drastic. For example, a US law called the Native American Graves Protection and Repatriation Act declares that museums must return human remains and grave goods to their tribal origins. For years, the Museum of Us in San Diego displayed Native American belongings and human remains behind glass, but after partnering with the Kumeyaay Nation it moved many of the human remains to burial grounds.[7]
2. Change the way museums interpret and display non-Western art and artifacts. For example, the Metropolitan Museum of Art has dozens of galleries dedicated to the paintings of Western Eu-

rope, while the arts of Africa, Oceania, and the Native Americas share a single space. Museums have tended to "other" non-Western cultures as "exotic" and "primitive."
3. Change the way museums approach and treat visitors. It is an unfortunate truth that museum visitor demographics in the United States skew to old, White, and female. Some museums are currently making an effort to capture more diverse audiences by developing programming that will appeal to a wider variety of visitors.

CONCLUSION

One important way to meet museum visitor needs is by creating an omni experience that includes cocreation, integration of institutional culture and community outreach, emotional impact, and a transformative experience that transcends the information the museum is trying to communicate. Tools to evaluate the museum omni experience include museum dashboards and museum stakeholder interviews.

NEXT STEPS

Select a museum customer group whose attendance you want to increase. For example, you might say, "We want to attract more twenty-somethings." Start by going out and actually speaking with your twenty-something visitors. Find out where they live, what they do, and what their interests are. Try to forget that you are interviewing them as part of a challenge and just have a conversation.

Now go out and talk to twenty-somethings in your community, using the same informal interview method. Twenty-something college students might not have time to visit a museum because of their college assignments and other commitments. Reframe the challenge: How can your museum help twenty-somethings with their assignments *and* increase visitation?

KEY CONCEPTS INTRODUCED IN THIS CHAPTER THAT ARE DEFINED IN THE GLOSSARY

decolonization
interactive transmedia exhibit
museum dashboard
omni experience
umbrella concept

ADDITIONAL RESOURCES

Astle, R. "Storyscapes: Tribeca Goes Interactive." *Filmmaker Magazine*, Apr. 23, 2013. https://filmmaker magazine.com/68946-storyscapes-tribeca-goes-interactive/#.Xgt9eUdKhPZ.
Chan, S. "On Storyworlds, Immersive Media, Narrative and Museums: An Interview with Mike Jones," Oct. 2, 2012, freshandnew.org. https://www.freshandnew.org/2012/10/storyworlds-immersive -media-narrative-interview-mike-jones/.
The Cleveland Museum of Art, dashboards. https://www.clevelandart.org/art/collection/dash board#page-1.
Devine, Catherine. "The Museum Digital Experience: Considering the Visitor's Journey," MWA2015: Museums and the Web Asia, Melbourne, Australia. 2015. https://mwa2015.museumsandtheweb .com/paper/the-museum-digital-experience-considering-the-visitors-journey/.
Fryett, Julia. "Transmedia Art Exhibitions, from Bauhaus to Your House." Aktionsart.org. 2013. http:// www.aktionsart.org/allprojects/2013/1/2/transmedia-art-exhibitions-from-bauhaus-to-your -house.

Hartig, Kasja. "Keynote: Re-Aligning Digital for the Responsive and Participatory Museum." SET Conference/ICOM General Conference, Milan, Italy. 2016. https://www.slideshare.net/kajhar /keynote-realigning-digital-for-the-responsive-and-participatory-museum.

Hatzipanagos, R. "The 'Decolonization' of the American Museum." *Washington Post*, Oct. 11, 2018. https://www.washingtonpost.com/nation/2018/10/12/decolonization-american-museum/.

Hegley, D. "Creating the Museum of the Future: Using Science to Reinvent the Museum Experience." Apr. 12, 2016. The Advertising Research Foundation. https://www.slideshare.net/dhegley/2016 -creating-the-museum-of-the-future-using-science-to-reinvent-the-museum-experience.

Institute of Museum and Library Services (IMLS) evaluation resources. https://www.imls.gov /research-evaluation/evaluation-resources.

The Met, Thomas J. Watson Library Dashboard. https://www.metmuseum.org/art/libraries-and -research-centers/thomas-j-watson-library/dashboard.

Museum of Us. https://museumofus.org/.

Smithsonian Metrics Dashboard. https://www.si.edu/dashboard.

Villaespesa, Elena. "Data Stories Centralized: A Digital Analytics Dashboard." The Met. 2015. https:// www.metmuseum.org/blogs/digital-underground/2015/data-stories-centralized.

Wong, A. "The Whole Story, and Then Some: 'Digital Storytelling' in Evolving Museum Practice." MW2015: Museums and the Web 2015, Chicago. https://mw2015.museumsandtheweb.com /paper/the-whole-story-and-then-some-digital-storytelling-in-evolving-museum-practice/.

Zorfas, A., and D. Leemon. "An Emotional Connection Matters More Than Customer Satisfaction." *Harvard Business Review*, Aug. 29, 2016. https://hbr.org/2016/08/an-emotional-connection -matters-more-than-customer-satisfaction.

NOTES

1. This quote has been edited to clarify museum application. See http://docubase.mit.edu/playlist /transmedia-101/ for the original quote: "a process where integral elements of a fiction get dispersed systematically across multiple delivery channels for the purpose of creating a unified and coordinated entertainment experience. Ideally, each medium makes its own unique contribution to the unfolding of the story."
2. Museum of Us, "Mission," accessed Nov. 4, 2020, https://museumofus.org/mission-vision-values/.
3. Ibid.
4. Andrew Emerson, Nathan Henderson, Jonathan Paul Rowe, Wookhee Min, Seung Y. Lee, James Minogue, and James C. Lester, "Early Prediction of Visitor Engagement in Science Museums with Multimodal Learning Analytics," *ICMI '20: Proceedings of the 2020 International Conference on Multimodal Interaction*, Oct. 2020, https://dl.acm.org/doi/pdf/10.1145/3382507.3418890.
5. Golam Rashed, Ryota Suzuki, Takuya Yonezawa, and Antony Lam, "Tracking Visitors in a Real Museum for Behavioral Analysis," Aug. 2016, 2016 Joint Eighth International Conference on Soft Computing and Intelligent Systems, https://doi.org/10.1109/SCIS-ISIS.2016.0030.
6. See https://vtshome.org/.
7. R. Hatzipanagos, "The 'Decolonization' of the American Museum," *Washington Post*, Oct. 11, 2018, https://www.washingtonpost.com/nation/2018/10/12/decolonization-american-museum/.

12

The Museum as a Hospitality Business

Hospitality means primarily the creation of free space where the stranger can enter and become a friend instead of an enemy. Hospitality is not to change people, but to offer them space where change can take place. It is not to bring men and women over to our side, but to offer freedom not disturbed by dividing lines.

—Henri J. M. Nouwen[1]

Some years ago, I taught skiing at Heavenly Mountain Resort in Lake Tahoe. I think I learned more about museum customer service as a ski instructor than I ever learned as a staff member at a museum.
My priorities at the ski resort, in order of importance, were as follows.

1. Safety. Make sure no one gets hurt, and that the kids were safely returned to their caregivers at the end of each lesson.
2. Fun. Give the kids such a good experience that they wanted to come back and ski again.
3. Learning. Teach the kids skills related to skiing.

You could adopt the same priorities for any museum: safety, fun, and learning, in that order. Many museums feel they are in the "education business." Some feel that they are in the business of protecting their collections ("Everything would be great if it weren't for those pesky visitors!"). Over the many years I have worked with museums and museum staff, I have thought repeatedly that museums need to recognize that they are in the hospitality business, not the education business. First and foremost, visitors need to have a good time, or they won't return. During my training at Heavenly Mountain, my supervisors drilled into me that the customer comes first, and that our job is to help the visitor have an experience of a lifetime. This is not a typical attitude for museum staff. Often, museum staff have an inward focus, thinking about the collection and museum politics first and the visitor last.
The idea that the visitor made plans to visit, got dressed for the occasion, drove there, and paid admission all before entering the museum is often lost on museum staff. As a staff member, it is your job to make their day special. You want the visitor to have the experience of a lifetime. Some advice that is relevant to both ski instructors and museum staff members, from directors to board members to floor staff, follows.

1. Take pride in the power of the uniform. As a museum staff member, you are in a privileged position of responsibility. People look up to you and value your opinion. That is a big responsibility, so take it seriously. If you don't know the answer to a visitor's question, go find out and get back to them. Museums don't like paying for uniforms, and museum staff don't like wearing them. However, you are there as an expert; you need to look the part and be easily identifiable.

2. Commit to training. As a first-year ski instructor, I went through three days of customer-service classroom training (for which I was paid minimum wage), one week of "on the snow" training, and three days of testing. I was often shadowed by more-experienced instructors and given feedback and advice. If I wanted to advance, there were opportunities for additional training; these were at my own expense but were tied to tiers of pay increases. I received more training as a part-time ski instructor than I ever received as a staff member at a museum.

3. Be selective. Heavenly Mountain is one of the best ski areas in the world. I was lucky to work there; the attitude of the management was that they only wanted the best; often the finest ski instructors are not great skiers but great teachers. Museum administrators should only hire the very best educators. Knowledge is important, but you have to know how to share it.

4. Offer tiers of certification. From my first day of ski-instructor training I knew how much I would be making (and I also knew how much everybody else was making). If I wanted to make more money, I could undergo additional training, with pay raises tied to the training. Typically, museum staff members are unclear of pay tiers or the criteria used to move from one tier to the next. On the first day of training, I was told about the Professional Ski Instructors of America certification website, and could start to study and learn about how I would be evaluated as a ski instructor and employee. The closest parallels in the museum world are the American Alliance of Museums Excellence Program[2] and the Museum Assessment Program (MAP).[3]

5. Participate in national organizations. Even as a first-year, part-time ski instructor, I was encouraged to join the national organization. Most museum staff only join the American Alliance of Museums or other organizations and participate in them if the museum pays. But how are employees expected to advance the field if they don't join a nationally recognized organization? Unfortunately, some associations, such as the Association of Science Technology Centers, allow only institutions—not individuals—to join; however, many others welcome individual members. For more information on museum associations, see part V.

6. Standardize and test. All ski instructors are judged by the same criteria and are tested on their ability to present the information. The same should be true of museum staff.

7. Value diversity. I taught kids from all over the world to ski. They came with many different skill levels, and I needed to meet them where they were. Some were athletic, some were overweight, and some did not speak English as their first language. Some were on scholarships and showed up with inappropriate equipment (it was my job to get them equipment for their day). It was my responsibility to make this a fun once-in-a-lifetime event for any kid under my care (and I always kept an extra set of mittens inside my jacket for kids who lost a mitten). As an instructor, I needed to lead the group, teach them to help one another, and learn from those who were different. This is why empathy (see chapter 2) is so important for museum staff—you need to learn how to put yourself in the visitor's shoes to give them the best experience.

8. Have systems in place. During Christmas week at Heavenly Mountain, we taught hundreds of kids each day. What made this easier were well-established systems for equipment rental and reservations. Most museums are good at providing school-group lunches and getting kids on and off buses. Museums are less good at administering programs and interacting with visitors; pay attention to these important aspects of the museum visitor experience.

9. Build on individuality. I often taught skiers who were quite shy. My first priority was to learn about them and discover their interests to put them at ease. Once trust was established, we could start

to ski. Without trust you can't teach, which is the primary job of museum staff. Emphasize to docents and staff that the visitor experience is informal learning and should be enjoyable.

10. Set clear expectations. As a ski instructor, I knew exactly what was expected of me: to help kids understand their equipment, be comfortable with it, learn basic skills, and practice those skills. In contrast, on my first day working at Liberty Science Center I was sent out onto the exhibit floor with no established expectations. All I was told was that I was there to answer questions. I was not equipped to answer questions about a cloud chamber (a particle detector used to detect ionizing radiation), but there I was trying to explain it. That lack of preparation is unfair to both the staff member and the visitor.

11. Share your passion. As you may have guessed, I am passionate about both museums and skiing, and I enjoy sharing those passions with others. Only hire staff who are passionate. Find people who are passionate about the subject area of the museum and encourage them to share their passion with visitors.

12. Come full circle. Train, evaluate, and provide feedback. As a ski instructor, I was given training, evaluated on my ability to present information, and given feedback by more-experienced instructors. Museum staff should undergo the same scrutiny to ensure the best visitor experience.

13. Encourage an independent-contractor attitude. I was encouraged to create my own systems and plans for teaching skiing. I was given guidelines, but also given the freedom to create my own lesson plans and teaching props, and my own style of interacting with students. Encourage museum staff members to be equally creative in their interactions with visitors.

14. Keep staff "on the hook." At the end of the ski season, I was not sure if I would be hired back the following season. You only want staff at their best. Test them continually, and let them know that if they are not performing at their best they may be let go.

15. Check your equipment daily. As a ski instructor, I was required to have annual physicals and equipment checks, and I was expected to check my own equipment at the start of every day. Make sure your staff does the same. Years ago, I had a disagreement with an architect with whom I was working on a new museum. The architect wanted a separate entrance for the museum staff, but I wanted the museum staff to walk through the front door every day to see what their visitors were seeing. Make sure that you can do everything you are asking your staff to do. Some museums require all staff, regardless of their position, to work on the floor at least once a month. This is a great idea! If you're not on the exhibition floor, you can't "check your equipment."

CONCLUSION

Museums can learn a lot from other institutions that are in the business of hosting and serving visitors. To ensure the highest-quality museum visitor experience, think hospitality first, and collections and politics second. Safety, fun, and education, in that order, should be the priorities for museum staff. Staff members should be given the opportunity to advance in their field, and should be evaluated regularly to ensure they are maintaining the highest level of service to those under their care. Finally, all staff members, regardless of status, should be given the opportunity to experience working the floor, so they understand how visitors are reacting to the space.

NEXT STEPS

Select one item from the fifteen listed above and apply it to the museum where you work, or to your favorite museum. What is the museum doing right? What could it do better?

ADDITIONAL RESOURCES

American Alliance of Museums (AAM): https://www.aam-us.org.

International Council of Museums (ICOM) standards. https://icom.museum/en/activities/standards
-guidelines/standards/.

NOTES

1. Henri J. M. Nouwen, *Reaching Out: The Three Movements of the Spiritual Life* (London: Fount, 1986).
2. "Accreditation and Excellence Programs," American Alliance of Museums, accessed Nov. 3, 2020, https://www.aam-us.org/programs/accreditation-excellence-programs/.
3. "Museum Assessment Program (MAP)," American Alliance of Museums, https://www.aam-us.org /programs/accreditation-excellence-programs/museum-assessment-program-map/.

Part IV

Future Museum Visitor Experiences (When)

13

Emerging Technologies and the Museum Visitor Experience

Content is king.

—Bill Gates[1]

The first time I heard this Bill Gates quote—the title of a 1996 essay published on the Microsoft website—was at a meeting with Andy Ackerman, director of the Children's Museum of Manhattan, where I served as director of exhibits from 1994 to 1997. That one phrase transformed my thinking about museums. It occurred to me that museum content should also be made accessible both in person and digitally. This is not limited to the internet, but should include other technologies that are playing a part in today's museum visitor experience. This chapter provides insights into how the digital revolution and emerging technologies have impacted museums and will continue to do so.

THE MUSEUM DIGITAL REVOLUTION

The COVID-19 pandemic and the resulting quarantine have accelerated the museum digital revolution and the fourth industrial revolution.[2] The museum digital revolution—the transformation from analog to digital—involves a tremendous increase in the capacity to store information, which is changing the way people relate to and visit museums. It is also changing what visitors require of museums.

Human–computer interaction is a key component of the content exchange between museum and visitor. Much of this revolution is being driven by Generation Z (Gen Z; people born between 1995 and the present), the first generation to have access to the internet from an early age. As of August 2015, 73 percent of thirteen- to seventeen-year-olds owned or had access to a smartphone,[3] and that figure is sure to increase.

Of all generations living today (including the Greatest Generation, 1901–1924; the Silent Generation, 1925–1945; Baby Boomers, 1946–1964; Generation X, 1965–1976; and Millennials/Gen Y, 1977–1995), Gen Z is the one most influenced by online communication and online education (see figure 13.1).

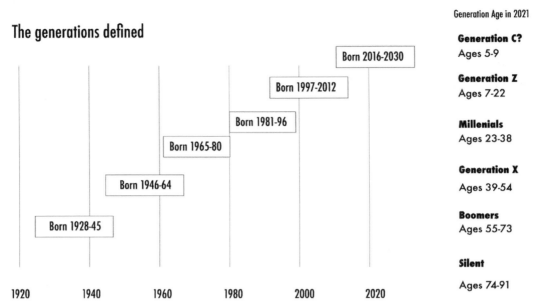

The generations defined

Generation Age in 2021

Generation C?
Ages 5-9

Born 2016-2030

Generation Z
Ages 7-22

Born 1997-2012

Millenials
Ages 23-38

Born 1981-96

Born 1965-80

Generation X
Ages 39-54

Born 1946-64

Boomers
Ages 55-73

Born 1928-45

Silent
Ages 74-91

1920   1940   1960   1980   2000   2020

Figure 13.1. Generations defined, 1920 to present, https://www.pewresearch.org/fact-tank/2019/01/17/where-millennials-end-and-generation-z-begins/.

Characteristics of Generation Z include the following.

- Hyperconnectedness. The proliferation of internet access allows everyone to have access to the same information, leveling the playing field.[4] It has also caused a shift from affluence to influence. It used to be that money was power, but these days influence, or a strong personal brand, is power.[5]
- Experience orientation. On-demand, mission-driven businesses such as food-delivery services have become common. Gen Zers are quick to notice any differences between a company's mission and the reality of the customer experience. They seek alignment of corporate images and their own objectives.[6]
- Social media expertise. Gen Zers cannot remember a time before social media. To them, social media is not media in the traditional sense, but *the* medium for "connecting, learning, showing off, expressing oneself, debating, dating and so much more."[7] In larger numbers than any other generation, Gen Zers think that social media affects how people see you. Forty-two percent of Gen Zers indicate that social media determines their happiness, well-being, and self-esteem.[8]
- Multiculturalism. According to the US Census Bureau, the country's Hispanic population grew at four times the rate of the total population between 2000 and 2010. The number of Americans self-identifying as mixed White and Black biracial rose 134 percent, and the number of Americans of mixed White and Asian descent grew by 87 percent.[9] Those who identify as being of two or more races is projected to increase from 7.5 million to 26.7 million from 2012 to 2060.[10]
- Blurring of gender roles. Seventy percent of Gen Zers support access to gender-neutral restrooms in public spaces, and 56 percent know someone who uses gender-neutral pronouns.[11]
- Inclusivity. Gen Zers tend to be inclusive and accepting, a quality that sets them apart from other generations.[12]
- Multidimensional, spatial thinkers. According to some research, because they are digital natives, Gen Z brains are structurally different from those of earlier generations. This is related not to genetics but to how they use their brains to respond to their environment. Because their brains

have become wired to sophisticated, complex visual imagery, the part of the brain responsible for visual ability is far more developed, making visual learning more effective. This age group strongly dislikes auditory learning (lecture and discussion). They appreciate interactive games, collaborative projects, advance organizers, challenges, and anything that they can try out and see.[13]

- Global social circles. Twenty-six percent of those in Generation Z would need to fly to visit most of the friends in their social networks.[14]
- Cocreation. Gen Zers gravitate toward livestreaming media and video conferences as preferred ways to communicate and generate content.[15]

To participate in the digital revolution and attract the museum visitors of the future, museums must recognize these characteristics and meet certain requirements of Generation Z:

- Personalized content that can facilitate visitor influence on others, tapping into their hyperconnectedness and social media expertise.
- Messages that include a call to action, encouraging visitors to get involved.
- CX-oriented information that is on demand, simple, and mission driven.
- A clear museum vision that allows the visitor to align themselves with the museum's objectives (or not).
- A social media presence that facilitates connecting, learning, showing off, and personal expression.
- A multicultural, multistory, and multi-history approach.
- Gender neutrality. This includes making restrooms gender neutral and evaluating exhibits to eliminate gender bias.
- Event-driven content. Special events are more likely to attract experience-oriented visitors and hold the decreased attention span of Gen Zers.
- Multidimensional exhibits. Exhibits must appeal to multiple types of learners, and interactive games, collaborative projects, advance organizers, and challenges should be developed.

A few museums that have begun to cater to the requirements of Generation Z include the Rijksmuseum, the Museum of Pop Culture, the New Museum, and Tate Modern.

CREATING AN ONLINE EXPERIENCE

What Is Your Question?

Perhaps more than anything else, the internet is a forum for answering questions. My website museumplanner.org is focused on answering two questions: "How do you design an exhibition?" and "How do you start a museum?" As I narrow my focus for a blog post, I often find that the topic broadens and I discover more and more to write about. Keep your online content narrow, decide what questions to answer, then let the ideas flow. Also, be a good sharer; answer as many questions as you ask. Your museum should have someone dedicated to checking online interaction at least once a day.

Be Local

The Arizona Science Center (Alexa ranking 751,289) is a local resource for science in Arizona and the Phoenix area. The Mobius Science Center (Alexa 5,000,000) requires association to the Spokane area. The lower the Alexa ranking of your museum, the better. Research into the correlation between the world's largest museums and their online rankings reveals that smaller museums often have higher rates of online visitation than their larger counterparts.[16]

Move People

Move people both literally and figuratively. Tell personal stories that include links to multiple platforms. Move people from Facebook to Twitter, from Twitter to YouTube, and from YouTube to LinkedIn. The internet is like a lint ball; as you move it around, it gathers more lint. Each time you move people from platform to platform, you gather more people.

Be Yourself

I think of my website museumplanning.com as a portfolio. It is a dynamic form of communication that serves as a repository of projects to which I can direct potential clients. In contrast, a blog is a conversation in which every participant has a voice. Of my time spent online, I spend about 20 percent working on my website backend (updating themes, making website design changes, and so on), and 80 percent updating content. If you are starting a new museum, the best use of your online time is developing content.

As with any conversation, it is important to be polite and communicate your point of view. One of my recurring themes is "built to last." I believe strongly that each museum has a personality that will attract like-minded customers and visitors. On the internet, your writing becomes your "voice"; make sure that it is a clear and consistent one. As a form of communication, the internet has grown into a forum of users, each of whom has or develops a persona.

Take Advantage of the Democratization of Content

One of the most important aspects of the internet is the "democratization of content," or how visitors vote with their clicks. Museums now compete for the number of online followers. A well-targeted, well-designed blog for a small museum can have many more online visitors than the less-focused website of a larger one. Consider the Corning Museum of Glass (Alexa 303,139) versus the Museum of Glass (Alexa 2,844,298). I continue to work on my "clicks versus bricks" theory, but I believe there is a correlation between the online experience and the in-person experience. A rough goal is to have three times as many visitors to your internet presence (clicks) as your in-person visitors (bricks).

Drive Your Visitors

Give your visitors, both online and in person, a reason to visit by creating new content on an ongoing basis. As long as the content is highly targeted, quick posts can be as successful as lengthier ones. Create online programming, online pre-visit materials, and online forums describing new exhibitions and new programs to drive traffic to your brick-and-mortar museum.

Remember, It's Still Virtual

As a sculptor by training, I strongly believe that an online experience will never replace an in-person experience, but it can be just as important. I like to think that providing an online pre-visit, visit, and post-visit experience can complement the in-person experience. Depending on the amount of time spent, a visitor's online experience can be as much as two-thirds of their entire museum experience.

MOBILE APPS

As we saw in chapter 3, the American Museum of Natural History (AMNH) has made many adjustments to enhance today's museum visitor experience. Perhaps AMNH's biggest outreach connected to learning and education is its mobile applications (apps). Museum executives realized early on that it is not always easy for people interested in a certain part of an exhibition to find additional information. One of its most successful apps was related to a special exhibit. "The Power of Poison" was a game that offered users the chance to investigate famous historical poisoning cases. The AMNH guide app allows access to interactive content related to physical exhibits, both inside and outside the museum. One of their goals is to use the power of the digital world to allow the public to see over thirty-three million artifacts, which could never be displayed at the same time in the museum's limited physical space.

Other museums are following the lead of AMNH in offering an interactive visitor-centric experience, both digital and physical. For example, the Art Lab app offered by the Museum of Modern Art (MoMA) provides visitors with the opportunity to work on their own piece of art following the style of famous artists.[17] The Cleveland Museum of Art's ArtLens app is a museum-wide app that includes every object on view.[18]

MUSEUM VR AND AR

You have probably heard the terms *virtual reality* (VR) and *augmented reality* (AR). Virtual reality (VR) is an immersive experience requiring a headset. For example, in the British Museum's VR tour with an Oculus headset, "high-resolution 360° photography has been combined with layers of additional content, including expert audio commentary from our curators and interactive 3D models of high-lighted objects."[19]

Another example of museum VR is the Met Cloisters's "Small Wonders: The VR Experience." After exploring the exhibition "Small Wonders: Gothic Boxwood Miniatures," which brought together for the first time some fifty rare boxwood carvings from museums and private collections across Europe and North America, visitors could don a VR headset and move through the "Last Judgment: Coronation of the Virgin (1500–1530)," a Gothic bead that fits inside the palm of one's hand. VR users were able to get up close and personal with the intricately carved saints and sinners.[20]

In contrast, augmented reality (AR) adds an effect to an experience without requiring a headset. In 2017, the Smithsonian Museum of Natural History used AR technology to add an additional dimension to the Bone Hall, one of its oldest exhibitions (many of the specimens have been on display since 1881). Visitors can use the Skin and Bone application to add a virtual image of the animals to the underlying skeleton.

In 2017, the Pérez Art Museum in Miami worked with artist Felice Grodin to create an ongoing AR art exhibition called "Invasive Species" (figure 13.2).[21] Digital sculptures were added to spaces throughout the museums and were visible through the use of the AR app on a smartphone or tablet.

While museum VR is more immersive, it requires more hardware in the form of the headset. Museum AR provides more freedom for the visitor, who uses a tablet, smartphone, or computer station to interact with the content.

3D TECHNOLOGY

Three-dimensional (3D) scanning, which is the process of capturing digital information about the shape of an object with equipment that uses a laser or light to measure the distance between the scanner and the object,[22] is becoming more popular in the museum world. It allows a museum to create digital collections that are available twenty-four hours a day, making them more accessible to the public. In addition, 3D printers allow objects to be reproduced easily. A 3D printer is a device that receives digital data from a computer as input and, instead of printing on paper as output, builds a three-dimensional model out of a custom material. For example, the Smithsonian is creating three-dimensional scans of many objects in its collections. A recent project was a compilation of

Figure 13.2. Felice Grodin's "Invasive Species" exhibit at the Pérez Art Museum Miami, 2017–ongoing. © *Pérez Art Museum Miami.*

three-dimensional scans of the skeleton of a woolly mammoth. The completed model is available online for 3D printing at home.[23]

IMPACT OF AI

Artificial intelligence (AI), which is the capability of a machine to imitate intelligent human behavior,[24] has impacted all spheres of our private and professional lives, so it naturally impacts the workings of museums today. A 2017 report by the American Alliance of Museums highlighted AI as one of the new trends to watch for regarding the functioning of museums.[25] In general, it is clear that museums could utilize the availability and accessibility of AI to improve how they work. These potentially game-changing modifications raise a number of questions regarding the ways in which museum staff will function in the future.

A number of museums have already begun to utilize AI. For example, the Norwegian National Museum has started using machine learning (the ability to automatically learn and improve from experience without being explicitly programmed)[26] and deep neural networks (multilayered neural networks that use sophisticated mathematical modeling to process data in complex ways)[27] to classify their collections. They create metadata (data that provides information about other data)[28] from the identification and tagging of images. In addition, they use an algorithm for mapping the collections to create new connections. This new and perhaps better understanding of the artifacts may lead to new discoveries. The computer programs are becoming so refined that they are now able to detect color similarities and patterns, understand color clusters, and quantify similarities and differences. All of this brings about more sophisticated ways in which art pieces and objects can be grouped for a better museum visitor experience.

In addition, as the machine learning engine is "trained," its "vision" becomes even better—that is, more accurate. Facial recognition can be utilized to read emotions from faces on the portraits, for example. Text recognition software, known as optical character recognition, has become widely available. Extracting text from documents allows them to become searchable and more easily analyzed.

In 2016, the United Kingdom's Tate Museum held a competition for the best digital innovation. The winning idea was a program called Recognition, which used AI to pair online news images with images from the Tate Museum's collection. It also analyzed the context to create written descriptions of the images.

AI researchers are testing ways to learn from people's reactions to the pairing of art and news. In Paris, the Musée du Quai Branly introduced an AI art critic on one of their exhibits, "Persona: Oddly Human." The idea behind the project was to explore how "intimate becomes animate," or how the relationships between people and objects are established. The AI, called the Berenson robot (after the late art critic Bernard Berenson), tracked visitors' reactions via facial expressions, and formed its opinion based on positive reactions such as smiles and movement toward the objects, and negative reactions like frowning and moving away (see figure 13.3).

More generally, AI can help with many aspects of museum management, including staff supplementation and performance enhancement. AI is already being used to help visitors plan their visits, book tickets, and accomplish other tasks, removing those burdens from staff members. Personal digital assistants like Apple's Siri or Microsoft's Cortana will certainly find their way into the functioning of museums.

However, the primary use of AI will be to help organize and present collections and resources more quickly and efficiently to provide better and more informed content. This will lead to a better

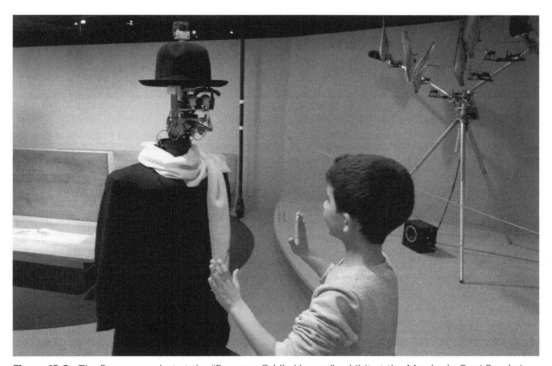

Figure 13.3. The Berenson robot at the "Persona: Oddly Human" exhibit at the Musée du Quai Branly in Paris. *Reuters/Alamy Stock Photo.*

Emerging Technologies and the Museum Visitor Experience

relationship with the public and a better museum visitor experience. The Brooklyn Museum already uses natural language processing (algorithms that help computers understand, interpret, and manipulate human language)[29] to help answer visitors' questions. In the near future, it may be possible for AI to recommend and connect visitors to resources based on these questions. AI will be an essential tool for managing all types of data, including that related to museums, in the twenty-first century. The biggest archives of the future will contain emails and social media posts, which are becoming so numerous that it will be impossible to gather and analyze them without the help of AI. For example, the William J. Clinton Presidential Library contains twenty million emails; the Barack Obama Presidential Library contains more than one billion.

Another useful application of AI is in the detection of art forgeries. Art authentication is a problematic field, and in the face of a number of lawsuits, many institutions now refuse to be involved in this kind of work. But AI can, in fact, analyze an artist's style and previous works in a deep way. It would have little problem in detecting whether the style of a newly discovered artwork corresponds to an already authenticated work, and it could potentially do so faster and more reliably than any art curator or expert.

AI can also help predict and analyze visitors' wants and needs. A 2020 research study from North Carolina State University used a machine-learning model to predict how long individual museum visitors would engage with a given exhibit.[30] This technology could undoubtedly help museums plan and allocate resources, attract more visitors, understand subscription rates, and fundraise. It could even automate donor outreach. Any kind of strategic planning should involve digital data analyses, and the smarter the better.

DOWNSIDES TO THE USE OF TECHNOLOGY IN MUSEUMS

The use of AI and other digital tools comes at a price. One of the primary concerns is its impact on the workforce of the future. If AI does an increasing amount of the work, what will happen to the museum staffers currently doing those jobs? In some areas, AI performs better than humans; when you take the cost savings and increased efficiency into account, the future of museum jobs becomes uncertain. As we saw in chapter 1, today's experience economy, like the switch from an agrarian economy caused by the industrial revolution, is changing all aspects of our lives. The 2016 *Economic Report of the President* speculated that 83 percent of those earning less than $20 an hour would soon lose their jobs to intelligent machines.[31] Even those earning twice as much per hour were estimated to have a 31 percent probability of being replaced. If this prediction comes to pass, it could lead to dramatic increases in unemployment and widen the gap between the rich and the poor.

Different options have been proposed to solve or at least mitigate these concerns. For example, Microsoft cofounder Bill Gates has proposed a "robot tax." For every human worker replaced by a robot, a company would pay taxes equivalent to the income taxes that human worker would have paid.[32] Gates proposed that the money collected should finance jobs that people are better at than machines, such as working with children or taking care of the elderly.

The European Parliament, the legislative branch of the European Union, appears to disagree. In 2017, the parliament rejected a tax that would finance support or retraining of workers who lost their jobs to robots, arguing that it would slow down research and technological advances. They called for a more general "robot law," which would regulate the rise of the number of robots, intelligent machines, and AI in industry and the workplace.[33]

Some, like Marco Annunziata, the chief economist at General Electric, are more optimistic regarding human–machine collaboration, part of what Annunziata calls the industrial internet. In his view, robots, AI, and intelligent machines will be helping workers to perform more efficiently. Advanced analytics and human creativity will work together to benefit everyone. Acknowledging that there may only be jobs for engineers and data scientists in the future, Annunziata suggests that we should not worry; the new generation will be prepared to meet these job requirements. He adds, "It will make life easier for workers of all skill levels. It's not going to be easy, but it is going to be worth it."[34]

CONCLUSION

COVID-19 and the resulting quarantine have accelerated the pace of the digitalization of museum experiences and a move to hybrid museum experiences (online/in person; virtual/real). However, a museum's mission, vision, and values should remain constant. What is changing is how museums implement and communicate their messages with specific visitors and selected audiences, increasing the importance of staff decision making.

The increasing popularity of blogs, websites, apps, and new exhibits embracing technology, and the Smithsonian's digitalization of their 137 million artifacts using 3D scanners, clearly indicate the direction that museums are taking in the new age. Combining educational opportunities for integrated and interactive learning with emerging technologies will continue to enhance the museum visitor experience. Museum staff are faced with the challenge of crafting messages for the cocreation of possible futures. And speaking of the future, the next and final chapter discusses visions of the future of the museum visitor experience.

NEXT STEPS

Which emerging technology or technologies should museums adopt to ensure the best museum visitor experience today and in the future, and why?

KEY CONCEPTS INTRODUCED IN THIS CHAPTER THAT ARE DEFINED IN THE GLOSSARY

artificial intelligence (AI)
deep neural network
human-computer interaction
machine learning
metadata
mobile applications (apps)
augmented reality (AR)
museum digital revolution
virtual reality (VR)
natural language processing
optical character recognition
3D printer
3D scanning

ADDITIONAL RESOURCES

Alexander, J. "Removing the Barriers of Gallery One: A New Approach to Integrating Art, Interpretation, and Technology." MW 2017: Museums and the Web 2017. Cleveland, OH, April 19–22, 2017. https://mw17.mwconf.org/paper/removing-the-barriers-of-gallery-one-a-new-approach-to-integrating-art-interpretation-and-technology/.
American Museum of Natural History Explorer App. https://www.amnh.org/apps/explorer.
Ashby, J. "Museums and Virtual Reality: VR in the Grant Museum." UCL Museums and Collections blog, Feb. 15, 2017. https://blogs.ucl.ac.uk/museums/2017/02/15/museums-and-virtual-reality-vr-in-the-grant-museum/.

Association for Computing Machinery (ACM) SIGGRAPH. https://www.siggraph.org. International community for those sharing an interest in computer graphics and interactive techniques.

Barack Obama Presidential Library. https://www.obamalibrary.gov.

Berger, B. "AI-Enabled Technologies Could Help Museums Survive the Digital Age." *Venture Beat.* Nov. 6, 2017. https://venturebeat.com/2017/11/06/ai-enabled-technologies-could-help-museums-survive-the-digital-age/.

Casa Batlló Augmented Guide. https://www.casabatllo.es/en/visit/.

Children's Museum of Manhattan. https://cmom.org.

Cooper Hewitt Immersion Room. https://www.cooperhewitt.org/events/current-exhibitions/immersion-room/.

Erlick, N. "20,000-Year-Old Artifacts, 21st-Century Technology," *The Verge*, May 6, 2017. https://www.theverge.com/2017/5/6/15563922/museums-vr-ar-apps-digital-technology.

French, A. "Service Design Thinking for Museums: Technology in Contexts." MW2016: Museums and the Web 2016, Los Angeles, Apr. 6–9, 2016. https://mw2016.museumsandtheweb.com/paper/service-design-thinking-for-museums-technology-in-contexts/.

Google Arts and Culture App, Museum Virtual Tours. https://artsandculture.google.com/theme/mwJiZHf_Y7FfLg

Ishii, H. "Tangible Bits: Beyond Pixels." MIT Media Lab, Feb. 18, 2008. https://www.media.mit.edu/publications/tangible-bits-beyond-pixels/.

The Met Cloisters. "Small Wonders: The VR Experience." http://cfccreates.com/news/pressroom/296-us-premiere-of-small-wonders-the-vr-experience-at-the-met-cloisters.

MIT Media Lab's Tangible Media Group. https://tangible.media.mit.edu.

Musée du Quai Branly. https://www.quaibranly.fr/.

Museum of Modern Art (MoMA). https://www.moma.org.

Museum of Pop Culture (MoPOP). https://mopop.org.

Museums and the Web. https://www.museweb.net.

The Natural History Museum. "London Tour with Sir David Attenborough." https://www.livescience.com/58784-david-attenborough-hologram-museum-tour.html.

New Museum. https://www.newmuseum.org.

Pangburn, D. J. "Take a Fantastic Virtual Reality Voyage into a 500-Year-Old Gothic Sculpture." *Vice*, Apr. 7, 2017. https://www.vice.com/en_us/article/nzgabb/500-year-old-gothic-sculpture-virtual-reality-voyage.

Rae, J. "Virtual Reality at the British Museum: What Is the Value of Virtual Reality Environments for Learning by Children and Young People, Schools, and Families?" Museums and the Web, 2016. https://mw2016.museumsandtheweb.com/paper/virtual-reality-at-the-british-museum-what-is-the-value-of-virtual-reality-environments-for-learning-by-children-and-young-people-schools-and-families/.

Rijksmuseum. https://www.rijksmuseum.nl/.

Sexton, C. "Exploring Key Trends in Digital Experience beyond the Museum Sector." MW2016; Museums and the Web, 2016. Los Angeles, Apr. 6–9, 2016. https://mw2016.museumsandtheweb.com/paper/exploring-key-trends-in-digital-experience-beyond-the-museum-sector/.

Smithsonian American Art Museum, Renwick Gallery. WONDER 360. https://americanart.si.edu/wonder360.

Smithsonian Museum of Natural History. Walk with Dinosaurs. https://www.smithsonianmag.com/videos/walk-with-dinosaurs-at-the-national-museum-o_1/.

Tangible, Embedded, and Embodied Interaction (TEI; international conference). https://tei.acm.org/2021/.

Tate Modern. https://www.tate.org.uk/visit/tate-modern.

Tate Museum (Recognition). recognition.tate.org.uk.

Westvang, E. "Deep Learning at the Museum." Jan. 5, 2016. http://bengler.no/blog/deep-learning-at
-the-museum.

William J. Clinton Presidential Library. https://www.clintonlibrary.gov.

NOTES

1. W. Gates, "Content Is King," Microsoft website, Jan. 3, 1996.
2. Brian Peccarelli, "Bend, Don't Break: How to Thrive in the Fourth Industrial Revolution," World Economic Forum, Jan. 13, 2020, https://www.weforum.org/agenda/2020/01/the-fourth-industrial-revolution-is -changing-all-the-rules/.
3. Amanda Lenhart, "A Majority of American Teens Report Access to a Computer, Game Console, Smartphone and a Tablet," Pew Research Center, Apr. 9, 2015, https://www.pewresearch.org/internet /2015/04/09/a-majority-of-american-teens-report-access-to-a-computer-game-console-smart phone-and-a-tablet/.
4. Jacob Morgan, "Generation Z and the Six Forces Shaping the Future of Business," *Inc.*, Jul. 5, 2016, http:// www.inc.com/jacob-morgan/generation-z-and-the-6-forces-shaping-the-future-of-business.html.
5. Ibid.
6. "Why Generation Z Wants Only Perfect Customer Service," Helprace, Jul. 14, 2016, https://helprace .com/blog/why-generation-z-wants-only-perfect-customer-service.
7. Jason Dorsey, *IGen Tech Disruption*, GenHQ, 2016, http://genhq.com/wp-content/uploads/2016/01 /iGen-Gen-Z-Tech-Disruption-Research-White-Paper-c-2016-Center-for-Generational-Kinetics.pdf.
8. Ibid.
9. Alex Williams, "Move Over, Millennials, Here Comes Generation Z," *New York Times*, Sep. 18, 2015, https://www.nytimes.com/2015/09/20/fashion/move-over-millennials-here-comes-generation -z.html.
10. See https://www.census.gov/newsroom/releases/archives/population/cb12-243.html, https://www .census.gov/prod/cen2010/briefs/c2010br-13.pdf.
11. Shepherd Laughlin, "Gen Z Goes Beyond Gender Binaries in New Innovation Group Data," Wunderman Thompson, Mar. 11, 2016, https://www.jwtintelligence.com/2016/03/gen-z-goes-beyond-gender-bina ries-in-new-innovation-group-data/.
12. "'Millennials on Steroids': Is Your Brand Ready for Generation Z?" Wharton, Sep. 28, 2015, http:// knowledge.wharton.upenn.edu/article/millennials-on-steroids-is-your-brand-ready-for-generation-z/.
13. Darla Rothman, "A Tsunami of Learners Called Generation Z," accessed Mar. 1, 2021, https://mdle.net /Journal/A_Tsunami_of_Learners_Called_Generation_Z.pdf.
14. "Meet Generation Z: Forget Everything You Learned About Millennials," Jun. 17, 2014, http://www.slide share.net/sparksandhoney/generation-z-final-june-17/40-They_are_less_active40This_generation.
15. "Teen Obesity Has Nearly Tripled," Jun. 17, 2014, https://www.slideshare.net/sparksandhoney/genera tion-z-final-june-17/43-Teen_obesity_has_nearly_tripled.
16. "20 Best Museum Website Designs for Inspiration 2020," Colorlib, Sep. 30, 2020, https://colorlib.com /wp/museum-website-design/.
17. Art Lab App, MoMA Design Studio, accessed Mar. 1, 2021, https://momadesignstudio.org/Art-Lab-App.
18. Artlens App, Cleveland Museum of Art, accessed Mar. 1, 2021, https://www.clevelandart.org /artlens-gallery/artlens-app.
19. See https://www.oculus.com/blog/new-webvr-experiences-entertain-educate-and-let-you-explore/.
20. "Encore Engagement at the Met: 'Small Wonders: The VR Experience,'" Canadian Film Centre, Mar. 26, 2017, http://cfccreates.com/news/739-encore-engagement-at-the-met-small-wonders-the-vr -experience.
21. "Felice Grodin: Invasive Species," Pérez Art Museum Miami, https://www.pamm.org/ar.
22. Absolute Geometries, accessed Mar. 1, 2021, http://absolutegeometries.com/3D-Scanning.html.
23. "Mammuthus primigenius (Blumbach)," Smithsonian, accessed Mar. 1, 2021, https://3d.si.edu /explorer/woolly-mammoth.
24. See https://www.merriam-webster.com/dictionary/artificial%20intelligence.

25. "TrendsWatch 2017, American Alliance of Museums, 2017, https://www.aam-us.org/programs/center -for-the-future-of-museums/trendswatch-2017/.
26. See https://expertsystem.com/machine-learning-definition/.
27. See https://www.techopedia.com/definition/32902/deep-neural-network.
28. See https://www.merriam-webster.com/dictionary/metadata.
29. See https://www.sas.com/en_us/insights/analytics/what-is-natural-language-processing-nlp.html.
30. Andrew Emerson, Nathan Henderson, Jonathan Paul Rowe, Wookhee Min, Seung Y. Lee, James Minogue, and James C. Lester, "Early Prediction of Visitor Engagement in Science Museums with Multimodal Learning," *ICMI '20: Proceedings of the 2020 International Conference on Multimodal Interaction*, Oct. 2020, https://doi.org/10.1145/3382507.3418890, https://dl.acm.org/doi/pdf/10.1145/3382507.3418890.
31. Jason Furman, Sandra Black, and Jay Shambaugh, "The 2016 Economic Report of the President," President Barack Obama White House, Feb. 22, 2016, https://obamawhitehouse.archives.gov/blog/2016 /02/22/2016-economic-report-president.
32. Kevin J. Delaney, "The Robot That Takes Your Job Should Pay Taxes, Says Bill Gates," *Quartz*, Feb. 17, 2017, https://qz.com/911968/bill-gates-the-robot-that-takes-your-job-should-pay-taxes/.
33. "European Parliament Calls for Robot Law, Rejects Robot Tax," Reuters, Feb. 16, 2017, https://www .reuters.com/article/us-europe-robots-lawmaking-idUSKBN15V2KM.
34. "Marco Annunziata: What Will Human-Machine Collaboration Mean for Our Jobs?" Apr. 21, 2017, https:// radio.wpsu.org/post/marco-annunziata-what-will-human-machine-collaboration-mean-our-jobs.

14

The Future of Museums

The future cannot be predicted, but futures can be invented.[1]

—Dennis Gabor, winner of the 1971 Nobel Prize in Physics for inventing holography

At the beginning of this book, we looked at the 2007 definition of a museum from the International Council of Museums (ICOM):

> A museum is a non-profit, permanent institution in the service of society and its development, open to the public, which acquires, conserves, researches, communicates and exhibits the tangible and intangible heritage of humanity and its environment for the purposes of education, study and enjoyment.[2]

At the ICOM's General Assembly on September 7, 2019, in Kyoto, Japan, the following definition was proposed (although the vote was postponed):

> Museums are democratizing, inclusive and polyphonic spaces for critical dialogue about the pasts and the futures. Acknowledging and addressing the conflicts and challenges of the present, they hold artefacts and specimens in trust for society, safeguard diverse memories for future generations and guarantee equal rights and equal access to heritage for all people.
>
> Museums are not for profit. They are participatory and transparent, and work in active partnership with and for diverse communities to collect, preserve, research, interpret, exhibit, and enhance understandings of the world, aiming to contribute to human dignity and social justice, global equality and planetary wellbeing.[3]

When you compare the 2007 definition to the 2019 proposed definition, there is clearly a shift in role: museums are becoming more visitor-centric. It is also clear that the role of a museum is changing from being a monolithic "expert" to becoming a shared authority: museums and visitors are now cocreators in content creation. In addition, "static history" is being transformed into a more fluid conception of changing histories. Museums are becoming ever-evolving institutions that are transparent about changes to facts and histories, acknowledging multicultural, multiperson interpretations of events.

Although the definition proposed in 2019 has yet to be ratified, the discussion and proposed changes make clear the shift to a more visitor-centric, multicultural experience that is representative of multiple perspectives. Also clear is that, in "aiming to contribute to human dignity and social justice, global equality and planetary wellbeing," museums must become future-oriented, active participants.

In the future, exhibitions will be transformed into digital hybrids[4] that can be experienced both in person and online. Museums themselves will become hybrid, existing both online and in person. Of course, the experiences will continue to differ, but one important goal is to create museum visitor experiences in which the digital, online experience drives in-person visitation and events.

Because this is a forward-looking book about creating visitor-centered experiences, we will not delve too much into the past, but an understanding of the past will lead to a better understanding of our views about the future. Before Reaganomics—the economic policies promoted by President Ronald Reagan in the 1980s—most museum directors were academics or curators. Reaganomics forced all museums to fundraise; a large part of their revenue had to come from sponsors, private donors, and grants rather than the federal government. This change in financing caused a seismic shift in the culture of museums. Instead of being academics or historians or curators, museum directors became fundraisers, and museum trustees judged them by their fundraising abilities. Today, museum directors are tasked with raising between one-third and two-thirds of museum revenues. This change to the financing model created an important side effect: Constant engagement in capital campaigns resulted in "the ever-expanding museum." Museum directors raised capital for constructing museum buildings, exhibitions, and other facilities, and earned income was used to cover operating costs. To keep covering costs, museums had to keep expanding.

Another side effect was the creation of a culture within museums of White people of privilege serving as museum staff. These were often young people who were wealthy enough that they could afford to work as unpaid interns. Museums often developed two cultures, with people of color working as floor staff at minimum wage and wealthy White young people working as unpaid interns or in lower-level management positions. The COVID-19 pandemic has pulled back the curtain on this inequity. With tens of thousands of museum staff furloughed or laid off, staffing inequities are easier to see: the ones who remain tend to be those in higher levels, and they tend to be White.

In Europe and most of the rest of the world, museums are predominantly government funded. In the United States, we assume that museums can continue to be ever-expanding and fundraise two-thirds of their revenue. In fact, most US museums have been barely surviving since Reaganomics. Museums are now going under the microscope as they are forced to answer the question "Are you providing for your local community?" As a result, it is becoming obvious that the museum financing model is broken. If the current funding model and staff inequities continue, museums will continue to serve only wealthy, well-educated, primarily White people.

On the other hand, with the recognition that this funding model is broken, I see a possible different future. If federal, state, and city governments step in and start to change the funding model for museums, they could go back to being more academic, more research-based, and more community oriented.

The majority of the thirty-five thousand museums in the United States are small local-history museums with one or no full-time staff members.[5] The lack of museum staff experience has made the adoption of digital technologies challenging. Often, museums are wary of digital content creation because they have little experience with it, but it requires the same process of achievement of the museum's mission and educational objectives, and development of content strategy. The digital sphere (including a website, social media, digital signage, and smartphone apps) forms an important vehicle of communication between a museum and its audience.

The experience economy[6] and the changing marketplace have forced museums to include digital experiences to enhance the museum visitor experience. In order to remain competitive, digital programming has become a necessary museum amenity.[7]

As noted earlier, the major differences between museums in the United States and those in the European Union are their funding models. Since the 1980s and the government's requirement that all museums raise funds for operating and capital costs, US museums have changed from being primarily government-funded organizations to being primarily private institutions funded by individual and corporate donors, a shift that will be exacerbated by the COVID-19 pandemic. In contrast, EU museums are primarily public organizations that continue to receive public (federal, state, and foundation) funding.

Some predictions about the future of museums in the United States follow.

MUSEUM CLOSINGS

In the United States, all museums are dependent on donations (including government-funded museums). Sadly, a large percentage of museums will close as a result of the COVID-19 pandemic. The majority of the closures will be of small local-history museums with no staff members, or just one or two.

MUSEUM STAFF, FREELANCERS, AND VENDORS

Since the 1980s, museums have decreased full-time museum staff, replacing them with independent contractors. Many freelance museum consultants (curators, art handlers, designers, registrars, and so on) will leave the museum field. Others will be unable to afford to return to museum work due to student loans and personal debt. In addition, many museum suppliers (including exhibit fabricators, art shippers, and art storage companies) will close because of a lack of business.

REDUCED MUSEUM SERVICES

Many museums that survive will be forced to reduce hours, close galleries, and increase online digital exhibits. In the short term, "blockbuster" exhibitions—large-scale, multimillion-dollar traveling exhibits—will be put on hold.

MUSEUM BOARDS OF DIRECTORS

Many boards of directors will be reorganized to include a greater number of "old money" members, due to the impact of COVID-19 and the loss of wealth of many younger board members. The downside to this will be the lack of input from younger members, and potentially a lack of diversity in the boards of directors.

TREND TOWARD NETWORKED AND DIGITAL

The financial costs of operating an in-person experience and concerns for both staff and visitor safety will be greater than those of operating digital online experiences. Museums that survive will increase their digital offerings.

GREATER RELIANCE ON METRICS

Due to the hesitant reopening of museums, there will be increases in the need for greater data regarding museum costs, museum revenue, visitor return rate, visitor dwell rate, and other metrics.

Smaller and more nimble local museums will find the transition to the new museum reality less challenging. Large encyclopedic museums will find it more difficult; they are more dependent on corporate sponsorships and have high operating costs. In the end, the new reality will benefit agile, visitor-centric museums that can operate lean, with artist-, scientist-, and historian-focused visitor experiences.

FUTURE SCENARIOS

The issues of the current and future pandemics, museum worker inequities, and museum survival are converging. The future of museums is tied directly to the country's political and economic future, as well as to issues related to economic and racial inequality, health insurance, and employment. The following sections present three possible scenarios that I envision for the future of museums.

Scenario One: Financial Conservatism

- One-third of museums in the United States close permanently.
- A racial and socioeconomic "cold war" sets in across the United States.
- Federal and state funding to museums is cut significantly.
- COVID-19 is followed by similar viruses; climate change impacts many communities.
- As people are affected by the climate-change-induced effects of drought, civil unrest increases and the numbers of walled cities and wealthy communes increase.
- The idea of democracy morphs into a combination of government and privatized services. The reach of the federal government is reduced, with greater authority given to individual states. Corporations are given a greater role as government services are privatized. Responsibility and authority continue in a new altered form, as a sort of "pay to play" relationship develops between government and privatized services.
- Museum endowments, and museums in general, are considered nonessential.
- Museums return to nonpublic status and are used by the wealthy as part of their children's education and for entertainment.

Scenario Two: Museums as Centrist

- The remaining two-thirds of museums become more insular, drawing inward into silos of points of view.
- Museums become more dependent on corporate and wealthy donors, and content is driven by corporate giving.
- Except for floor staff, museum staffs remain mostly White. Museum floor staff hire people of color as needed and pay them minimum wage.
- Museums as a whole lose their trustworthiness; it becomes accepted that certain museums represent certain points of view.
- Museums continue in a state of stasis and lose relevance to many audiences.
- Museums experiment with digital and online exhibitions, but due to costs and a lack of funding only a small percentage are deemed successful.
- The distinction between "museum" and for-profit entertainment becomes blurred.
- As many corporations close retail stores, museums become corporate marketing and retail sales centers.
- Museums are considered "boring" and are thought of as storage facilities that are no longer relevant.
- As stasis sets in, many question whether museums should be closed.

Scenario Three: Green Transparency

- Museums accept and encourage inclusivity.
- A new digital model of "museum" flourishes.
- Museums become central to both the operation of civil society and formal and informal education.
- Approximately 40 percent of the US workforce continues to work from home post–COVID-19.[8] All parents receive six weeks of paid vacation time to spend with their families.
- Museums create and adopt a digital standard, allowing sharing of museum content across digital platforms, similar to Creative Commons.[9]
- A Green New Deal incorporates museums as civic hubs for education and family enjoyment.
- All museums institute a standard of transparency regarding curation, museum collections, and education about contemporary art.
- Museums and universities become part of an initiative in which all digital content is shared freely.
- Museums and universities sign an agreement providing free digital education with transparent degree standards.
- Museum collections are centralized to allow greater access to all people.
- A wealth tax is instituted to limit wealth; the tax is used to institute the above changes.
- All companies and nonprofits are required to represent the racial mix of their local communities (within a thirty-mile radius).
- All companies are required to contribute 10 percent of profits to benefit civil society.

My hope is that society and GLAMs (galleries, libraries, archives, and museums) move toward the future outlined in scenario three, with greater societal equality and a more earth-centered point of view. The future is our own. Even better than predicting a future of museums is active participation in creating the desired museum of the future.

BLUE SKY

I often do an exercise with students called "blue sky," in which I ask how they would design a product, experience, or service without any restrictions. Now, at the end of this book, it is my turn to do the exercise. For me, the perfect museum would be a combination art museum, science center, children's museum, library, local history museum, and natural history museum. The museum would include a public museum school for middle school and high school students; the students from the school would need to volunteer and work part-time at the museum for both class credit and a small stipend.

The museum would not be large—maybe thirty thousand square feet. It would be located in the center of a small city. Car traffic would be restricted to outside the city center, with parking on the outer edge of the city square. The museum would be part of a downtown complex including walking paths and municipal buildings (fire department, city hall, and courthouse). Surrounding the museum on the city square would be a combination of restored buildings, new construction, and local shopping. Large corporate retailers would be restricted from being part of the city center. The museum would have a pay-as-you-wish policy and a membership program, but memberships would be used more often than individual pay-as-you-wish ticket sales. The museum would be "digital-first": exhibits, programs, and educational content would be almost 100 percent digital and event based. Schedules of events, programs, and classes would exist both online and in person, creating a hybrid experience. "Visitors" could take a class one night at home and then go to the museum the following night for an in-person experience. The most important staff members would be a small group of volunteers and paid staff composed of full-stack developers, educators, and designers. Floor staff could work with this core group on upcoming projects after meeting a certain number of volunteer hours.

Much of the museum and the school would be project-based learning. Almost all of the exhibitions would be developed and built in house, using staff and volunteer labor.

Unlike most current museums, the building and facility would be designed by a local architect and builder. The complex would never be finished; it would be iterative and updated continually. Visiting artists could stay with local families for one or two months while creating on-site artwork in collaboration with the public. The museum would include a maker space staffed by local university and museum school students. The director of the museum, who would be more like the leader of a band than a typical museum director, would live locally and arrive in jeans ready to work with other staff members and with the public. The museum endowment would be sufficient to underwrite operating costs, and new programs and exhibitions would be underwritten through memberships, contributions by local donors, and support from the city.

Most importantly, the museum would belong to everyone and everyone would want to cherish it. The museum visitor experience would be as important as the content, and would consist of a mixture of quiet, meditative, and introspective experiences and highly interactive kinetic experiences.

Note that, so far, this "blue sky" picture includes almost no mention of content or exhibition materials, because the most important part of the museum is a sense of ownership and pride. It is a given that the exhibitions would be excellent and would emerge from the local community. The museum would have a small collection of local artists, local history, and artwork created by the artists, designers, and scientists in the residence program. The artwork would be stored in a combination of open and off-site storage.

The information in this book should help you create your own "blue sky" museum project. If I have done my job right, you should be able to check off all the items in the following list of museum objectives to create your own meaningful museum visitor experience.

MUSEUM OBJECTIVES

Visitor-centered
Personalized
Accessible to all
Event-driven
Always new
Activist
Based on narratives, not objects
Multicultural and inclusive
Encourages visitors to have a sense of ownership and responsibility
Grounded in the local environment and community
Incorporates digital technology
Transparent
Without walls (pre-visit, visit, and post-visit)
Embraces customer-centered service design

CONCLUSION

Almost all of the ideas included in my "blue sky" museum already exist. Achieving them would only be a matter of combining the different attributes into a single facility. Constructing a building and creating a collection are not difficult; the mission, vision, and values require the most effort. I often say to clients and students that raising the money and erecting the building are relatively easy; creating a vibrant institutional culture is the most challenging aspect of providing a meaningful museum visitor experience.

NEXT STEPS

Visit a local museum and imagine how you might transform the museum using the objectives outlined above.

Write a one-to-two-page paper describing your vision of a local museum that meets all the museum objectives outlined above. Have friends and family read your paper, ask for feedback, and revise the paper based on that feedback.

ADDITIONAL RESOURCES

Please visit the Museum Visitor Experience Toolbox at https://www.museum-experiences.com/ for additional resources on the future of museums.

"Is This the World's Most Accessible Museum?" *New York Times*, Sept. 6, 2019. https://www.nytimes.com/2019/09/06/arts/design/disabled-access-wellcome-collection.html.
American Visionary Art Museum. http://avam.org/.
Beacon New York. https://www.diaart.org/visit/visit-our-locations-sites/dia-beacon-beacon-united-states/main/lightningfield.
Big Car. https://www.bigcar.org.
Boulder Library. https://boulderlibrary.org/.
City Museum. https://www.citymuseum.org/.
Eli Whitney Museum. http://www.eliwhitney.org/.
Fernbank. https://www.fernbankmuseum.org/experiences/outdoor-experiences/.
Indianapolis Art Center. https://www.indplsartcenter.org/.
Invention Studio. https://www.news.gatech.edu/features/invention-studio.
Lightning Fields, Quemado, NM. https://www.diaart.org/visit/visit-our-locations-sites/walter-de-maria-the-lightning-field/main/lightningfield.
MakerFaire. https://makerfaire.com/.
Marfa, Texas. https://www.npr.org/2012/08/02/156980469/marfa-texas-an-unlikely-art-oasis-in-a-desert-town.
Palo Alto Junior Museum. https://www.destinationpaloalto.com/junior-museum-and-zoo.
Polk Interactive Museum. https://copolkmuseum.org/.
Reno Art Museum. https://www.nevadaart.org/.
Santa Cruz. https://www.santacruzmah.org/.
Solar Decathlon. https://www.solardecathlon.gov/.
The Upswing by Robert D. Putnam. http://robertdputnam.com/the-upswing/.

NOTES

1. Dennis Gabor, *Inventing the Future* (London: Penguin, 1964).
2. "Museum Definition and Code of Ethics," International Council of Museums, Jan. 11, 2021, https://www.imls.gov/assets/1/AssetManager/MUDF_TypeDist_2014q3.pdf.
3. Kate Brown, "What Defines a Museum? The Question Has Thrown the Art World's Leading Professional Organization into Turmoil," Artnet, Aug. 10, 2020, https://news.artnet.com/art-world/icom-museums-definition-resignation-1900194.
4. "Sculpture Lens—Strike a Pose," video, Cleveland Museum of Art, accessed Aug. 19, 2020, https://vimeo.com/60866008.
5. Colleen Dilen Schneider, "How Much Do Building Expansions Increase Attendance—And for How Long?" Dec. 11, 2019, https://www.colleendilen.com/2019/11/12/the-data-informed-difficulties-of-building-expansions-for-newer-museums-data/.

6. B. Joseph Pine II and James H. Gilmore, *The Experience Economy* (Cambridge, MA: Harvard Business School Press, 1999).

7. Daniel Grant, "Amenities Galore!: Museums Are Upping the Extras but to What End?" *Observer*, Sep. 8, 2016, https://observer.com/2016/09/amenities-galore-museums-are-upping-the-extras-but-to-what-end/.

8. May Wong, "Stanford Research Provides a Snapshot of a New Working-From-Home Economy," *Stanford News*, Jun. 29, 2020, https://news.stanford.edu/2020/06/29/snapshot-new-working-home-economy/.

9. "Attribution—NonCommercial—ShareAlike 4.0 International," accessed Aug. 19, 2020, https://creativecommons.org/licenses/by-nc-sa/4.0/legalcode.

Part V

Visitor Experience Toolbox

Museum Visitor Experience Toolbox

ADDITIONAL TOOLS

1. Project Brief
2. Community Canvas
3. Umbrella Concept
4. Ethnographic Profiles
5. Context Map Canvas
6. Culture Canvas
7. Project Charter
8. User Requirements
9. Value Proposition Canvas
10. Importance/Influence Matrix
11. SWOT Analysis
12. Task Analysis
13. Vision Board
14. Keyword Matrix
15. Mission, Vision, and Values Statements
16. Scenario Canvas
17. "What You Don't Know"
18. Touchpoint Matrix
19. Storyboard
20. Lamina
21. Product Canvas
22. Museum Institutional Planning Diagram

Project Brief

The **project brief** is a written document with the goal of outlining the objectives, scope, and deliverables of a project. A typical project includes the following.

1. Project title
2. Project participants, including the project manager and sponsor
3. Project background
4. Parameters and assumptions
5. Planning considerations
6. Project objectives
7. Visitor experience goals

8. Scope of work
9. Stakeholders
10. Constraints, budget, schedule, and risks
11. Floor plans and technical descriptions

You can find a sample project brief at https://www.museum-experiences.com/museum-toolbox/.

Community Canvas

A **community canvas** is a framework intended to help build strong communities or to improve the operation of established ones. These communities are not limited to museums; they can include human-resources departments, startup incubators, chambers of commerce, religious organizations, academic institutions, sports clubs, and any other places where people gather for a common purpose.[1] The community canvas has three sections: Identity, Experience, and Success. *Identity* establishes who the community is and what it wants to believe. *Experience* is what happens in the community from the perspective of its members. *Structure* relates to the long-term stability of the community and how it is achieved and sustained.

- Identity: purpose, identity, values, brand, success definition
- Experience: selection, rituals, rules, shared experiences, content, roles, transition
- Structure: organization, governance, financing, channels and platforms, data management

For a visual representation of the relative importance of these components and the relationships among them, see figure 15.1.

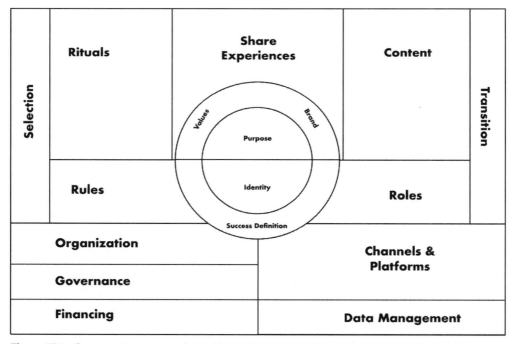

Figure 15.1. Community canvas, adapted from "Community Canvas," created by Nico Luchsinger, Fabian Pfortmüller, and Sascha Mombartz: https://community-canvas.org/.

Umbrella Concept

An **umbrella concept** proposes ideas in groups of three to show various conceptual frameworks for a visitor. We'll use the example of a science exhibition.

- Option 1: The visitor has been transported to a remote space station; from their new location, they have the tools and gain the experience to understand space from a new perspective.
- Option 2: Visitors are tasked with planning and executing a rocket launch to Mars, using the tools in the gallery to plan their journey.
- Option 3: Visitors enter a magical house. Within it, they discover secret doors and a slide that can transport them anywhere in the galaxy.

Umbrella concepts are often used as part of team discussions to help participants understand how different approaches might meet the requirements of different user groups. Written descriptions are usually presented with mood boards to help each team member understand the look and feel of each solution.

Ethnographic Profiles

An excellent way to understand your museum customers' goals and needs is through conducting ethnographic studies, commonly known as field studies. Such studies involve visiting people in their own environment and result in the creation of **ethnographic profiles** of visitors and potential visitors. These tools can help us understand people and groups as they go about their normal lives, including how they interact and how they develop. One source describes ethnography as the social equivalent of technology's usability testing: "Where usability is about how people directly interact with a technology in the more traditional sense, ethnography is about how people interact with each other."[2] Each of us creates and curates ourselves through our decisions about what we buy, where we live, and how we behave. To understand your museum customer, you must first understand why they make the decisions that they do. Through understanding their decisions, project teams can better encourage behavioral change. Ethnographic profiles are especially useful if you are starting a new museum in an unfamiliar location and want to know who your museum visitors might be. See figure 15.2.

Figure 15.2. Creating ethnographic profiles.

Context Map Canvas

A **context map canvas** can help demonstrate where a business lies within the general environment. See figure 15.3. It looks at a number of issues:

- Demographic trends. What social shifts, employment trends, or other changes might affect the business?
- Technology trends. What technologies impact the business, and how?
- Rules and regulations. How do current or possible future regulations affect the business?
- Economic climate. How is the larger economy changing, and how might those changes affect the business?
- Customer needs. What particular requirements do customers or potential customers have?
- Competitors. What is the current competition in the market? How might unknown competitors change the market in the future?
- Uncertainties. What changes might affect the future market?

Culture Canvas

The **culture canvas** is a tool in the form of a hierarchical pyramid with segments that answer a number of questions. Value Propositions (What values are being satisfied?) and Customer Segments (Who are the customers?) appear at the base. Just above the base are Values (Which values are shared, and which are personal?) and Actions (Which actions support the values?). Above that are Stories and Metrics, which include stories that best describe values and ways to record those values. At the apex of the pyramid are Purpose and Impact (What are the results?). See figure 15.4.

Project Charter

A **project charter** is a contract to be signed between client (or other stakeholder), project team, and user to achieve the desired results. It identifies project resources and includes descriptions of the roles of all members of the project team. See figure 15.5.

User Requirements

The **user requirements** document contains a detailed "nuts and bolts" description of the final deliverables for a project. This document is often used when writing a request for vendor proposals to confirm vendor adherence to contract requirements. You can find sample user-requirements documents and research at https://www.museum-experiences.com/museum-toolbox/.

Value Proposition Canvas

A **value proposition canvas** is a CX tool divided into two segments: a value map and a customer profile map. Designed by Swiss business-management theorist Alexander Osterwalder, it helps you visualize how value is created for your customer. Its goal is to design a product that customers really want. The customer profile map includes three parts: customers' tasks (what they are trying to accomplish), their pains, and their gains. The value map also includes three parts: your products and services, "pain relievers" (how they solve issues), and "gain creators" (how they add value). The two segments should interact. The "pain relievers" should address customer pains, and the "gain creators" should match as many of the customer gains as practically possible. See figure 15.6.

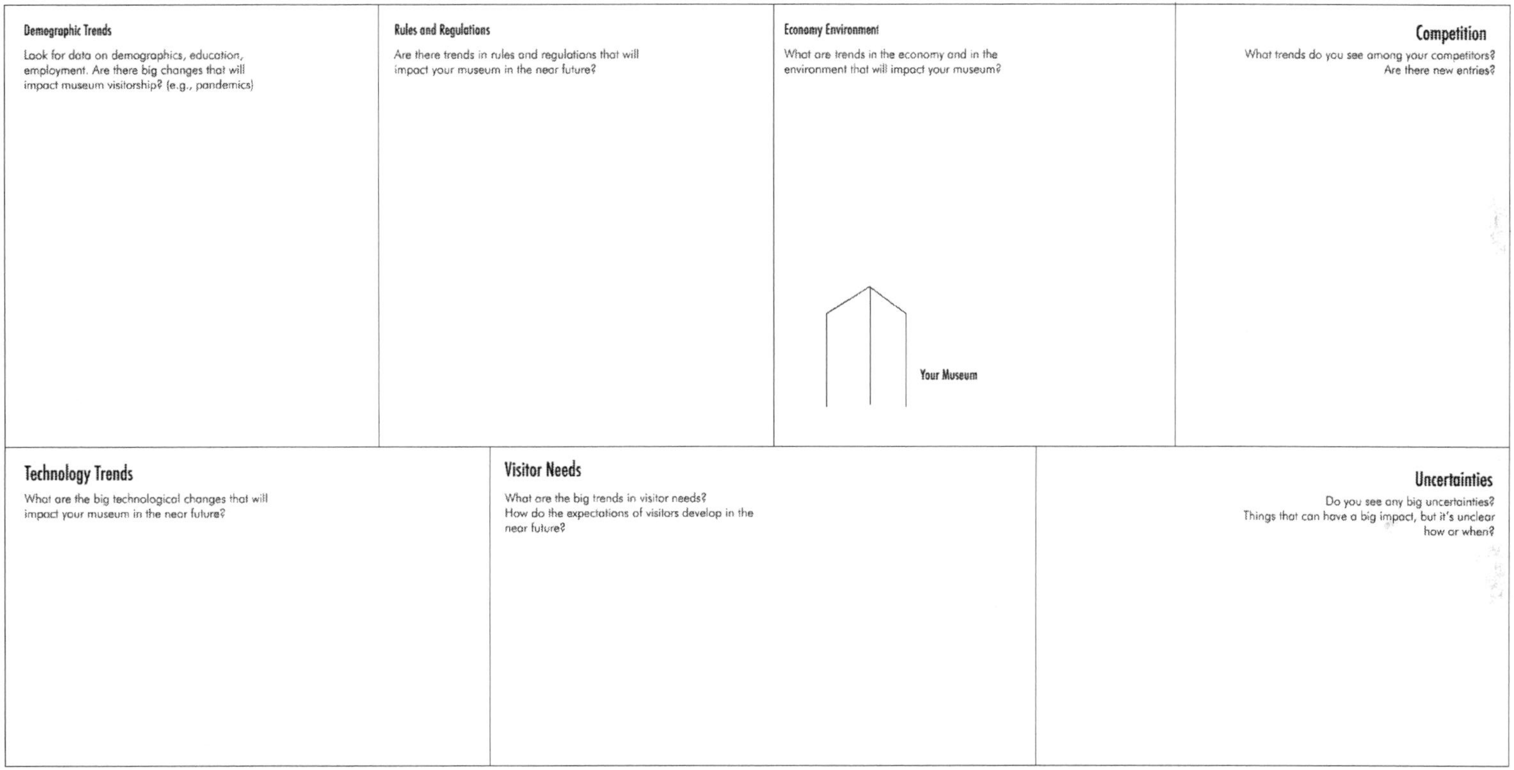

Demographic Trends

Look for data on demographics, education, employment. Are there big changes that will impact museum visitorship? (e.g., pandemics)

Rules and Regulations

Are there trends in rules and regulations that will impact your museum in the near future?

Economy Environment

What are trends in the economy and in the environment that will impact your museum?

Competition

What trends do you see among your competitors? Are there new entries?

Your Museum

Technology Trends

What are the big technological changes that will impact your museum in the near future?

Visitor Needs

What are the big trends in visitor needs? How do the expectations of visitors develop in the near future?

Uncertainties

Do you see any big uncertainties? Things that can have a big impact, but it's unclear how or when?

Figure 15.3. Context map canvas, adapted from "Context Map Canvas," created by David Sibbet of Grove Consulting: https://davidsibbet.com/about/.

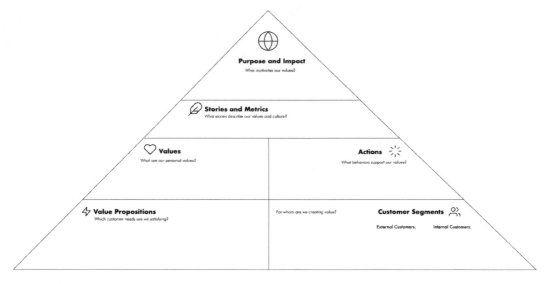

Figure 15.4. Culture canvas, adapted from "The Culture Canvas" by Javier Muñoz, https://blog.deliver inghappiness.com/blog/how-to-keep-the-culture-conversation-going.

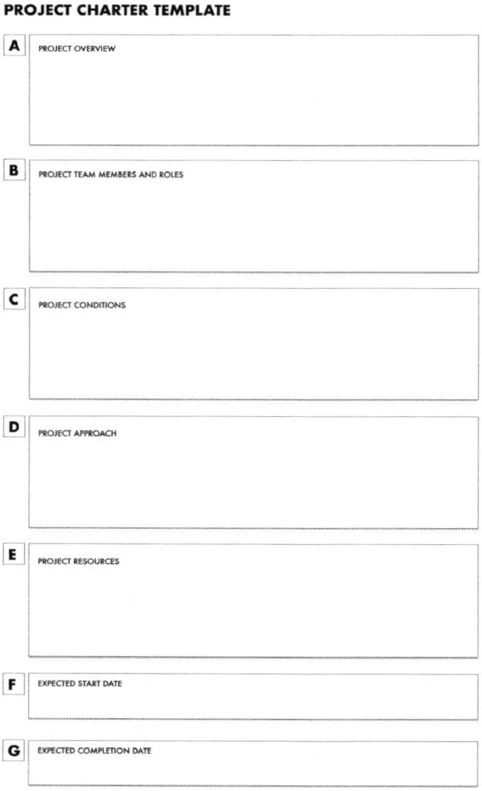

PROJECT CHARTER TEMPLATE

A PROJECT OVERVIEW

B PROJECT TEAM MEMBERS AND ROLES

C PROJECT CONDITIONS

D PROJECT APPROACH

E PROJECT RESOURCES

F EXPECTED START DATE

G EXPECTED COMPLETION DATE

Figure 15.5. Project charter template, adapted from the Project Management Institute, https:// www.pmi.org/learning/library/charter-selling -project-7473.

Value Proposition

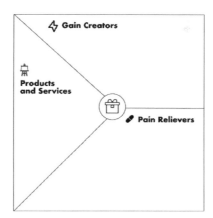

Gain Creators

Products and Services

Pain Relievers

Visitor Segment

Gains

Visitor Task(s)

Pains

Figure 15.6. Value proposition canvas, adapted from "Value Proposition Canvas" by Alex Osterwalder: https://www.strategyzer.com /canvas/value-proposition-canvas.

Importance/Influence Matrix

An additional method of stakeholder analysis is the **importance/influence matrix**. The matrix is a graph with two axes. The vertical axis shows the rising level of importance; the horizontal access shows the rising level of influence. Importance is the priority given to a shareholder's interests and needs. Influence is the power of a shareholder in achieving an objective. The matrix has four quadrants: high importance/low influence, high importance/high influence, low importance/low influence, and low importance/high influence. Once the influence and importance of a stakeholder have been determined, they can be assigned a quadrant. Knowing your stakeholders' quadrants allows you to see which of their needs and interests are fulfilled and allows you to evaluate your goals. See figure 15.7.

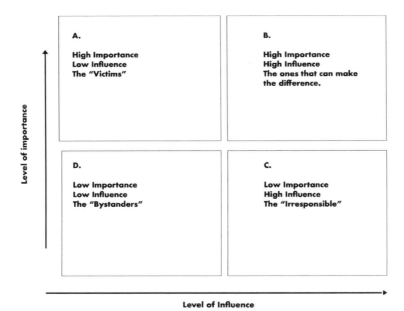

Figure 15.7. Importance/influence matrix, adapted from "APMAS Knowledge Network," http://www.mspguide.org/tool/stakeholder-analysis -importanceinfluence-matrix.

SWOT Analysis

SWOT stands for strengths, weaknesses, opportunities, and threats. **SWOT analysis** uses a matrix to identify internal and external factors that are important for achieving organizational goals. The internal factors include strengths and weaknesses; the external factors include opportunities and threats.

Write a list of prominent factors within the categories, and then situate them on the matrix. This will allow you to explore initiatives and understand possibilities for changing organizational goals as you develop your project. As an example, in creating a SWOT analysis, a group might recognize an opportunity to increase visitation of younger visitors by perceiving a weakness of having few younger staff and volunteers currently working at the museum. See figure 15.8.

Figure 15.8. SWOT analysis, adapted from SWOT Analysis by Albert Humphrey.

Task Analysis

Task analysis is the process of learning about ordinary users by observing them in action to understand in detail how they perform their tasks and achieve their intended goals.[3] This CX tool helps identify a task from two points of view: the customer and the project team. The customer point of view should answer the question "What tasks does the customer need to complete to achieve the desired results?" The project team point of view should answer the question "How can we create a repeatable process to achieve desired results?" See figure 15.9.

TASK ANALYSIS

CUSTOMER POINT OF VIEW

What do I need to do in order to complete or achieve the desired results?

TASKS

A

B

C

PROJECT TEAM POINT OF VIEW

How do we create a repeatable process to achieve the desired results?

TASKS

A

B

C

Figure 15.9. Task analysis, adapted from "Task Analysis: Support Users in Achieving Their Goals," Nielsen Norman Group, https://www.nngroup.com/articles/task-analysis/.

Vision Board

A **vision board** is a CX tool that helps visualize product vision and strategy. It includes visual answers to questions regarding the project's vision statement, target group, the needs the product is intended to fill, product description, unique selling point, and product value (how the product helps the company). Additional questions relate to competition, channels, and price. A vision board is similar in purpose to a mood board but is based more on text than on images.

Keyword Matrix

A **keyword matrix** is a table that cross-references user intent and search volume. It is used to focus the core intent of a project.

Understanding keywords and their usage is essential for success. The keyword matrix helps determine if the interests of the public are aligned with the intent of the project. With the advent of online searches, the keywords of a museum or museum exhibition are vital to the success of in-person and online traffic. When working with a keyword matrix, it is important to remember the *sales funnel*[4]—the steps searchers take in going from an online search to the desired in-person result.[5] I keep a list of keyword searches (my own and those of clients) in a spreadsheet and update the list once a month to review how the keywords are performing. See figure 15.10.

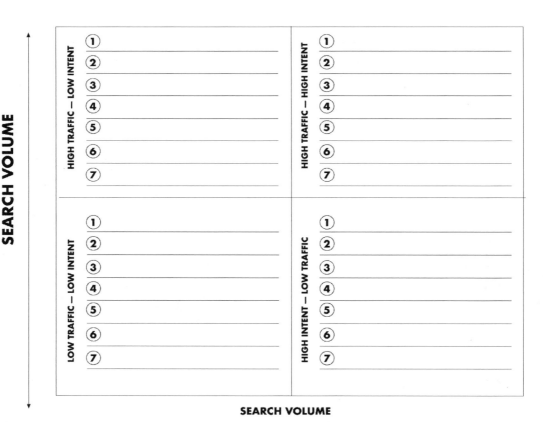

Figure 15.10. Keyword matrix, adapted from "The SEO Keyword Research Master Guide," https://moz.com/keyword-research-guide.

Mission, Vision, and Values Statements

Core to the management of any organization are mission, vision, and values statements. A museum's **mission statement** identifies its purpose. It is the answer to the question "What problem will the museum solve?" Its **values statement**, also called its *code of ethics*, defines what the museum believes in and how its stakeholders are expected to behave.[6] It answers the questions, "How does the museum plan to achieve the solutions to the problem it is facing?" or "If the museum were an individual, what would be its personal attributes?" A **vision statement** is an overarching statement about what the organization hopes to achieve.[7] It is goal-oriented, and attempts to answer the question, "One hundred years from now, how will the museum be operating?" Together, the answers to these questions capture the essence of the museum. Creating mission, values, and vision statements is invaluable when starting a new museum. See figure 15.11.

MISSION

"What 'problem' will the museum solve?"

Identify the museum's purpose

VISION

"One hundred years from now, how will the museum be operating?"

Identify the museum's goals

VALUES

"How does the museum plan to achieve the solutions to the problem it is facing?"

Identify the museum's ethics

Figure 15.11. Museum mission, vision, and values.

Scenario Canvas

A **scenario canvas** is a CX tool that provides a single context in order to help you describe an event and understand its users, the goals they envision, the actions they take, and the desired product. This tool will help you determine whether the desired outcome or product will occur with a particular user in a particular context who takes certain actions. See figure 15.12.

"What You Don't Know"

Project teams often become overly confident about their knowledge, falsely believing that they understand a topic or user completely. As Mark Twain said, "It ain't what you don't know that gets you into trouble. It's what you know for sure that just ain't so." A *business assumptions exercise* can be used as a reality check to bring the focus back to the identified user by identifying the following.[8]

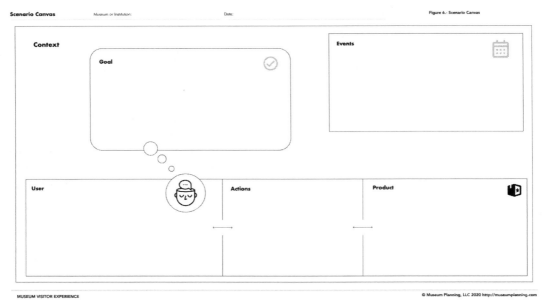

Figure 15.12. Scenario canvas, adapted from *Business Model Generation* by Alexander Osterwalder.

- The customer pain points
- The solution being offered
- Who the customer is
- Customer acquisition channels
- The business model
- Competitors and the current market
- Product risks and business assumptions

In an article about working through design challenges in product design job interviews, author Tanner Christenson presented the following questions to begin exploring what you don't know.[9]

- If you know the problem primarily affects a certain type of person, what does their "user journey" look like and how can a digital product influence that experience?
- Are there any existing solutions you can reference for guidance?
- What might possible new solutions look like?
- Where might new solutions fail, and where might they succeed?
- What trade-offs will you need to consider while working toward a solution?
- What extreme cases can you think of?
- What tools or resources might you leverage in building out solutions?
- How does technology play a role in the problem you're exploring, and what facets of digital tools can help create a solution to the problem?

In the end, you can never completely understand any given user. You are always making assumptions, but undertaking these exercises can help you make better ones.

Touchpoint Matrix

A **touchpoint matrix** is a visual guide that helps you understand the user experience and their interactions within the product-service system. The vertical axis lists different devices and contexts, and the horizontal axis lists main actions supported by the system. A museum designer can use the touchpoint matrix to imagine a particular person inside the system and think about how they would journey through the touchpoints. Examples would include touchpoints between the museum and the donor of a major gift, online touchpoints between an eight-year-old and the museum's digital presence, and touchpoints between the museum and a seventy-six-year-old living in a care facility. See figure 15.13.

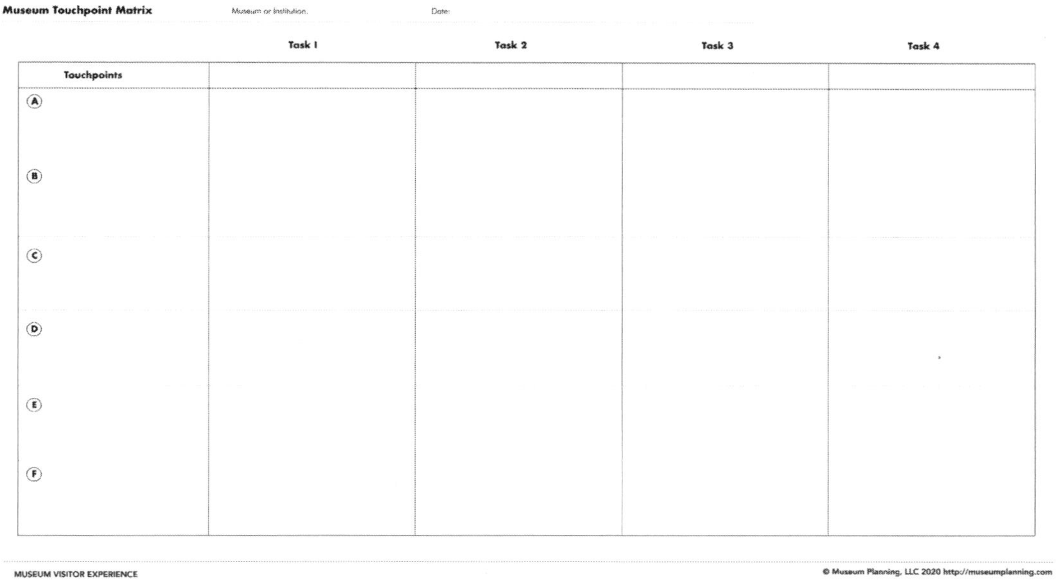

Figure 15.13. Museum touchpoint matrix, adapted from "New Representation Techniques for Designing in a Systemic Perspective" by Nicola Morelli (2007), https://servicedesigntools.org/tools/system-map.

Storyboard

A **storyboard** or *user scenario* is the fictitious story of a user who accomplishes an action or goal via a product or service. It focuses on a user's motivations and documents the process of using a design.[10] The storyboard includes a number of pictures to give a narrative sequence and should represent all touchpoints and their relationships with the users. See figure 15.14.

Lamina

A **lamina** is a poster that offers an overall understanding of a project. It includes the project name, design brief, persona, context, visual overview and treatment, mood board, and examples of low-fidelity prototyping. See figure 15.15.

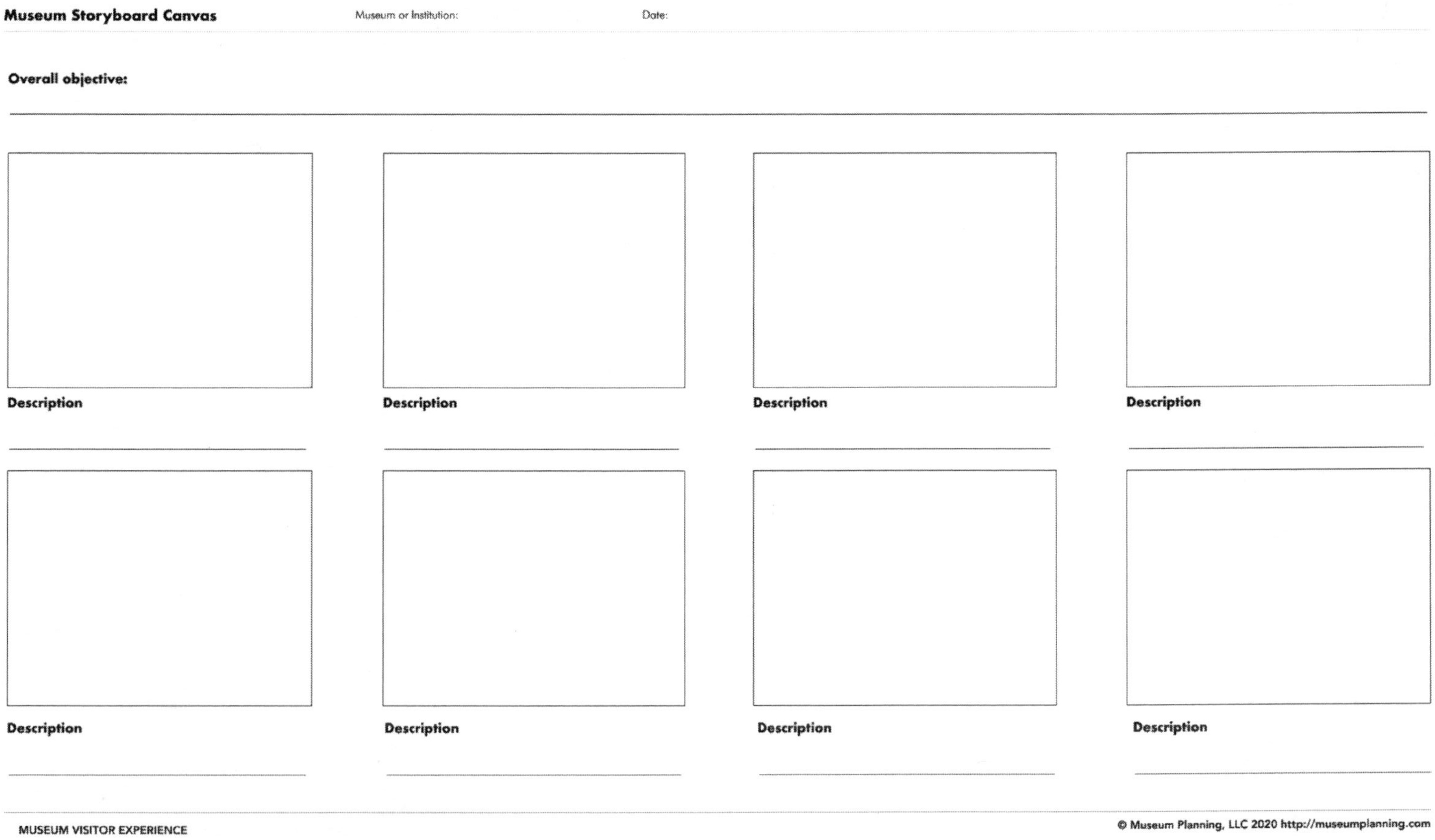
Museum Storyboard Canvas
Museum or Institution:
Date:
Overall objective:
Description
Description
Description
Description
Description
Description
Description
Description
MUSEUM VISITOR EXPERIENCE
© Museum Planning, LLC 2020 http://museumplanning.com

Figure 15.14. Museum storyboard canvas, adapted from "The Story Canvas," created by Denise Withers: https://www.denisewithers.com/story-design/.

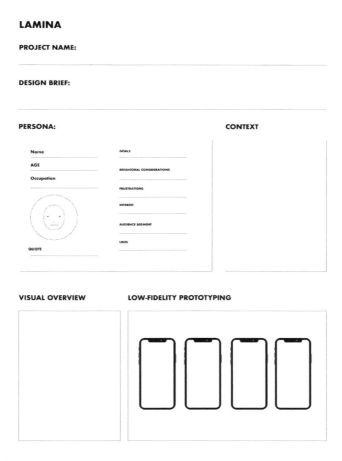

LAMINA

PROJECT NAME:

DESIGN BRIEF:

PERSONA: CONTEXT

Name   GOALS

AGE   BEHAVIORAL CONSIDERATIONS

Occupation
                              FRUSTRATIONS

                              INTEREST

                              AUDIENCE SEGMENT

                              LIKES

QUOTE

VISUAL OVERVIEW   LOW-FIDELITY PROTOTYPING

Figure 15.15. Lamina.

Product Canvas

A **product canvas** is a one-page template that can help capture the features and key components of a product quickly. It includes the following segments.

- Customers. This segment should identify the user for whom the product is solving a problem or creating value, and should include early adopters.
- Problems. Three to five problems facing targeted customers.
- Existing Alternatives. This segment should identify product alternatives already on the market.
- Unique Value Propositions. A clear message about the value of the product, what makes it different, and why it is worth buying.
- Channels. How will customers be acquired and retained?
- Solutions. Ways in which the three to five problems will be solved.
- Key Stakeholders. Important stakeholders who need to be persuaded should be identified, as well as those who can do the persuading.
- Key Success Factors. This should include measurements of success.
- Key Resources and Partners. Determine what resources—internal or external—are needed, and whether the product requires partners.

At the bottom of the product canvas are Revenue/Business Value, Cost Structure (which determines the most important costs), and Key Resources and Activities.

"Product" is a different way for museums to think about their work; as an example, an educational program is a product with associated costs, potential revenue, and a value proposition. The "product" also increases the soft power[11] of the museum and has an associated value.

Museum Institutional Planning Diagram

A museum institutional planning diagram is an overview of the institutional planning process. It is inclusive of communities and is used to create bidirectional flow of content (see figure 15.16).

NOTES

1. "About," Community Canvas, accessed Mar. 9, 2021, https://community-canvas.org/about.
2. Nathanael Boehm Coyne, "Ethnography in UX," UX Matters, June 21, 2010, https://www.uxmatters.com/mt/archives/2010/06/ethnography-in-ux.php.
3. "Task Analysis," Usability.gov, accessed Mar. 9, 2021, https://www.usability.gov/how-to-and-tools/methods/task-analysis.html.
4. Claire Axelrad, "The Donor Pyramid and Marketing Funnel Have Changed," GuideStar, Jun. 5, 2019, https://trust.guidestar.org/the-donor-pyramid-and-marketing-funnel-have-changed.
5. Tom Treanor, "How to Get Brilliant Ideas for Top of Funnel Content," Alexa, accessed Mar. 9, 2021, https://blog.alexa.com/get-brilliant-ideas-top-of-funnel-content/.
6. "Mission, Vision, and Values," Lumen, accessed Mar. 9, 2021, https://courses.lumenlearning.com/wm-principlesofmanagement/chapter/reading-mission-vision-and-values/.
7. Ibid.
8. Jess Eddy, "UX Facilitation Methods," Prototypr, Jan. 15, 2017, https://blog.prototypr.io/ux-facilitation-methods-ecfb87f4fcf4.
9. Tanner Christensen, "Working through Design Challenges in Product Design Interview," *UX Design*, Mar. 19, 2018, https://uxdesign.cc/working-through-design-challenges-in-digital-product-design-interviews-d4b118df4265.
10. "What Are User Scenarios?" *Interaction Design*, accessed Mar. 9, 2021, https://www.interaction-design.org/literature/topics/user-scenarios.
11. Gail Lord, "The Soft Power of Museums," The Soft Power 30, Aug. 11, 2017, https://softpower30.com/soft-power-museums/.

Museum Planning Process

The museum visitor experience planning
process is an iterative, user-centric process that
has integrity and museum communities at
heart.

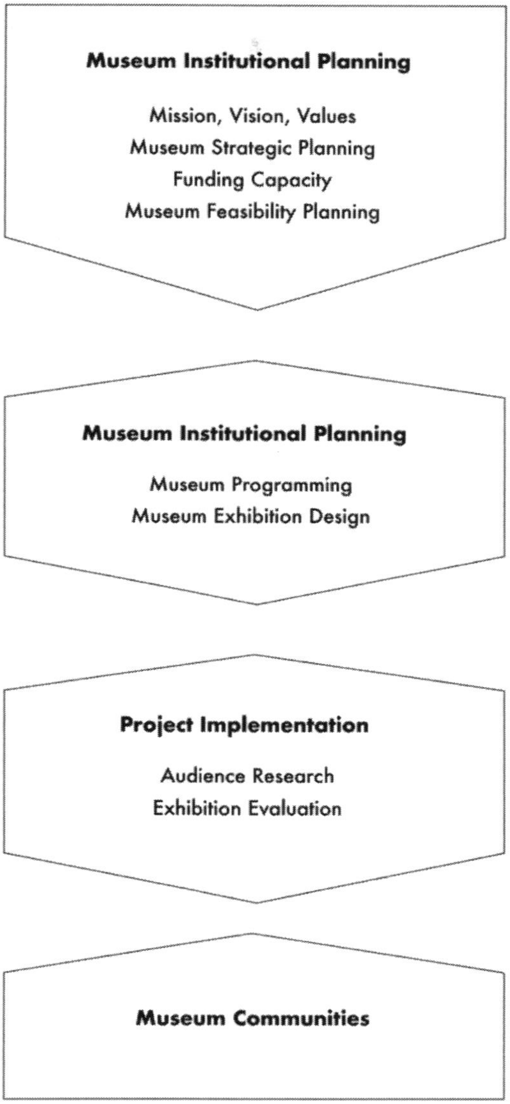

Museum Institutional Planning

Mission, Vision, Values
Museum Strategic Planning
Funding Capacity
Museum Feasibility Planning

Museum Institutional Planning

Museum Programming
Museum Exhibition Design

Project Implementation

Audience Research
Exhibition Evaluation

Museum Communities

Museum 360°

A bidirectional flow from communities
and visitors (users)
to institutional mission.

Figure 15.16. Museum planning process, adapted from *The Manual of Museum Planning* by Barry Lord, Gail Dexter Lord, and Lindsay Martin (2012).

Resources

FREE ONLINE MUSEUM DESIGN THINKING COURSES, RECOMMEND TAKING AS A GROUP

Acumen Facilitator's Guide to Human-Centered Design
    https://www.plusacumen.org/courses/facilitator%E2%80%99s-guide-human-centered-design.
Acumen Human-Centered Design 201: Prototyping
    https://www.plusacumen.org/courses/prototyping.
Acumen Introduction to Human-Centered Design
    https://www.plusacumen.org/courses/introduction-human-centered-design.
d. School Virtual Crash Course in Design Thinking
    https://dschool.stanford.edu/resources-collections/a-virtual-crash-course-in-design-thinking.
Stanford Online Design Thinking Action Lab
    http://online.stanford.edu/course/design-thinking-action-lab.

PAID ONLINE MUSEUM DESIGN THINKING COURSES

Design Kit

IDEO U
    https://www.ideou.com/.
IDEO.org
    http://www.designkit.org/.
Interaction Design Foundation
    https://www.interaction-design.org/.

RESOURCE GUIDES

Adobe Kick-box
    https://innov8rs.co/news/adobe-kickbox-innovation-kit/.
Design Thinking for Educators
    https://designthinkingforeducators.com/.
Design Thinking for Libraries
    http://designthinkingforlibraries.com/.
18F Design Methods Cards
    https://methods.18f.gov/.
Equity-Centered Design Framework
    https://dschool.stanford.edu/resources/equity-centered-design-framework.
Google Ventures Design Sprint
    http://www.gv.com/sprint/.

IDEO Method Cards
   https://www.ideo.com/post/method-cards.
Inclusive Design at Microsoft
   https://www.microsoft.com/en-us/design/inclusive.
Innovating for People: Human-Centered Design Planning Cards
   http://www.deckaholic.com/lib/innovating-for-people.
New York Times Product Discovery Activity Guide
   https://medium.com/@al.ming/the-nyt-product-discovery-activity-guide-fd27af3efd54.
Service Design Tools
   http://www.servicedesigntools.org/.
UX Magazine
   https://uxmag.com.

WEBSITES

American Alliance of Museums (AAM), Media & Technology Network
   http://www.aam-us.org/resources/professional-networks/media-technology.
American Alliance of Museums (AAM) Public Trust
   https://www.aam-us.org/programs/ethics-standards-and-professional-practices/public-trust
   -and-accountability-standards/.
Center for the Future of Museums
   http://futureofmuseums.blogspot.mx/.
Constructivist Learning Theory
   https://www.exploratorium.edu/education/ifi/constructivist-learning.
Ergonomics (human factors)
   https://www.osha.gov/ergonomics.
Hackerspaces
   https://wiki.hackerspaces.org.
Hatch Act
   https://osc.gov/Services/Pages/HatchAct.aspx.
Howard Gardner, The Good Project
   https://www.thegoodproject.org/.
Human-Computer Interface (HCI), International Conference
   http://www.hci.international/.
Industrial Designers Society of America (IDSA)
   http://www.idsa.org/.
Institute of Electrical and Electronics Engineers (IEEE), Robotics and Automation Society (RAS)
   http://www.ieee-ras.org/.
International Association of Engineers (IAENG), Society of Mechanical Engineering (ISME)
   http://www.iaeng.org/ISME.html.
Museum Computer Network
   http://mcn.edu/.
Museums and the Web
   https://www.museumsandtheweb.com/.
Myers-Briggs
   https://www.myersbriggs.org/.
National Association of Schools of Art and Design (NASAD)
   https://nasad.arts-accredit.org/.

National Endowment for the Arts (NEA)
    https://www.arts.gov/.
National Endowment for the Humanities (NEH)
    https://www.neh.gov/.
Project Management Institute (PMI)
    https://www.pmi.org/.
Society for Experiential Graphic Designs (SEGD)
    https://segd.org/.
Special Interest Group on Computer Graphics and Interactive Techniques (SIGGRAPH)
    http://www.siggraph.org/.
STEAM (science, technology, engineering, the arts, and mathematics)
    https://scholarship.claremont.edu/steam/.
STEM (science, technology, engineering, and mathematics)
    https://www.ed.gov/stem.

ASSOCIATIONS

American Association for State and Local History (AASLH)
    https://aaslh.org/.
Association of Children's Museums (ACM)
    https://www.childrensmuseums.org/.
Association of Science and Technology Centers (ASTC)
    https://www.astc.org/.
Industrial Designers Society of America
    http://www.idsa.org/.
International Council of Societies of Industrial Design
    http://www.icsid.org/.
Leonardo/ISAST
    https://www.leonardo.info/.
Network of European Museum Organizations (NEMO)
    https://www.ne-mo.org/.
Tangible, Embedded and Embodied Interactions
    https://tei.acm.org/.

ONLINE RESOURCES

Lean Canvas
    http://leanstack.com/app/.
SDT
    http://www.servicedesigntools.org/repository.
The Toolkit Project
    http://thetoolkitproject.webflow.io/.

TREND RESEARCH

Antad
    http://www.antad.net/.
Coolhunting
    http://www.coolhunting.com/.

Fashion Channel Youtube
   http://www.youtube.com/channel/UCepVy23t8l-CEaASZzfo9Jg.
Millward Brown
   http://www.millwardbrown.com/.
WGSN
   http://www.wgsn.com/en/.

DEMOGRAPHIC INFORMATION

Guidestar
   http://www.guidestar.org/.
Pew Research
   http://www.pewresearch.org/.
Sperlings
   http://www.bestplaces.net/.
Worldbank Data
   http://www.worldbank.org/en/country/.

OTHER FAVORITES

Artnet
   http://www.artnet.com/.
e-flux
   http://www.e-flux.com/.
Hyperallergic
   http://hyperallergic.com/.

People on Medium

Dan Nessler
   https://medium.com/@dan.nessler.
Jim Fishwick
   https://medium.com/@FimJishwick.

Placemaking

Creative Placemaking
   https://www.arts.gov/sites/default/files/How-to-do-Creative-Placemaking_Jan2017.pdf.
Creative Placemaking
   https://www.arts.gov/sites/default/files/CreativePlacemaking-Paper.pdf.
Placemaking
   https://uploads-ssl.webflow.com/5810e16fbe876cec6bcbd86e/5a6a1c930a6e6500019faf5d
   _Oct-2016-placemaking-booklet.pdf.

Bibliography

ESSENTIAL BIBLIOGRAPHY

American Alliance of Museums. "Facing Change: Report from the American Alliance of Museums' Working Group on DEAI." July 02, 2018. https://www.aam-us.org/wp-content/uploads/2018/04/AAM-DEAI-Working-Group-Full-Report-2018.pdf.

Dunne, Anthony, and Fiona Raby. *Speculative Everything: Design, Fiction, and Social Dreaming*. Cambridge, MA: MIT Press, 2013.

Falk, John H. *Identity and the Museum Visitor Experience*. Walnut Creek, CA: Left Coast Press, 2009.

Gutwill, Joshua P., and Thomas Humphrey. *Fostering Active Prolonged Engagement: The Art of Creating APE Exhibits*. San Francisco, CA: Exploratorium, 2005.

Kim, Eundeok, Ann Marie Fiore, and Hyejeong Kim. *Fashion Trends Analysis and Forecasting*. New York, NY: Bloomsbury, 2013.

Kumar, Vijay. *101 Design Methods: A Structured Approach for Driving Innovation in Your Organization*. Hoboken, NJ: John Wiley & Sons, 2013.

Maurya, Ash. *Running Lean Iterate from Plan A to a Plan That Works*. Beijing: OReilly, 2012.

Merritt, Elizabeth E. *National Standards and Best Practices for U.S. Museums*. Washington, DC: American Association of Museums, 2008.

Norman, Donald A. *The Design of Everyday Things*. NY, NY: Basic Books, 2013.

Osterwalder, Alexander, and Yves Pigneur. *Business Model Generation a Handbook for Visionaries, Game Changers, and Challengers*. New York: Wiley & Sons, 2013.

Pine, B. Joseph., and James H. Gilmore. *The Experience Economy*. Boston, MA: Harvard Business Review Press, 2011.

Senge, Peter M. *The Fifth Discipline*. London: Random House Business, 2006.

Simon, Norma. *The Participatory Museum*. Santa Cruz, CA: Museum 2.0, 2010.

Stickdorn, Marc, and Jakob Schneider. *This Is Service Design Thinking: Basics—Tools—Cases*. Amsterdam: BIS Publishers, 2011.

Walhimer, Mark. *Museums 101*. Lanham, MD: Rowman & Littlefield, 2015.

Weaver, Stephanie. *Creating Great Visitor Experiences: A Guide for Museums, Parks, Zoos, Gardens & Libraries*. Walnut Creek, CA: Left Coast Press, 2007.

BIBLIOGRAPHY

"Accreditation and Excellence Programs." American Alliance of Museums. Accessed Nov. 3, 2020. https://www.aam-us.org/programs/accreditation-excellence-programs/.

Alexander, Moira. "Agile Project Management: 12 Key Principles, 4 Big Hurdles." *CIO*, Jun. 19, 2018. https://www.cio.com/article/3156998/agile-project-management-a-beginners-guide.html.

Angel, David W. "The Four Types of Conversations: Debate, Dialogue, Discourse, and Diatribe." *Medium*, Dec. 31, 2016. https://medium.com/@DavidWAngel/the-four-types-of-conversations-debate-dialogue-discourse-and-diatribe-898d19eccc0a.

Art Lab App. MoMA Design Studio. App. Accessed Mar. 1, 2021. https://momadesignstudio.org
/Art-Lab-App.

Artlens App. Cleveland Museum of Art. App. Accessed Mar. 1, 2021. https://www.clevelandart.org
/artlens-gallery/artlens-app.

"Attribution—NonCommercial—ShareAlike 4.0 International." Creative Commons. Accessed Aug. 19,
2020. https://creativecommons.org/licenses/by-nc-sa/4.0/legalcode.

Black, Graham. *The Engaging Museum: Developing Museums for Visitor Involvement.* Philadelphia: Routledge, 2001.

Bowley, G. "Museums Chart a Response to Political Upheaval: In a Tumultuous Era, Some Museums
Are Rushing to Embrace the Political Moment, While Others Deliberately Retreat." *New York Times,*
Mar. 13, 2017. https://www.nytimes.com/2017/03/13/arts/design/museums-politics-protest
-j20-art-strike.html.

Brown, Jeffrey. "Can This Rural Town Go from a Youth Exodus to an Art Epicenter?" PBS. Apr. 17,
2018. https://www.pbs.org/newshour/show/can-this-rural-town-go-from-a-youth-exodus-to-an
-art-epicenter.

Bullard, Giuliana. "Government Doubles Official Estimate: There Are 35,000 Active Museums in the
U.S." Institute of Museum and Library Services. Oct. 13, 2015. https://www.imls.gov/news/govern
ment-doubles-official-estimate-there-are-35000-active-museums-us.

Callimachus. *Aetia Iambi Hecale and Other Fragments; Musaeus; Hero and Leander.* Translated by C. A.
Trypanis, T. Gelzer, and C. Whitman. Loeb Classical Library, vol. 421. Cambridge, MA: Harvard
University Press, 1973.

Callimachus. *Hymns and Epigrams; Lycophron; Aratus.* Translated by A. W. Mair and G. R. Mair. Loeb
Classical Library, vol. 129. Cambridge, MA: Harvard University Press, 1921.

Campbell, Gary, and Laurajane Smith. "Fostering Empathy through Museums." *Museum Management
and Curatorship* 32, no. 3 (2017): 298–300. https://doi.org/10.1080/09647775.2017.1326450.

"Can We Really Say That?" Bolder Advocacy. Accessed Nov. 14, 2017. https://www.bolderadvocacy
.org/wp-content/uploads/2017/01/Can-We-Really-Say-That.pdf.

"Citizenship Now." City University of New York. Accessed Feb. 28, 2021. http://www1.cuny.edu/sites
/citizenship-now.

"The Citizenship Project." New York History. Accessed Feb. 28, 2021. https://www.nyhistory.org
/education/citizenship-project.

"Conanp impulsa el diseño para la artesanía hecha en áreas naturales protegidas." https://www.gob
.mx/conanp/prensa/conanp-impulsa-el-diseno-para-la-artesania-hecha-en-areas-naturales
-protegidas.

Connell, Bettye Rose, Mike Jones, Ron Mace, Jim Mueller, Abir Mullick, Elaine Ostroff, Jon Sanford, Ed
Steinfeld, Molly Story, and Gregg Vanderheiden. "The Principles of Universal Design." Jan. 4, 1997.
https://projects.ncsu.edu/ncsu/design/cud/about_ud/udprinciplestext.htm.

Costa, Tony, and Joana de Quintanilha. "Mapping the Customer Journey: Four Approaches to Customer Journey Mapping; When and How to Use Them." *Forrester.* Nov. 16, 2015. https://www
.forrester.com/report/Mapping+The+Customer+Journey/-/E-RES55987#.

Cotter, Holland. "Got an Hour? See the Met These Four Ways." *New York Times,* Dec. 8, 2016. https://
www.nytimes.com/2016/12/08/arts/design/got-an-hour-see-the-met-these-4-ways.html.

Culture Track '17. Culture Track. 2017. https://2017study.culturetrack.com/.

"Customer Experience." McKinsey. Accessed Nov. 13, 2017. https://www.mckinsey.com/global
-themes/customer-experience.

de Boer, Victor. "Semantic Technologies for Digital Humanities." Semantics Online. Mar. 29, 2019.
https://2020-eu.semantics.cc/semantic-technologies-digital-humanities.

Delaney, Kevin J. "The Robot That Takes Your Job Should Pay Taxes, Says Bill Gates." *Quartz,* Feb. 17,
2017. https://qz.com/911968/bill-gates-the-robot-that-takes-your-job-should-pay-taxes/.

Dercon, Chris. "What Is the Museum of the Future?" Tate Museum. 2015. https://www.tate.org.uk
/tate-etc/issue-35-autumn-2015/what-museum-future.

Discovery Center at Murfree Spring. https://explorethedc.org/.

Dorsey, Jason. *IGen Tech Disruption.* GenHQ. 2016. http://genhq.com/wp-content/uploads/2016/01
/iGen-Gen-Z-Tech-Disruption-Research-White-Paper-c-2016-Center-for-Generational-Kinetics
.pdf.

"Emerging Museum Professionals." Mountain-Plains Museums Association. Accessed Nov. 30, 2020.
https://mpma.net/Emerging-Museum-Professionals.

Emerson, Andrew, Nathan Henderson, Jonathan Paul Rowe, Wookhee Min, Seung Y. Lee, James
Minogue, and James C. Lester. "Early Prediction of Visitor Engagement in Science Museums with
Multimodal Learning Analytics." ICMI '20: Proceedings of the 2020 International Conference on
Multimodal Interaction. Oct. 2020. https://dl.acm.org/doi/abs/10.1145/3382507.3418890.

"Encore Engagement at the Met: 'Small Wonders: The VR Experience.'" Canadian Film Centre. Mar.
26, 2017. http://cfccreates.com/news/739-encore-engagement-at-the-met-small-wonders-the-vr
-experience.

"Epicenter: Our Futures." Utah Museum of Fine Arts. Accessed Nov. 6, 2020. https://umfa.utah.edu
/our-futures.

"European Parliament Calls for Robot Law, Rejects Robot Tax." Reuters. Feb. 16, 2017. https://www
.reuters.com/article/us-europe-robots-lawmaking-idUSKBN15V2KM.

Falk, J. H. *Identity and the Museum Visitor Experience.* Walnut Creek, CA: Left Coast Press, 2009.

Falk, J. H., and L. D. Dierking. *The Museum Experience Revisited.* Walnut Creek, CA: Left Coast Press,
2013.

"Felice Grodin: Invasive Species." Pérez Art Museum Miami. https://www.pamm.org/ar.

Furman, Jason, Sandra Black, and Jay Shambaugh. "The 2016 Economic Report of the President."
President Barack Obama White House. Feb. 22, 2016. https://obamawhitehouse.archives.gov
/blog/2016/02/22/2016-economic-report-president.

Gabor, Dennis. *Inventing the Future.* London: Penguin, 1964.

Gates, W. "Content Is King." Microsoft website. Jan. 3, 1996.

Grant, Daniel. "Amenities Galore!: Museums Are Upping the Extras but to What End?" *Observer*, Sep.
8, 2016. https://observer.com/2016/09/amenities-galore-museums-are-upping-the-extras-but
-to-what-end/.

Grant, Daniel. "Pandemic Pushes Museums Deeper into Digital Age." *Wall Street Journal*, Jul. 31, 2020.
https://www.wsj.com/articles/pandemic-pushes-museums-further-into-digital-age-11596196801.

Hatzipanagos, R. "The 'Decolonization' of the American Museum." *Washington Post*, Oct. 11, 2018.
https://www.washingtonpost.com/nation/2018/10/12/decolonization-american-museum/.

"History of Benesse Art Site Naoshima | Benesse Art Site Naoshima." Benesse Art Site Naoshima.
Accessed Nov. 13, 2017. http://benesse-artsite.jp/en/about/history.html.

IDEO. *The Field Guide to Human-Centered Design.* Palo Alto, CA: IDEO, 2015.

"Information and Technical Assistance on the Americans with Disabilities Act." Accessed Feb. 27,
2021. https://www.ada.gov/ada_intro.htm.

Internal Revenue Service. "Common Tax Law Restrictions on Activities of Exempt Organizations."
Sept. 23, 2020. https://www.irs.gov/charities-non-profits/common-tax-law-restrictions-on-activ
ities-of-exempt-organizations.

"Introducing Museum 2040." Center for the Future of Museums blog. American Alliance of Museums.
Oct. 31, 2017. https://www.aam-us.org/2017/10/31/introducing-museum-2040/.

Jones, Jonathan. "The Drop in Museum Visitors Reveals a Nation without Aspiration or Hope." *Guardian*, Feb. 2, 2017. https://www.theguardian.com/artanddesign/jonathanjonesblog/2017/feb/02
/all.

Kaplan, Sarah. "Museums and Libraries Fight 'Alternative Facts' with a #DayofFacts." *Washington Post*, Feb. 17, 2017. https://www.washingtonpost.com/news/speaking-of-science/wp/2017/02/17/museums-and-libraries-fight-alternative-facts-with-a-dayoffacts/.

Kennedy, Randy. "Is It Art, Science, or a Test of People?" *New York Times*, Oct. 25, 2011. https://www.nytimes.com/2011/10/26/arts/design/carsten-holler-exhibition-at-the-new-museum.html.

Korzun, Dmitry G., Aleksey Varfolomeyev, Svetlana E. Yalovitsyna, and Valentina Volokhova. "Semantic Infrastructure of a Smart Museum: Toward Making Cultural Heritage Knowledge Usable and Creatable by Visitors and Professionals." *Personal and Ubiquitous Computing* 21, no. 2 (Apr. 2017): 345–54. https://doi.org/10.1007/s00779-016-0996-7.

Lake, Franki. "Human Centered Design vs Design Thinking vs Service Design vs UX. . . . What Do They All Mean?" LinkedIn. Jun. 8, 2016. https://www.linkedin.com/pulse/human-centred-design-vs-thinking-service-ux-what-do-all-simonds/.

Laughlin, Shepherd. "Gen Z Goes Beyond Gender Binaries in New Innovation Group Data." Wunderman Thompson. Mar. 11, 2016. https://www.jwtintelligence.com/2016/03/gen-z-goes-beyond-gender-binaries-in-new-innovation-group-data/.

Lenhart, Amanda. "A Majority of American Teens Report Access to a Computer, Game Console, Smartphone and a Tablet." Pew Research Center. Apr. 9, 2015. https://www.pewresearch.org/internet/2015/04/09/a-majority-of-american-teens-report-access-to-a-computer-game-console-smartphone-and-a-tablet/.

"Lobbying." Internal Revenue Service. Accessed Nov. 14, 2017. https://www.irs.gov/charities-non-profits/lobbying.

Makienko, Igor. "Effective Frequency Estimates in Local Media Planning Practice." *Journal of Targeting Measurement and Analysis for Marketing* 20, no. 1 (Feb. 2012): 57–65. https://link.springer.com/article/10.1057/jt.2012.1.

"Mammuthus primigenius (Blumbach)." Smithsonian. Accessed Mar. 1, 2021. https://3d.si.edu/explorer/woolly-mammoth.

"Marco Annunziata: What Will Human-Machine Collaboration Mean for Our Jobs?" Apr. 21, 2017. https://radio.wpsu.org/post/marco-annunziata-what-will-human-machine-collaboration-mean-our-jobs.

Matthews, Chris. *Hardball: How Politics Is Played, Told by One Who Knows the Game*. New York: Simon and Schuster, 1999.

Maurya, Ash. "The LEAN Sprint." Oct. 1, 2015. https://blog.leanstack.com/the-lean-sprint-bc3f9f8caafd.

Maurya, Ash. *Running Lean*. Sebastopol, CA: O'Reilly, 2012.

McKnight, John L. *The Four-Legged Stool*. Kettering Foundation, 2013. https://www.kettering.org/catalog/product/four-legged-stool.

"Meet Generation Z: Forget Everything You Learned About Millennials." Jun. 17, 2014. http://www.slideshare.net/sparksandhoney/generation-z-final-june-17/40-They_are_less_active40This_generation.

Mereu, Sebastiano. "Applying the Experience Economy Model to the Periscope Channel of a Football Club." Sports Business Research. Mar. 9, 2016. https://sportsbusinessresearch.blog/2016/03/09/applying-the-experience-economy-model-to-the-periscope-channel-of-a-football-club/.

"'Millennials on Steroids': Is Your Brand Ready for Generation Z?" Wharton. Sep. 28, 2015. http://knowledge.wharton.upenn.edu/article/millennials-on-steroids-is-your-brand-ready-for-generation-z/.

"Mission." Museum of Us. Accessed Nov. 4, 2020. https://museumofus.org/mission-vision-values/.

Morgan, Jacob. "Generation Z and the Six Forces Shaping the Future of Business." *Inc.*, Jul. 5, 2016. http://www.inc.com/jacob-morgan/generation-z-and-the-6-forces-shaping-the-future-of-business.html.

"Museums around the World in the Face of COVID-19." UNESCO. 2020. https://unesdoc.unesco.org
/ark:/48223/pf0000373530.

"Museum Assessment Program (MAP)." American Alliance of Museums. Accessed Oct. 31, 2017.
https://www.aam-us.org/programs/accreditation-excellence-programs/museum-assessment
-program-map/.

"Museum Facts." American Alliance of Museums. Accessed Oct. 31, 2017. http://www.aam-us.org
/about-museums/museum-facts.

National Trust for Historic Preservation. "Reclaiming the Past in Bricks and Mortar: New Study Reveals
Millennials' Desire to Connect with Historic Places." Saving Places. 2017. https://savingplaces
.org/press-center/media-resources/new-study-reveals-millennials-desire-to-connect-with-histo
ric-places#.Xc2bVldKhPY.

Nouwen, Henri J. M. Reaching Out: The Three Movements of the Spiritual Life. London: Fount, 1986.

"Our Town." National Endowment for the Arts. Accessed November 6, 2020. https://www.arts.gov
/grants/our-town.

Peccarelli, Brian. "Bend, Don't Break: How to Thrive in the Fourth Industrial Revolution." World Economic Forum. Jan. 13, 2020. https://www.weforum.org/agenda/2020/01/the-fourth-industrial
-revolution-is-changing-all-the-rules/.

"Personas." Service Design Tools. Accessed Nov. 10, 2020. https://servicedesigntools.org/tools
/personas.

Pine, B. Joseph II, and James H. Gilmore. The Experience Economy. Cambridge, MA: Harvard Business
School Press, 1999.

Pine, B. Joseph II, and James Gilmore. "Welcome to the Experience Economy." Harvard Business Review,
Jul. 1, 1998. https://hbr.org/1998/07/welcome-to-the-experience-economy.

"The Placemaking Process." Project for Public Spaces. Dec. 21, 2017. https://www.pps.org/article/5
-steps-to-making-places.

Project for Public Spaces. "Placemaking: What If We Built Our Cities around Places?" Oct. 2016.
https://dn60005mpuo2f.cloudfront.net/wp-content/uploads/2016/10/Oct-2016-placemak
ing-booklet.pdf.

"Project Implicit." Harvard University. Accessed Feb. 24, 2021. https://implicit.harvard.edu/implicit/.

"Quick Facts, Murfreesboro City." Census.gov. Jul. 1, 2019. https://www.census.gov/quickfacts/mur
freesborocitytennessee.

Rashed, Golam, Ryota Suzuki, Takuya Yonezawa, and Antony Lam. "Tracking Visitors in a Real Museum
for Behavioral Analysis." Aug. 2016. 2016 Joint Eighth International Conference on Soft Computing
and Intelligent Systems. https://doi.org/10.1109/SCIS-ISIS.2016.0030.

"Resources." OF/BY/FOR ALL. Accessed Feb. 28, 2021. https://www.ofbyforall.org/.

"The Restriction of Political Campaign Intervention by Section 501(c)(3) Tax-Exempt Organizations."
Internal Revenue Service. Accessed Feb. 28, 2021. https://www.irs.gov/charities-non-profits/char
itable-organizations/the-restriction-of-political-campaign-intervention-by-section-501c3-tax
-exempt-organizations.

Rodney, Seph. "Is Art Museum Attendance Declining Across the U.S.?" Hyperallergic, Jan. 18, 2018.
https://hyperallergic.com/421968/is-art-museum-attendance-declining-across-the-us/.

Rothman, Darla. "A Tsunami of Learners Called Generation Z." Accessed Mar. 1, 2021. https://mdle
.net/Journal/A_Tsunami_of_Learners_Called_Generation_Z.pdf.

Rothstein, Edward. "A Touch of the Toxic, for Good or Ill." New York Times, Nov. 14, 2013. https://www
.nytimes.com/2013/11/15/arts/design/the-power-of-poison-at-american-museum-of-natural
-history.html.

Russeth, Andrew. "Protesting Trump, Wellesley's Davis Museum Will Remove from View Works Made
or Donated by Immigrants to the United States." ARTnews, Feb. 15, 2017. https://www.artnews
.com/art-news/news/protesting-trump-wellesleys-davis-museum-will-remove-from-view-works
-made-or-donated-by-immigrants-to-the-united-states-7781/#!

Samis, Peter, and Mimi Michaelson. *Creating the Visitor-Centered Museum*. Milton Park: Routledge, 2016.

Santa Cruz Museum of Art and History. https://www.santacruzmah.org/.

"Sculpture Lens—Strike a Pose." Cleveland Museum of Art. Video. Accessed Aug. 19, 2020. https://vimeo.com/60866008.

Senge, Peter M. *The Fifth Discipline*. New York: Doubleday, 1990.

Shanks, Michael. An Introduction to Design Thinking: Process Guide. Stanford. Accessed Oct. 30, 2020. http://web.stanford.edu/~mshanks/MichaelShanks/files/509554.pdf.

Silber, Bohne, and Tim Triplett. "A Decade of Arts Engagement: Findings from the Survey of Public Participation in the Arts, 2002–2012." National Endowment for the Arts. Jan. 2015. https://www.arts.gov/sites/default/files/2012-sppa-feb2015.pdf.

Solomon, Micah. "How to Think Like Apple about the Customer Service Experience." *Forbes*, Nov. 11, 2014. https://www.forbes.com/sites/micahsolomon/2014/11/21/how-apple-thinks-differently-about-the-customer-service-experience-and-how-it-can-help-you/.

Steinbeck, John. *East of Eden*. New York: Viking, 1952.

Styles, Cath. "Museum Experience Design: Lessons from across the Field." *Semantics Scholar*, 2010. https://pdfs.semanticscholar.org/d8ed/a250ecad163538cc41ecce39a41cdf29c747.pdf.

"Sublime Ideas: Drawings by Giovanni Battista Piranesi." Morgan Library and Museum. Jun. 24, 2020. https://www.themorgan.org/programs/sublime-ideas-drawings-giovanni-battista-piranesi.

"Teen Obesity Has Nearly Tripled." Jun. 17, 2014. https://www.slideshare.net/sparksandhoney/generation-z-final-june-17/43-Teen_obesity_has_nearly_tripled.

Teixeira, Thales. "Products Don't Disrupt Markets; Customers Do." Podcast. Accessed Oct. 27, 2020. https://podcasts.apple.com/us/podcast/s5e9-thales-teixeira-products-dont-disrupt-markets/id1359935118.

TrendsWatch 2017. American Alliance of Museums. 2017. https://www.aam-us.org/programs/center-for-the-future-of-museums/trendswatch-2017/.

"20 Best Museum Website Designs for Inspiration 2020." Colorlib. Sep. 30, 2020. https://colorlib.com/wp/museum-website-design/.

"Want to Make Your Organization Of, By, and For Your Diverse Community?" OF/BY/FOR ALL. Accessed Feb. 28, 2021. https://www.ofbyforall.org/.

"What Is a Project Charter in Project Management?" Wrike. https://www.wrike.com/project-management-guide/faq/what-is-a-project-charter-in-project-management/.

"What Is Premises Liability?" NOLO. Accessed Feb. 27, 2021. https://www.nolo.com/legal-encyclopedia/what-premises-liability.html.

"What Makes a Successful Place?" Project for Public Spaces. https://www.pps.org/article/grplacefeat.

"Why Generation Z Wants Only Perfect Customer Service." Helprace. Jul. 14, 2016. https://helprace.com/blog/why-generation-z-wants-only-perfect-customer-service.

Williams, Alex. "Move Over, Millennials, Here Comes Generation Z." *New York Times*, Sep. 18, 2015. https://www.nytimes.com/2015/09/20/fashion/move-over-millennials-here-comes-generation-z.html.

Wong, May. "Stanford Research Provides a Snapshot of a New Working-From-Home Economy." *Stanford News*, Jun. 29, 2020. https://news.stanford.edu/2020/06/29/snapshot-new-working-home-economy/.

Wünsch, Silke. "The Museum That Changed a Whole City: Guggenheim Museum Bilbao Turns Twenty." *Deutsche Welle*, Oct. 19, 2017. https://www.dw.com/en/the-museum-that-changed-a-whole-city-guggenheim-museum-bilbao-turns-20/a-41013716.

Zorfas, Alan, and Daniel Leemon. "An Emotional Connection Matters More Than Customer Satisfaction." *Harvard Business Review*, Aug. 29, 2016. https://hbr.org/2016/08/an-emotional-connection-matters-more-than-customer-satisfaction.

Glossary

3D printer: Programmable device used to manufacture three-dimensional objects by layering a hardening material.

3D scanning: Analyzing a three-dimensional object in a way that acquires transferable data.

A

Accessibility: Giving equitable access to everyone along the continuum of human ability and experience. Accessibility encompasses the broader meanings of compliance and refers to how organizations make space for the characteristics that each person brings.[1]

Advisory group: A collection of individuals who bring unique knowledge and skills that complement the knowledge and skills of the formal governing authority. The advisory group does not have authority to govern the museum; it cannot issue directives that must be followed. Rather, the advisory group serves to make recommendations or provide key information to the formal governing authority. The advisory group can be standing (on-going) or ad hoc (one time) in nature.

Americans with Disabilities Act (ADA): A civil rights law, enacted in 1990, that prohibits discrimination against individuals with disabilities.

Annual pass program: A purchased pass that allows unlimited visits during the year (or another set time period). Pass Programs can also be set up as a local partnership program which allows purchasers free admission to several participating venues in the area. Often coordinated through a chamber of commerce or welcome wagon type of organization, these can be set up to allow one visit to each venue, or unlimited visits during a set time period.

Artificial intelligence (AI): Computers or systems that simulate human intelligence.

Audience: Groups of people who use the museum's services by attending or participating at an event, exhibit, program, or other presentation. Audiences can be defined by using categories, such as the types of services they use and how they use them (e.g., visitors, members, researchers, program participants, Web site users), or by their demographic characteristics (e.g., families, school groups, seniors, culturally specific groups) or their interests and motivations for participating.

Audience survey/study: Collecting data from the museum's actual and potential audiences to determine their composition and receive feedback. Used to assess the effectiveness of the museum's activities and services.

Audience, target: A sub-group of a community with shared demographics or interests that has been chosen as a group to engage with or attract.

Augmented reality (AR): Digital effects added to a real-life experience.

Auxiliary group: See **Friends/auxiliary group.**

Awareness: In a museum setting, a visitor's knowledge of the museum prior to the visit.

B

Behavioral design: Design that influences or shapes human actions and character.

Bubble diagram: In a museum design context, visual representations of the visitor's literal path through a museum and the associated content along the way.

Benchmark: A point of reference used in measuring and judging quality or value.

Best practices: Commendable actions and philosophies that successfully solve problems, can be replicated, and demonstrate an awareness of standards.

C

Civic: Describes an entity as having to do with a city or town.

Civil: Describes an object or a person relating to citizenship or a citizen, as opposed to the military or religious leadership.

Code of ethics: Professional standards of conduct for staff, governing authority members, and volunteers carrying out the mission of the museum. A code puts the interests of the public ahead of the interests of the institution or of any individual and encourages conduct that merits public confidence. A code of ethics acknowledges applicable laws and appropriate discipline-specific professional practices in order to help museums meet or exceed them. For more information see: AAM Standards regarding an institutional code of ethics.

Collections plan: A plan that guides the content of the collections and leads staff in a coordinated and uniform direction over time to refine and expand the value of collections in a predetermined way. Plans are time-limited and identify specific goals to be achieved. They also provide a rationale for those choices and specify how they will be achieved, who will implement the plan, when it will happen, and what it will cost.

Community: Each museum self-identifies the community or communities it serves. These may be geographically defined, may be communities of common interests, or may be communities formed around identities or a combination of these types.

Community engagement: Engaging with and collaborating with diverse groups to jointly meet needs articulated by the community and taking actions that truly benefit the community.

Content map: A method of designing content based on where you are and where you want to be.

Core Standards: The AAM Core Standards were developed in collaboration with other museum organizations and are grouped into the following categories: Public Trust and Accountability, Mission & Planning, Leadership and Organizational Structure, Collections Stewardship, Education and Interpretation, Financial Stability, and Facilities and Risk Management.

Creative placemaking: A process where community members, artists, arts and culture organizations, community developers, and other stakeholders use arts and cultural strategies to implement community-led change.

Culture: A group of people with shared experiences, beliefs, values, practices, and norms.

Curatorial activism: The active participation of the curator in creating impactful experiences between museum and visitor.

Curriculum plan: A written plan containing the framework, goals, and policies that guide the development and delivery of a curriculum.

Customer experience (CX): The overall impact of the interactions between a person and a company at all touchpoints.

D

Decolonization: The long, slow, painful, and imperfect process of undoing some of the damage inflicted by colonial practices that remain deeply embedded in our culture, politics, and economies.[2]

Deep neural network: Multilayered neural networks that use sophisticated mathematical modeling to process data in complex ways.

Democratization of content: Making museum content accessible to all.

Design Thinking: The process of creating customer experiences; a creative problem-solving approach to providing a service or building a product.[3]

Diversity: All the ways that people are different and the same at the individual and group levels. Even when people appear the same, they are different. Organizational diversity requires examining and questioning the makeup of a group to ensure that multiple perspectives are represented.[4]

Docent/guide: A volunteer or paid staff person who provides interpretation to visitors through a guided tour, talk, or presentation. The museum field appears to be transitioning from the more traditional model of docents as volunteer tour guides to an increasing number of institutions using paid guides. The National Docent Symposium Council now uses the term docents/guides to be inclusive and refer to the education and interpretation function or role, not to employment status.

E

Education master plan: A written plan that identifies education goals, audiences, content, delivery methods, data gathering, and evaluation methods for all education programs and services.

Educational ecosystem: The formal and informal learning organizations within a community, the roles they each play, who they serve, the dynamics between them, and areas of intersection or overlap in the community.

Effective frequency: How many times a potential visitor needs to see a notice or advertisement to reach awareness.

Emotional design: Driven by behavioral change and human response.

Empathy: In a museum context, understanding and being aware of the emotions of the visitor.

Empathy map: Starts with the observable phenomena of things the user sees, says, does, and hears, and ends at the center with what it feels like to actually be them.

Equity: The fair and just treatment of all members of a community. Equity requires commitment to strategic priorities, resources, respect, and civility, as well as ongoing action and assessment of progress toward achieving specific goals.[5]

Ethnographic research: Gathering cultural and demographic data from a particular area or population.

Evaluation: Obtaining valid and reliable information from visitors that helps in the planning of exhibitions, activities, and programs and in determining the extent to which the activities are meeting their intended objectives. Can include observation (tracking) studies, questionnaires, interviews, community meetings, and focus groups. Visitor evaluation can be carried out before (front end), during (formative), and after (summative) exhibition or program development.

Exhibit: The localized grouping of objects and interpretative materials that form a cohesive unit within a gallery and relate a message or idea.[6]

Exhibition: Exhibitions use a combination of objects, text, graphics, interactives, and/or props to create a physical space dedicated to the exploration of specific themes, messages, and ideas. An exhibition is a comprehensive grouping of all elements (including exhibits and displays) that form a complete public presentation of collections and information for public use.[7]

Exhibit/exhibition plan or policy: A written plan that identifies exhibition schedules, goals, interpretive guidelines, and policies and procedures, as well as policies applying to any object loans, and care and documentation of objects in temporary custody.

Experience design: In a museum context, all the efforts to shape the customer experience.

Experience economy: A business environment in which memorable events are created for customers, and the memory of the experience becomes the product.

F

Financial resources: The income and expenses of the museum.

Focus group: Interview studies involving a carefully selected sample of eight to 10 individuals whose demographic and psychographic characteristics are of special interest to the museum. A planned but informal discussion carried out with the small group of visitors or community members to discuss a predetermined topic in their own terms.

Forecasting: Using data to identify trends and project the future state of a variable. Variables might include broad topics such as the local economy or the demographics of a community, or more specific topics such as available volunteers, school tours attendance, or Wifi bandwidth needs.

Friends/auxiliary group: A support organization that is separately incorporated and whose primary purpose is the support of the museum. This may involve financial support, volunteers, or expertise.

Full-time staff: Employees who work 35 hours or more per week.

G

Governing authority: The entity that has legal and fiduciary responsibility for the museum (this body may not necessarily own the collection or the physical facility) and may include not-for-profit boards, appointed commissions, governmental bodies, and university regents.

Names of governing authority include advisory council, board of commissioners, board of directors, board of managers, board of regents, board of trustees, city council, commission, or tribal council.

Head of governing authority: The elected or appointed head of the executive body to which the director reports. For institutions that are part of a larger non-museum parent organization, the head of the governing authority is considered to be the individual within the institution's larger parent organization to whom the director reports/is responsible (e.g., dean or provost of a university, director of parks and recreation for a city government, military post commander, etc.).

Guide: See **Docent/guide**.

H

Half-listening: Listening for the reasons behind people's decisions when interviewing them.
Head of governing authority: See **Governing authority.**
Human-computer interaction: The interface between a person and a digital system.
Human resources: All of the people, paid and unpaid, who regularly work at the museum.

I

IDEO design thinking process: A planning methodology that goes through the following steps: empathize, define, ideate, prototype, test.

Immersive experience: Feeling deeply absorbed, involved, and engaged.

Implicit bias: Unconsciously held opinions, attitudes, and expectations that shape decisions, actions, and understandings without full awareness of this influence, which limits the ability to be objective.

Inclusion: The intentional, ongoing effort to ensure that diverse individuals fully participate in all aspects of organizational work, including decision-making processes. It also refers to the ways that diverse participants are valued as respected members of an organization and/or community. While a truly "inclusive" group is necessarily diverse, a "diverse" group may or may not be "inclusive."[8]

Inquiry based learning: A pedagogical method that uses questions, problems, and/or scenarios to trigger curiosity and critical thinking.

Institutional plan: See **Strategic plan**.

Interactive transmedia exhibit: A narrative dispersed across multiple channels for the purpose of creating a unified experience.

Intern: A student or trainee who works to gain experience for a career or profession. Some internships are paid, some are unpaid, and some are done in exchange for school credit, housing, or other compensation.

Interpretation: The media/activities through which a museum carries out its mission and educational role:

- Interpretation is a dynamic process of communication between the museum and the audience.
- Interpretation is the means by which the museum delivers its content.
- Interpretation media/activities include but are not limited to exhibits, tours, websites, classes, school programs, publications, and outreach.
- Interpretation methods and design are based upon museum and educational learning theories. Knowledge of cognitive development, educational theory, and teaching practices are applied to the types of voluntary, personal, and life-long learning that occurs in museums.

Interpretive plan: A document that outlines what stories and messages the museum wants to convey through a variety of media, such as exhibits, programming, and publications. It may include the institution's interpretive philosophy, educational goals, and target audiences. A museum may develop an overall institutional interpretive plan, or an interpretative plan for an individual component of its operation—for example, for its permanent exhibits or for one of its historic sites.

J

Journey map: A visual representation of customer touchpoints; the interactions of a customer with the product or service.

L

Lateral thinking: A method for solving problems by making unusual or unexpected connections between ideas.

Lean canvas: A one-page planning document that helps define problems and connect to solutions.

Lean startup: A methodology for developing products that uses curtailed product-development cycles.

Learning, formal: Structured learning that typically focuses on teaching specific, predetermined skills and/or knowledge. Learning outcomes are frequently measured or evaluated, usually through testing.

Learning, informal: Learning environments or systems that offer self-directed opportunities that can lead to unexpected or unplanned learning, impacts, and outcomes.

Learning, self-directed: Learning in which an individual takes ownership of their learning process (with or without guidance); also known as *independent learning*. The free-choice environment of many museums can be a foundation for creating self-directed learning opportunities through interpretive scaffolding and visitor choices that offer multiple points of access.

Learning organizations: Organizations that value continuous knowledge and skills development and actively support ongoing learning for all members as well as for the organization as a group.

Learning styles: Categorizations that differentiate the manner in which a person most effectively comprehends and processes new information. Designing educational materials and approaches to either match an individual's learning style or to be inclusive of all learning styles is one educational strategy or pedagogical approach.

Linear thinking: A step-by-step approach to solving a problem or completing a task.

Lobbying: Attempts by a person or organization to influence legislation.

Logic model: A model (usually depicted in the form of a table or diagram) used to plan the resources, activities, outputs, outcomes, and impact for a program or event.

M

Machine learning: The ability to automatically learn and improve from experience without being explicitly programmed.

Marketing: The wide range of activities involved in making sure that you're continuing to meet the needs of your customers and getting value in return. These activities include market research to find out, for example, what groups of potential customers exist, what their needs are, which of those needs you can meet, and how you should meet them. Marketing also includes analyzing the competition, positioning your new product or service (finding your market niche), pricing your products and services, and promoting them through continued advertising, promotions, public relations, and sales.

Material culture: Objects, materials, and spaces created by people to sustain, perpetuate, or enjoy life as defined by their particular culture or society.

Membership program: A program that offers specific privileges, perks, and discounts in exchange for payment of dues or fees (usually annually) as a charitable contribution. A well-thought-out membership program can support fundraising and marketing, and can encourage member feelings of belonging, stewardship, and loyalty.

Memorandum of agreement/memorandum of understanding: A written agreement spelling out the terms of the relationship between two entities, such as a museum and a support organization, or a museum and a municipality. It is signed by the governing authorities of the organizations.

Metadata: Data that provide information about other data.

Mission: A statement approved by the museum's governing authority that defines the purpose of a museum—its reason for existence. The mission statement establishes the museum's identity and purpose, provides a distinct focus for the institution, and identifies its role and responsibilities to the public and its collections.

Mobile applications (apps): Small programs that are usually accessed via smartphone.

Mood board: A two-dimensional visual statement that indicates a project's visual aesthetic.

Multiple intelligences: A learning theory that suggests humans have eight possible different types of intelligence that impact learning styles and capabilities.

Multi-year plan: See **Strategic plan**.

Museum dashboard: An online snapshot of metrics regarding the performance of museum strategy and tactics.

Museum digital revolution: The movement of museum content from analog to digital (primarily online) spaces.

N

Names of governing authority: See **Governing authority.**

Natural language processing: Algorithms that help computers understand, interpret, and manipulate human language.

Nonoperating income and expenditures: Income and expenditures related to temporarily or permanently restricted funds, such as endowment contributions and pledges; capital campaign contributions and pledges; all realized capital gains and losses that are rolled back into principal; income from capital campaigns; and capital expenditures.

O

Omni experience: A unified experience at all touchpoints between user and museum.

Open storage: Placing stored collections on public view without interpretative materials.

Operating income and expenditures: Income generated by or expenditures supporting the museum's general operations in a given fiscal year, including exhibitions, education, conservation, collections management, acquisitions, research, training, development, and administration. It includes any portion of income from the endowment that is applied to operating expenses in a given year. It does not include capital expenditures. See also **Nonoperating income and expenditures**.

Operational plan: See **Strategic plan.**

Optical character recognition: Software that facilitates pulling text from documents.

Organizational capacity: The ability to effectively use resources to successfully fulfill its mission and goals while honoring its values and maintaining positive social impact.

P

Parent organization: The overseeing organization (such as a historical society or university) that is responsible for the fiduciary control of the museum.

Part-time staff: Staff who work less than 35 hours per week.

Pedagogy: A method and practice of teaching.

Persona: A representation of a type of user, based on clusters of behaviors and needs.

Persona diagram: Visual and textual imagery evoking a type of user.

Placemaking: A multifaceted approach to the planning, design, and management of public spaces that is grounded in the local community.

Planning: The creation of policy and written plans. Thomas Wolf (*Managing a Nonprofit Organization*, 1990) lists two essential prerequisites of planning as 1) an evaluation/assessment of the organization's current position, and 2) a clear vision of the organization's future expressed through a statement of mission and goals. These prerequisites apply to all types of planning, whether it is long-range, disaster, exhibition, marketing, or program.

Positionality: Uncovering implicit bias.

Professional practice: A practice generally accepted in the field as a reliable method or technique for achieving a desired result; also known as *best practice*.

Public trust: The obligation and duty to serve the public interest rather than individual interest or institutional interest.

Purpose: The museum's broad guiding principle as stated in its governing documents.

R

Reflective design: A process that seeks to create a deep emotional relationship between user and product.

S

Service design: A holistic view of all related actors, their interactions, and supporting materials and infrastructures.

Social media: Forms of electronic communication (like websites for social networking and microblogging) through which users create online communities to share information, ideas, personal messages, and other content (such as videos).

Special events: Concerts, festivals, or special seasonal programs.

Special exhibitions: Usually short-term, temporary exhibitions.

Staff: Unless otherwise noted, refers to full- and part-time staff (paid or unpaid) of your organization.

Stakeholder analysis: A list of the people in the process with disproportionate influence as well as those who have little influence.

Stakeholder canvas: A visual representation of the people who influence a process.

Stakeholders: People who have influence on your institution or are impacted by your institution.

Standard: Generally accepted level of attainment that all museums are expected to achieve.

Stereotype: An inaccurate generalization about a person or group based on oversimplified or limited information.

Strategic plan: Comprehensive plan that broadly delineates where the institution is going and provides sufficient detail to guide implementation. Sets priorities and guides important decisions that are oriented towards the future. Some museums split this into two parts:

- **Multi-year plan:** Big-picture plan that sets strategies, goals, and priorities. Sometimes referred to as a strategic or long-range plan.
- **Operational plan:** Plan that provides the details needed to implement the decisions in the strategic or long-range plan. Usually focuses on a short period of time and is typically geared to the museum's budget year. Sometimes referred to as an implementation plan. For more information see the AAM Standards regarding an institutional plan.

Sustainability: A way of operating that supports the organization's current needs and can be continued without reducing resources or opportunities for the future.

System map: A visualization of the ecosystem of the museum, including galleries, libraries, archives, and art service and art storage firms.

T

Threshold: In a museum context, the front doors and the area surrounding the entrance.

Time-box: An agreed-upon period during which a person or a team works steadily toward the completion of a goal.

Tours: Any type of tour of the exhibitions, grounds, buildings, or surrounding area. This includes school, self-guided, audio, and guided tours.

Triangulation: The strategic placement of amenities in order to encourage social interaction.

U

Umbrella concept: The way in which an organization will accomplish its goal.

Universal design: The design of products and environments to be usable by all people, to the greatest extent possible, without the need for adaptation or specialized design.

User experience (UX): The emotional impact of product, experience, or service on a person.

User interface: Everything designed into an information device with which a person may interact.

V

Values: The core belief system that provides a moral compass and framework for an organization's goals, priorities, and decisions.

Virtual reality (VR): An immersive, digitally created experience requiring a headset.

Visceral design: Based on initial user reactions to certain environments and contexts.

Vision statement: An aspirational declaration of a museum's intentions that may include a description of the ideal scenario or successful future.

Visitors: Groups and individuals who go to the museum's physical facilities to use the museum services.

Visitor-centered approach: Making museums accessible to new and existing audiences, regardless of age or background.

Visitor experience: All interfaces or points of contacts a visitor has with the museum and its facility, services, and products. A visitor experience begins when a decision is made to visit, and continues through the planning and research, the onsite experience at the museum, and then post-visit activities such as online research or conversations with others about the visit.

Visitor motivation: The reason why someone visits a museum, an exhibition, or a program. A visitor's expectations and needs are part of a visitor's motivation to attend or not attend.

Visitor services: Facilities or services that provide comfort to visitors, including assistive devices, baby changing stations, checkrooms, dining area/food service, first aid stations, information desks, nursing areas, restrooms, seating, signage, water fountains, wheelchairs, and Wi-fi® access.

Visitor studies: The use of data collection, research, and evaluation to better understand and improve the visitor experience.

Visitor survey: A set of questions designed to gather information from visitors that will help a museum improve its programs and services. Surveys may be done using different methods: verbally, online, on paper, or by email.

Visual literacy: The ability to observe, interpret, analyze, and make meaning from a still or moving image. A shared vocabulary used to describe and discuss an image is generally considered a foundation for literacy.

Visual thinking strategies: A pedagogical method that uses structured facilitation to help students observe and engage with visual art.

Volunteer: An individual who offers time and service to the museum for no salary or wage.

W

Wayfinding: How a visitor determines his or her location and the best route to take to get to a destination within the museum. Maps and signage are some ways museums help visitors stay physically oriented and aid in wayfinding.

Glossary Copyright 2020 American Alliance of Museums, Arlington, VA. Reprinted with permission. For more information, visit https://www.aam-us.org.

NOTES

1. From *Facing Change: Insights from the American Alliance of Museums' Diversity, Equity, Accessibility, and Inclusion Working Group Report*, 2018. Full Report available in the MAP Portal.
2. From TrendsWatch 2019, the American Alliance of Museums.
3. Added by author.
4. From *Facing Change: Insights from the American Alliance of Museums' Diversity, Equity, Accessibility, and Inclusion Working Group Report*, 2018. Full Report available in the MAP Portal.

5. From *Facing Change: Insights from the American Alliance of Museums' Diversity, Equity, Accessibility, and Inclusion Working Group Report*, 2018. Full Report available in the MAP Portal.
6. Adapted from David Dean, *Museum Exhibition: Theory and Practice* (London: Routledge, 1994), 161.
7. Adapted from David Dean, *Museum Exhibition: Theory and Practice* (London: Routledge, 1994), 161.
8. From *Facing Change: Insights from the American Alliance of Museums' Diversity, Equity, Accessibility, and Inclusion Working Group Report*, 2018. Full Report available in the MAP Portal.

Index

European Network of Science Centres and Museums, 33. *See also* Ecsite

evaluation, 26, 39, 45, 102–104, 165

exhibit, 165

exhibit/exhibition plan or policy, 3–4, 7, 18, 32–34, 39, 55–56, 75, 83–85, 99, 102–105, 115, 121, 125, 129, 165, 167

exhibition, 22–27, 32–34, 38, 68, 78–79, 83–85, 102–104, 126–127, 137, 144, 165, 170, 171

experience design, 6–8, 26–27, 35–38, 40, 43–45, 48, 53–56, 147, 165. *See also* reflective design

experience economy, 6–8, 120, 126, 165

Falk, John H., 37–38

feedback, 26, 47, 48, 53, 56, 58, 79, 99, 101, 102–104, 108–109, 131, 163. *See also* audience survey/study

financial resources, 166

flow experience, 10. *See also* Csikszentmihalyi, Mihaly

focus group, 103–104, 166. *See also* audience study

forecasting, 166

friends, 163, 166. *See also* auxiliary group

full-time staff, 126–127, 166, 170. *See also* staff

funding, 21, 126–128

fundraising, 38, 44, 68, 126, 168. *See also* development

Gardner, Howard, 154. *See also* emotional intelligence

generations, 31, 34, 113–114

governing authority, 163, 164, 166, 168

handshake, 76

Hatch Act of 1939, 154. *See also* political issues

high-fidelity, 45. *See also* prototyping

hospitality, 107, 109

human-centered design, 53, 153, 154

human-computer interaction (HCI), 113, 121, 166

human factors, 154. *See also* ergonomics

human resources, 136, 166

immersive experience, 3, 53, 99, 117, 166

implicit bias, xx, 16, 18, 63, 166, 169

inclusion, xix, 40, 166

inequity, 126

informal learning, 109, 165, 167. *See also* learning, self-directed

inquiry-based learning, 167

Institute of Museum and Library Services (IMLS), 21

institutional plan, 135, 150–151, 167, 170. *See also* strategic plan

Integrated Museum Approach (IMA), 121. *See also* Inclusive Museum Process (IMP)

interactive, 55, 84, 85, 99, 103, 105, 115, 117, 121, 130, 165, 167

intern, 126, 167

International Council of Museums (ICOM), 4, 33, 110, 125, 131

institutional plan, 167, 169, 170. *See also* operational plan

interpretation, 5, 23, 26, 125, 165, 167

interpretive plan, 167, 171. *See also* visitor experience

journey map, xxi, 56, 61, 68–69, 73, 75, 77, 79, 167

key performance indicator (KPI), 101

lean methodology, 45, 56–58, 59, 167

lean startup, xvii, 56–57, 59, 167

learning: formal, 165, 167; informal, 109, 165, 167; self-directed, 167

learning organizations, 165, 168

learning styles, 168. *See also* multiple intelligences

logic model, 168

low-fidelity, 47, 147. *See also* prototyping

machine learning, 31, 118, 119, 120–121, 168

maker space, 130

marketing, xx, 38, 48, 100, 104, 128, 168, 169

massive open online course (MOOC), 31

material culture, 168

membership program, 129–130, 168

memorandum of agreement, 168. *See also* memorandum of understanding

memorandum of understanding, 168. *See also* memorandum of agreement

mission, 7, 26, 100, 102, 114–115, 121, 126, 130, 135, 145, 164, 167, 168, 169, 171. *See also* purpose

mood board, 61, 62, 63, 73, 137, 144, 147, 168

multiple intelligences, 168

multi-year plan, 168, 170. *See also* strategic plan

museum CX, xvii, xix, xx, 7, 8, 44, 53–56, 58–59, 61, 68, 95, 143–145, 164

museum planning, 14, 16–17, 38, 150–151

museum services, xx, 7, 49, 127, 138, 141, 163, 168, 171

Museum Visitor Experience Toolbox, xx, 18, 48, 50, 61, 131, 135–136, 138

Myers-Briggs, 154

National Endowment for the Arts (NEA), 155

National Endowment for the Humanities (NEH), 155

Network of European Museum Organizations (NEMO), 155

net promoter score (NPS), 101

nonoperating income and expenditures, 169

About the Author

Mark Walhimer is a managing partner of Museum Planning, LLC, a museum consultancy, and a part-time industrial design professor. He splits his time between the United States and Mexico City.

His company, Museum Planning, LLC, specializes in the planning, design, and management of interactive educational experiences. Walhimer started his firm in 1999 to assist start-up and expanding museums with feasibility studies, strategic planning, museum master planning, exhibition design, exhibition project management, fabrication supervision, installation supervision, and staff training. His firm has completed more than forty projects worldwide, including science centers, art museums, history museums, libraries, and corporations.

Walhimer is the founder of Museum Courses, an online platform for museum courses, and has taught at Georgia Institute of Technology in Atlanta, Georgia; Tecnológico de Monterrey in Mexico City; and Universidad Iberoamericana in Mexico City.

Projects include providing "turnkey" museum services for the C. O. Polk Interactive Museum in McDonough, Georgia; project manager and National Park Service liaison for the "Alcatraz: Life on the Rock" traveling exhibition; project manager for Museo Interactivo de Economía (MIDE) in Mexico City; and master planning and exhibition design for Trans Studio Science Center in Bandung, Indonesia. Prior to starting his company, Walhimer held positions at Discovery Science Center in Santa Ana, California; the Children's Museum of Indianapolis; the Tech Museum in San Jose, California; and Liberty Science Center. He has also been Chief Operating Officer of a museum exhibition design and fabrication firm, and is the author of *Museums 101* (2015), a how-to guide for creating and organizing all varieties of museums.

Mark Walhimer has been a three-time juror for the US Department of Energy Solar Decathlon, an American Alliance of Museums Museum Assessment Program (MAP) peer reviewer, and an Institute of Museum and Library Services peer reviewer.

He holds a bachelor's degree in studio art from Skidmore College in Saratoga Springs, New York, and a master's degree in industrial design and exhibition design from Pratt Institute in Brooklyn, New York.

Museum Visitor Experience website: https://www.museum-experiences.com/.
Portfolio: https://museumplanning.com.
Museum Planner blog: https://museumplanner.org.
Teaching: https://markwalhimer.com.
Online Museum Courses: *Museums 101*, Introduction to Museums, and a book companion online
    course *Museum Visitor Experience* (with project) https://museumcourses.com/.
Museums 101 website: https://museums101.com.